WHITE COLLAR CRIME

WHITE COLLAR CRIME

THE UNCUT VERSION

EDWIN H. SUTHERLAND

WITH AN INTRODUCTION BY
GILBERT GEIS AND COLIN GOFF

YALE UNIVERSITY PRESS
NEW HAVEN AND LONDON

Designed by Sally Harris
and set in Primer type.
Printed in the United States of America by
Vail-Ballou Press, Binghamton, N.Y.

Library of Congress Cataloging in Publication Data

Sutherland, Edwin Hardin, 1883–1950.
    White collar crime.

    Includes bibliographical references and index.
        1. White collar crime—United States.
2. Corporations—United States—Corrupt practices.
I. Title.
IIV6769.S93   1983   364.1′68′0973   82–48911
ISBN 0–300–02921–7
(pbk.) 0–300–03318–4

10 9 8 7 6 5 4 3 2

CONTENTS

LIST OF TABLES

INTRODUCTION

Gilbert Geis and Colin Goff

The thirty-fourth annual meeting of the American Sociological Society—convened in Philadelphia in 1939 during the academic recess between Christmas and New Year—was held jointly with the fifty-second gathering of the American Economic Association. On December 27, at eight P.M., Jacob Viner of the University of Chicago, president of the AEA, addressed the assembled group.[1] Viner was followed to the podium by Edwin H. Sutherland of Indiana University, president of the sociological society.

Sutherland's talk was entitled "The White Collar Criminal,"[2] and it altered the study of crime throughout the world in fundamental ways by focusing attention upon a form of lawbreaking that had previously been ignored by criminological scholars. Sutherland's targets were several: First, he ridiculed theories of crime which blamed such factors as poverty, broken homes, and Freudian fixations for illegal behavior, noting that healthy upbringings and intact psyches had not served to deter monstrous amounts of lawbreaking by persons in positions of power. Thereafter, Sutherland documented in detail derelictions by corporations, concluding that their "rap sheets" resembled, at least in length and frequency, those of many professional predators, such as con men and bank robbers, persons who by choice prey upon the public. He focused on such representative corporate offenses as antitrust violations,

Some of this material was presented at the Conference on White-Collar and Economic Crime, Potsdam College of Arts and Science, Potsdam, N.Y., in February 1980, and published in the conference proceedings (Peter Wickman and Timothy Daily, eds., *White-Collar and Economic Crime: Multidisciplinary and Cross-National Perspectives* [Lexington, Mass.: D. C. Heath, 1982], pp. 3–21).

1. Jacob Viner, "The Short View and The Long in Economic Policy," *American Economic Review*, 30 (1940), 1–15.

2. Edwin H. Sutherland, "The White Collar Criminal," *American Sociological Review*, 5 (1940), 1–12.

false advertising, theft of trade secrets, and bribery in order to obtain special privileges.

That inadequate attention had been paid to the crimes of the powerful was tied by Sutherland most particularly to the close relationship between the white-collar offenders and those in our midst who call attention to what they regard as especially heinous behavior. Newspapers, for instance, themselves skirting the spirit if not the letter of child labor laws by employing minors as delivery boys and girls and labeling them "independent contractors," would hesitate to highlight violations of regulatory laws by other business enterprises lest their own tactics come under disapproving scrutiny. The papers also depend upon advertiser goodwill and will be reluctant to bite the hands that feed them. Judges, often benefactors of political processes that are less than wholesome, understandably would see the business and professional violations of those who had attended the same colleges, belonged to the same churches, and lived in the same neighborhoods as they did as a good deal less serious than the street offenses committed so disproportionately by members of minority groups and others in dispossessed statuses. Sutherland insisted that the white-collar behaviors he detailed were criminal, not civil, offenses, and that the persons who committed them ought to receive the same kind of scorn and punishment that attends other kinds of property and personal crime. He regarded white-collar crime as in many instances more consequential than run-of-the-mill street offenses, insisting that it was more apt to tear at the core of a social system and render citizens cynical and selfish.

Sutherland labored for another decade following his presidential address to write his manuscript on white-collar crime, which fleshed out the details and the theoretical notions of his talk before the sociological society. The monograph was accepted and ultimately published (1949) by Dryden Press, where Sutherland had recently been appointed sociology editor. At the last moment, fearful that the volume was too statistical, Sutherland added the final chapter, on theory. Dryden, however, then demanded that the names of the companies be eliminated from the book. Its counsel insisted that Dryden would be liable for damages because the book called certain corporations "criminal" although they had not been dealt with under criminal statutes. At Indiana University too, Sutherland came under pressure from the administration to delete the names of the corporate offenders, in part, he believed, because the university feared alienating some of its wealthy business contributors. Sutherland agonized over the question of whether to make

the excisions. He often invited students and colleagues into his office
to discuss the issue. Donald Cressey, one of those advisers and later
Sutherland's collaborator, has recalled his reaction to Sutherland's di-
lemma:

> Had the original manuscript been published, and had a libel suit
> been initiated, then Sutherland's contention that the listed offenses
> are in fact crimes might have been tested in a court of law—a cor-
> poration might have argued that the statement is libelous because
> its behavior is not a crime, with Sutherland giving the arguments
> presented in his book. I was one of Sutherland's research assistants
> at the time, and I urged that the original manuscript be published
> for this reason, if for no other. However, my idealistic desire to see a
> scientific principle tested in a court of law was not tempered by any
> practical consideration such as having money riding on the legal va-
> lidity of the scientific principle. This was not the case with either
> the publisher or Professor Sutherland.[3]

Sutherland finally acceded to Dryden's request, rationalizing his decision in part on the ground that elimination of the names of the offend-
ing companies, and of a chapter entitled "Three Case Histories," made
the book more "objective" and "scientific." Persons who wrote to him
after *White Collar Crime* was published requesting the names of the
corporations did not get them; instead, they were sent citations to the
relevant court cases. Sutherland, however, had looked into the question
of when the statute of limitations would protect him from liability. It
proved to be 1953. Sutherland died in 1950, and by 1953 McCarthyism
was rampant. Criminologists by then had warily turned their attention
to matters other than wrongdoing by persons with power.

White Collar Crime, absent the identities of the corporate malefactors
and the case histories, remained in print for more than thirty years. It
was translated into Japanese in 1955 by Ryuichi Hirano, now president
of Tokyo University, and Koji Iguchi, and into Spanish in 1969 by Roso
del Omo of the faculty of economic and social science at the Central University of Venezuela. The term *white-collar crime* was incorporated into
the language of scholarly work overseas as well as in the United States.
In France, it became *crime en col blanc,*[4] in Italy, *criminalitá in colletti*

3. Donald R. Cressey, "Preface," in Edwin H. Sutherland, *White Collar Crime*
(New York: Holt, Rinehart, and Winston, 1961), p. vii.
4. André Normandeau, "Les Deviations en Affaires et la 'Crime en Col Blanc,' "
Review of International Criminal and Police Technology, 19 (1965), 247–58.

bianchi,[5] and in Germany, *weisse-kragen-kriminalität*.[6] In the Netherlands, there has been a call for "a good Dutch word" to denote white-collar crime, and the suggestion of an offer of a prize for the best submission.[7]

In the United States, Sutherland's pathbreaking work had an immediate influence on the research focus of a number of young scholars. In 1953 Cressey published *Other People's Money*, a study of embezzlers imprisoned in federal penitentiaries;[8] Marshall Clinard carried out an investigation of the violations of the rules of the Office of Price Administration during the Second World War;[9] and Frank E. Hartung examined the pattern of cheating in the wholesale-meat industry in Detroit during wartime rationing.[10] Thereafter there was a hiatus in concern with white-collar crime, then a great surge during recent years. Today, there are several collections of scholarly articles on the subject,[11] numerous monographs,[12] and a number of proceedings of symposia devoted exclusively to white-collar crime.[13]

Not the least of Sutherland's achievements with this book was to add

5. Guiseppe G. Loschiavo, "La Mafia della Lupara e Quella dei 'Coletti Bianchi,' " *La Giustizia Penale*, 68 (1952), 336–44.

6. Markus Binder, "Weisse-Kragen-Kriminalität," *Kriminalistik* (Hamburg), 16 (June 1962), 251–56.

7. Jan van Weringh, "White Collar Crime, een Terreinverkenning," *Nederlands Tijdschrift voor Criminologie*, 11 (1969), 133–44.

8. Donald R. Cressey, *Other People's Money: A Study in the Social Psychology of Embezzlement* (Glencoe, Ill.: Free Press, 1953).

9. Marshall B. Clinard, *The Black Market* (New York: Rinehart, 1952).

10. Frank E. Hartung, "White-Collar Offenses in the Wholesale Meat Industry in Detroit," *American Journal of Sociology*, 56 (1950), 25–32.

11. M. David Ermann and Richard J. Lundman, eds., *Corporate and Governmental Deviance: Problems of Organizational Behavior in Contemporary Society*, 2d ed. (New York: Oxford University Press, 1982); Gilbert Geis and Robert F. Meier, eds., *White-Collar Crime: Offenses in Business, Politics, and the Professions*, rev. ed. (New York: Free Press, 1977); John M. Johnson and Jack D. Douglas, *Crime at the Top: Deviance in Business and the Professions* (Philadelphia; Lippincott, 1978). See also J. T. Skip Duncan and Marc Caplan, *White-Collar Crime: A Selected Bibliography* (Washington, D.C.: National Institute of Justice, U.S. Department of Justice, 1980).

12. See, e.g., Herbert Edelhertz and Marilyn Walsh, *The White-Collar Challenge to Nuclear Safeguards* (Lexington, Mass.: D. C. Heath, 1978); Robert K. Elliott and John J. Willingham, *Management Fraud: Detection and Deterrence* (New York: Petrocelli, 1980); Pawel Horoszowski, *Economic Special-Opportunity Conduct and Crime* (Lexington, Mass.: D. C. Heath, 1978).

13. See, e.g., Herbert Edelhertz and Charles Rogovin, eds., *A Strategy for Containing White-Collar Crime* (Lexington, Mass.: D. C. Heath, 1980); "Symposium on White-Collar Crime," *Temple Law Quarterly*, 53 (1980), 975–1146.

the term *white-collar crime* to the American vocabulary. Take the phrase's usage in the *New York Times*, for example. A judge is reported to have assailed the growing number of programs under which nonviolent as well as "white-collar criminals" are sentenced to perform community service work as an alternative to prison.[14] Attorney General William French Smith sets forth his office's priorities as targets: first, violent crime, closely followed "in due course by white-collar crime."[15] The United States Attorney for New Jersey tells a congressional committee that "white-collar crime" is a "cancer which is eroding society from the inside,"[16] and a story detailing an offense involving knowing possession of stolen bonds carries the subhead: "White-Collar Crime is Easy."[17] So common is the usage that a defense lawyer pleads for a light sentence for his client by insisting that he ought not to be regarded as an ominous Mafia leader but rather should be treated in "conformity with people who have been convicted of a white-collar crime."[18] There now also exists a comic book providing renderings of the histories of the more infamous corporate crimes. The news story reporting its publication is headed "White-Collar Villains."[19] Overseas, a headline in Australia from the *Sydney Morning Herald* points out that the State Attorney-General of New South Wales "Predicts Rapid Increase in White-Collar Crime."[20] Most people, seemingly in most places, now have come to understand the meaning of the designation that Sutherland in this book placed upon perpetrators of a variety of criminal and regulatory offenses that are related to their business or professional position.

Readers who compare the present volume with the 1949 edition will be struck by the sense of authenticity that pervades the unexcised text because of the inclusion of the corporate names and the case histories. The book had been written to highlight such information. Beyond his own assiduous plowing of library materials, Sutherland had gathered

14. Joseph P. Fried, "Judge Assails Alternative Sentencing," *New York Times,* Feb. 21, 1982.

15. Robert Pear, "Smith Seeks Effort on Violent Crimes," *New York Times*, Jan. 16, 1981.

16. Alfonso A. Narvaez, "White-Collar Crime Deterrents Urged," *New York Times,* Dec. 2, 1978.

17. John H. Allan, "The Case of the Albuquerque Eights," *New York Times*, June 11, 1972.

18. Gay Talese, *Honor Thy Father* (New York: World, 1971), p. 479.

19. "New Comic Book Portrays Corporate Crimes," *Arizona Republic,* Feb. 25, 1973.

20. *Sydney Morning Herald,* Feb. 2, 1979.

his data on white-collar crime by hiring graduate students for about
$60 a month from a university grant to record all decisions made against
a corporation or a group of companies. Each decision was copied verba-
tim by the student and sometimes annotated by Sutherland before being placed in an appropriate file. The original materials can still be seen
in the Lilly Library at Indiana University. Not only does this book restore
the Sutherland study to its original state, but the material included per-
mits further investigation of the criminal (or law abiding) careers of the
corporate offenders, perhaps by using data such as those provided
in *Corporate Crime* by Clinard and Peter C. Yeager,[21] and the similar
but briefer documentation of big business violations published by *Fortune.*[22]

Besides the matter of identities and the case histories, there are a
number of minor differences between the shortened version of *White
Collar Crime* and the present text. In the Dryden edition, Sutherland
remarked that he had excluded public utility, transportation, and communications companies from his roster of the top 70 corporations in the
country, as well as "the corporations in one other industry." Here he
identifies that other industry as petroleum; why he altered the original
language is not clear to us. Also, a phrase describing corporations as "rationalistic, a-moral, and non-sentimental" was eliminated from the 1949
version, very likely as part of an attempt to render the book less polemi-
cal.

There are only sparse clues regarding the route by which Sutherland
came to the study of white-collar crime and to the labeling of the topic
that he had chosen to investigate. He was fifty-six years old at the time of
his presidential address to the American Sociological Society. Little in
his earlier work would have prepared the audience for his strong indictment of the practices he discussed. Sutherland was best known at the
time for his writing of a very highly regarded textbook, *Criminology,* and
for tightly argued essays on the need to employ scientific methods for
dealing with criminal offenders. Nor would that earlier work have allowed anticipation of the occasional expressions of indignation and vitu-
peration that he allowed himself when discussing white-collar crime.
Note, for instance, this example from the pages that follow:

21. Marshall B. Clinard and Peter C. Yeager, *Corporate Crime* (New York: Free
Press, 1980).
22. Irwin Ross, "How Lawless are Big Companies?," *Fortune,* Dec. 1, 1980,
57–64.

[T]he utility corporations for two generations or more have engaged in organized propaganda to develop favorable sentiments.
They devoted much attention to the public schools in an effort to
mold the opinion of children. Perhaps no groups except the Nazis
have paid so much attention to indoctrinating the youth of the land
with ideas favorable to a special interest, and it is doubtful whether
even the Nazis were less bound by considerations of honesty in
their propaganda.[23]

This seems surprising from a person who is uniformly described by
those who knew him well as "imbued with sincerity and objectivity,"
"soft-spoken," a man of "paternal wisdom" who "never taught in terms
of sarcasm, ridicule, or abuse."[24] Jerome Hall, a colleague of Sutherland's at Indiana University, observed that Sutherland was "distinguished by an attitude of extraordinary objectivity and thorough inquiry
maintained on a high level" and was an individual who "knew how to
keep his feelings and personality from intruding into the discussion."[25]

Obviously, Sutherland harbored some very deep feelings about white-
collar crime, feelings which he was willing to let loose at times, and feelings that did not mark his other professional work. Some hint that he
was angered by the selfishness and greed he believed underlay white-
collar offenses particularly can be found in correspondence that he exchanged in late 1942 with the secretary-manager of the Hoosier Motor
Club in Indianapolis, a man who had advocated that state residents petition their congressional representatives to vote to postpone national gas
rationing. Sutherland found the arguments put forward in support of
the proposal "absurd" and pointed out that its proponent and those he
represented had a "financial interest in promoting the driving of automobiles," and that they were "placing personal interest ahead of the national interest." In fiery tones, Sutherland concluded:

This is an effort to interfere with the successful prosecution of the
war and is subversive. I feel that the government is entirely justified
in sending the F.B.I. to investigate you. They may find that your action is directed from Berlin, or they may find that it is merely selfish
interest in your own welfare; the effects are the same.[26]

23. Edwin H. Sutherland, *White Collar Crime* (New York: Dryden, 1949), p. 210.
24. Howard Odum, "Edwin H. Sutherland, 1883–1950," *Social Forces*, 29
(1951), 348.
25. Jerome Hall, "Edwin H. Sutherland, 1883–1950," *Journal of Criminal Law
and Criminology*, 41 (1950), 394.
26. Edwin H. Sutherland to Todd Stoops, Nov. 13, 1942.

Sutherland wrote the letter as a private citizen; he did not use Indiana University stationery, and he gave his home address. The secretary-manager replied with a flood of literature and the observation that Sutherland owed him an apology for "probably the most insulting . . . letter I have ever received."[27]

Sutherland quickly recanted on the personal attack, though he did so in a letter which launched a further assault on the motives of the Hoosier Motor Club. "I apologize for the personal reference in my former letter," Sutherland now wrote. "My letter was written in anger against your movement but I know nothing whatever about you as a person and had no justification in making personal statements about you." But he would "retract nothing . . . regarding the organized effort to delay the rationing program" and insisted that when rationing came, as it most surely would, "all of the literature you are distributing will encourage the blackmarkets and crookedness which you so freely predict."[28]

Despite his intense support of government control of gasoline consumption during wartime, Sutherland fundamentally was an advocate of free enterprise. He believed, however, that the government had to regulate economic affairs in order to maintain fair competition. Otherwise, corporations would engage in cutthroat predatory activity to the disadvantage of consumers. Sutherland's economic views are represented in a paragraph in an unpublished article regarding the A & P food stores:

Free enterprise can be maintained in a society only if the economy is controlled by free and fair competition. When free and fair competition breaks down, the society must control by legislation either in the form of regulation or of public ownership. A & P is an illustration of the corporations which have grown big because of profits acquired illegally. If the illegal practices of this corporation continue and expand, they will ruin the independent grocers. . . . A & P . . . has attained its ambition of 25 percent of the grocery trade in many communities. . . . They may raise their sights to 40 percent or 60 percent and then expand to other communities. This would be similar to socialism except that the public would have no

27. Stoops to Sutherland, Nov. 15, 1942.
28. Sutherland to Stoops, Nov. 16, 1942.

voice in the industry. . . . A & P . . . is driving the United States . . .
away from free enterprise into a socialistic economy.[29]

Just as his work on white-collar crime was a striking departure from
both the content and the lack of emotional involvement that marked
Sutherland's earlier work, the term *white-collar crime* itself represented
an initial usage both for Sutherland and for the field of sociology.

In a speech at DePauw University, Sutherland would say that he had
been collecting materials on white-collar crime since 1928,[30] though
there are virtually no published clues to his interest in the subject before
the presidential address. In a 1932 article advocating the use of the concept of *culture* for understanding the crime patterns of immigrants,
Sutherland observed in passing that his idea "certainly does not explain
the financial crimes of the white-collar classes."[31] And in a 1936 book,
written with Harvey J. Locke (one of Sutherland's very few collabora-
tors), the term *white collar worker* is used as a classificatory category to
distinguish those residents of Chicago's shelters for unemployed men
who had been "professional men, business men, clerks, salesmen, accountants, and men who previously held minor political positions."[32]
Obviously the terms *crime* and *white collar* were prominent in Sutherland's professional vocabulary. Their linkage first surfaced in the 1934
edition of Sutherland's textbook in criminology when he used the term
white-collar criminaloid. (*Criminaloid* was a coinage of Edward A.
Ross, employed to designate "those who prosper by flagitious practices
which have not yet come under the effective ban of public opinion."[33])
In the present book Sutherland points out in a footnote that he means
to employ the term *white collar* in the sense that Alfred A. Sloan, Jr. did—
that is, "principally" to refer to business managers and executives.
(Oddly, Sutherland, who was a meticulous scholar in such respects, in-

29. Edwin H. Sutherland, "A & P, Propaganda, and Free Enterprise," unpublished manuscript in possession of Karl Schuessler, Department of Sociology, Indiana University.

30. Edwin H. Sutherland, "Crime of Corporations," in Albert Cohen, Alfred Lindesmith, and Karl Schuessler, eds., *The Sutherland Papers* (Bloomington: Indiana
University Press, 1956), pp. 78–96.

31. Edwin H. Sutherland, "Social Process in Behavior Problems," *Publications of
the American Sociological Society,* 26 (1932), 59–60.

32. Edwin H. Sutherland and Harvey J. Locke, *Twenty Thousand Homeless Men:
A Study of Unemployed Men in Chicago Shelters* (Philadelphia: Lippincott, 1936), p.
62.

33. Edward A. Ross, "The Criminaloid," *Atlantic Monthly,* 99 (1907), 44–50.

correctly cites the title of Sloan's book, which actually was *Adventures of a White Collar Man,* not *An Autobiography of a White Collar Worker.*[34])

The term *white-collar crime* served to focus attention on the social position of the perpetrators and added a bite to commentaries about the illegal acts of businessmen, professionals, and politicians that is notably absent in the blander designations, such as "occupational crime" and "economic crime," that sometimes are employed to refer to the same kinds of lawbreaking that occupied Sutherland's attention. For Sutherland, intent upon both pressing a political viewpoint and invigorating theories of criminal behavior, the phrase *white-collar crime* proved to be a particularly felicitous choice.

What is there in Sutherland's heritage that helps to locate his work on white-collar crime in terms of his time and personal experiences?

Details of Sutherland's family background are readily recaptured. In 1935 his father, a Baptist educator and minister, then eighty-seven years old, completed three book-length manuscripts, one of them an account of his own life. The typescripts were deposited by their author in the library of the Baptist Historical Society in Rochester, New York.

A reading of these materials, as well as Sutherland's own work, indicates that both father and son were intellectually demanding, sharply critical of the work of colleagues which failed to meet their rigorous standards, as well as unstintingly self-critical.[35] Most prominently, there is a religious commitment that, at its best, demands that the ethics of Christianity be maintained in human and business relationships. At times, the tone of Sutherland's work on white-collar crime is reminiscent of the preaching of outraged biblical prophets. There is a theological insistence that something other than strict legal denotation demark the realm of acceptable behavior, a matter that would involve Sutherland in considerable debate with those who adhered more firmly to lawbook codes as the only criteria by which criminological judgments should be made.[36] In the fourth edition of his textbook, *Principles of Criminology,* published in 1947, Sutherland went so far as to argue that

34. Alfred P. Sloan, Jr., and Boyden Sparkes, *Adventures of a White-Collar Man* (New York: Doubleday Doran, 1941).

35. Edwin H. Sutherland, "Critique of Sheldon's *Varieties of Delinquent Youth,*" *American Sociological Review,* 16 (1951), 10–13; George Sutherland, "Reminiscences," manuscript (Rochester, N.Y.: American Baptist Historical Society, 1935), p. 19.

36. Edwin H. Sutherland, "Is 'White-Collar Crime' Crime?" *American Sociological Review,* 10 (1945), 132–39.

the definition of white-collar crime should include behaviors which "are not even a violation of the spirit of the law, for the parties concerned have been able by bribery and other means to prevent the enactment of laws to prohibit wrongful and injurious practices."[37] The abuse of power constitutes for Sutherland a kind of behavior of uppermost importance, deserving of special scrutiny. By Sutherland's account, for example, "a murder committed by a manufacturer in strike-breaking activities would be a white-collar crime."[38]

Sociologist Jon Snodgrass has pointed out that "Edwin Sutherland grew up to love bridge, golf, cigarettes, magazines, movies and jigsaw puzzles," and that he was not particularly religious as an adult, despite his family background. But he remained, Snodgrass notes, "a man of compulsive virtue and integrity. . . . While he may have given up the orthodoxy of his Baptist upbringing, he never lost its scruples."[39] Edwin's father was religious about his Baptist faith; Edwin retained the ethics of his upbringing and became religious about his sociology. *White Collar Crime* fuses these twin elements of Sutherland's personality and patrimony.

We have located only a few hints regarding the nature of the father–son relationship. Relatives testify that George Sutherland was a stern disciplinarian, but they believe that Edwin, something of a favorite, was more indulged than the other children.[40] In one of his writings, Sutherland discusses "professions in which the problem is to control human behavior" and offers as examples of such professions precisely the four occupations his father had followed: "salesmanship, teaching, preaching, and social work."[41] In *White Collar Crime* Sutherland observes caustically that "in the earlier years the religious journals were notorious as accessory to misrepresentation in advertising"; his father several times was responsible for publication of such newspapers, including the *Nebraska Baptist*.[42]

Throughout his life Sutherland was extremely reticent in regard to

37. Edwin H. Sutherland, *Principles of Criminology*, 4th ed. (Philadelphia: Lippincott, 1947), p. 37.
38. Edwin H. Sutherland, "Crime and Business," *Annals of the American Academy of Political and Social Science*, 217 (1941), 112.
39. Jon Snodgrass, "The Gentle and Devout Iconoclast," in Snodgrass, "The American Criminological Tradition: Portraits of Men and Ideology in a Discipline," Ph.D. dissertation, University of Pennsylvania, 1972, p. 223.
40. Ibid.
41. Edwin H. Sutherland, "Crime and the Conflict Process," in Cohen, Lindesmith, and Schuessler, eds., *Sutherland Papers*, p. 109.
42. Sutherland, *White Collar Crime*, p. 126.

discussing personal matters and rarely mentioned his upbringing to associates. At one point, though, in a letter to Luther Bernard, who had been a fellow graduate student at the University of Chicago, Sutherland noted, perhaps sarcastically, that he hoped he would come up to the religious standards at William Jewell College, where he had been employed, since his father was "a praying man and may lead me through the difficulties."[43]

The pattern that shows itself is familiar: a strict father with children who rebel to the extent of casting aside some of the more superficial aspects of the parent's behavior and values. As grown men, Sutherland and his brothers would sneak away from their parents' house during visits in order to enjoy a cigarette, undoubtedly finding the need for secrecy either silly or stupid. But the father's fundamental attitudes and commitments permeated the ethos of the son. At one point, with the bluntness and immodesty that characterized him, George Sutherland said of one of his jobs: "I was asked to withdraw from the teaching force of the college for the reason that my personality was so striking and impressive that no president could stand up against me."[44] Edwin Sutherland would never have lapsed into such public conceit, but the impress of his father's strong personality was bred into him; so were the sense of righteousness and toughness. Psychiatrists might insist that Sutherland's work on white-collar crime contains strong oedipal traces: the hostile son turning against the strong and omnipresent father, represented by the powerful corporations. Be that as it may, there is no questioning that the emotional roots of *White Collar Crime* lie deep in the midwestern soil of Sutherland's early home life.

The independence of the frontiersman also constituted an essential aspect of Sutherland's heritage. In his study of homeless men in Chicago, Sutherland points out how migration from the protective rural countryside into the jungle of the city had been disconcerting for so many shelter residents.[45] Later, he would write that he "loathed Chicago as a place in which to live."[46] The ruses and rudeness, the predation and pitilessness—all must have been unnerving for the Baptist

43. Edwin H. Sutherland to Luther Bernard, Nov. 24, 1912, Luther Bernard Papers, Pennsylvania Historical Collections, Pennsylvania State University, University Park, Pa.

44. G. Sutherland, "Reminiscences," p. 177.

45. Sutherland and Locke, *Twenty Thousand Homeless Men.*

46. Edwin H. Sutherland to Dean Johnson, Mar. 30, 1930, Bureau of Social Hygiene, Rockefeller Foundation Archives, New York.

minister's son from Nebraska when he first came to the big city. The novelist Willa Cather, raised in a Nebraska rural setting in about the same years as Sutherland, would find the city exhilarating. Cather, of course, was different—a creative artist and a lesbian, who found the freedom of metropolitan life liberating. For Sutherland, the immorality and self-interest of impersonal predation, the target of *White Collar Crime,* were singularly identified with the large financial enterprises located in the centers of the big cities.

Sutherland's mixture of rural integrity and self-reliance, his combined fear and scorn of city-bred sophistication, and his zeal for social reform were characteristics he shared with a large number of the early leaders of American sociology. In time, Sutherland was indoctrinated by the prevailing imperatives of the sociological trade into the ethos of "scientific" objectivity. His writings are unsparing in their exposure of the false syllogism, sloppy logic, the unsupported inference, and the generalization rooted in fancy rather than fact. But behind this lay his Nebraska Baptist heritage, a heritage that would break through as well, combining with his scientific imperatives when Sutherland in his later years came to study and to write about white-collar crime.

Most of Edwin Sutherland's formative years, up to the age of twenty-one, were spent in Grand Island, Nebraska. This city, which had a population of about 6,000 in Sutherland's time, owed its original growth to a favorable position as a railroad distribution point. It is located almost in the center of the United States and was founded in 1866 (less than two decades before the Sutherlands arrived), partly in the quixotic belief that its location would persuade the federal government to place the national capital in Grand Island.[47]

Sutherland's great-grandparents had migrated to Canada from Scotland about 1840 and settled in the fishing and lumbering village of St. George, New Brunswick. George Sutherland, Edwin's father, was born there in 1848. In the 1850s depressed economic conditions drove the family to settle on a farm on the outskirts of Eau Claire, Wisconsin. From his mother, George Sutherland acquired a strong religious sense; from his father, a fervid antagonism toward liquor, "the great corrupter of mankind."[48] A maternal uncle, Peter McVicar, may have helped point

47. Federal Writers Project, *Nebraska: A Guide to the Cornhusker State* (New York: Viking Press, 1939), p. 163.
48. G. Sutherland, "Reminiscences," p. 155.

the boy toward education: he was an instructor at Beloit College and
later became president of Washburn College in Topeka, Kansas.

In 1877 Sutherland's father received a divinity degree from the Baptist Union Theological Seminary of the University of Chicago, and in
1881 he was appointed to teach Greek and bookkeeping at the Nebraska
Baptist Seminary in Gibbon, a frontier town in the southeastern part of
the state where Edwin H. Sutherland was born on August 13, 1883.
Less than a year later the family relocated in Kansas. For the next nine
years George Sutherland served as head of the history department at Ot-
tawa College. "It is my judgment," he would later write, "that for a man
who likes books and young people, teaching in a college is the height of
human bliss."[49] The father's point was taken to heart by a number of the
Sutherland children. Edwin, of course, spent his adult life in an academic career. His older brother, Arthur, an educational psychologist,
taught at the University of Illinois, Yale, and the City College of New
York, among other places. A sister, Nellie, became Dean of Women at
Sioux Falls College in South Dakota. George, Jr. served as a pediatrician
on the faculty of Rush Medical College in Philadelphia.

When the Nebraska Baptist Seminary moved in 1893 thirty miles east
to become Grand Island College,[50] George Sutherland became its president. He remained in the position for eighteen years, from 1893 to 1911.
During this period, the college was in incessant financial difficulty, a
predicament that it managed to survive, according to the school historian, only because of the extraordinary energy and personality of its
president.[51] After leaving Grand Island, Sutherland accepted a position
in St. Louis with the Society for the Friendless, a group dedicated to aid-
ing former prison inmates. In 1929, when he was 81, Sutherland again
was named president of Grand Island College. He held that position for
the next two years, until Grand Island was absorbed by Sioux Falls College in South Dakota.

Sutherland mentions his wife only once in the 181 pages of his autobiography. He states that he married Lizzie T. Pickett in 1877 and that she
was from Connecticut (they had met in Chicago), "active in Christian
service," "a good Sunday school teacher," and "one who led the singing

49. Ibid., p. 144.
50. Pauline S. Woodruff, "President George Sutherland: A Tribute," *Grand Island College Advance,* 7 (1929).
51. Herbert E. Hinton, *A Brief History of Grand Island College* (Rochester, N.Y.:
American Baptist Historical Society, 1970), p. 13.

and prayer meetings."[52] That is all that we learn about Edwin's mother from her husband.

The final line of George Sutherland's reminiscences reads: "Perhaps my executors will complete this autobiography by writing here an account of my decease."[53] No one did. George Sutherland died at the age of ninety-five, on December 11, 1943, four years after his son's presidential address on white-collar crime to the American Sociological Society.

Edwin Sutherland received his A.B. degree in 1904 from Grand Island College, while his father was president there. He played football: there is a picture of him in the yearbook in uniform, looking suitably fierce and formidable. He tied for a Rhodes scholarship nomination that ultimately went to his competitor. Immediately after graduation, Sutherland went to Sioux Falls College, Grand Island's sister Baptist institution, where he taught Greek, Latin, and shorthand.

While he was at Sioux Falls, a stay that lasted from 1904 to 1906, Sutherland enrolled in a correspondence course through the Home Study Department of the University of Chicago. The course was in sociology, a prerequisite for graduate study in history, the field Sutherland intended to pursue. It was taught by Annie Marion MacLean, a Chicago Ph.D. with a strong activist bent. She had worked as a hop picker in Oregon, as a department store clerk in Chicago, and as an employee in a New York sweat shop while carrying out research on the working conditions of women.[54]

In the summer of 1906 Sutherland took up residence at the University of Chicago, enrolling in three courses in the Divinity School: "Introduction to the Books of the New Testament," "Outlines of Church History," and "Psychology of Conduct." MacLean prevailed upon him to register also for "Social Treatment of Crime," offered by Charles R. Henderson. In short order, Sutherland changed his academic emphasis to sociology and began that interest in criminal behavior that was to culminate in his study of white-collar crime. Sutherland's explanation of his change in major subject anticipates the close relationships that he himself would form with some outstanding graduate students who later worked with him:

52. G. Sutherland, "Reminiscences," p. 100.
53. Ibid., p. 181.
54. Virginia K. Fish, "Annie Marion MacLean: A Neglected Part of the Chicago School," *Journal of the History of Sociology*, 3 (1981), 54.

> When I entered Dr. Henderson's course, I received personal attention. He spoke to me, knew me, was interested in me. Consequently, I was interested in pursuing sociology, and interested in the type of sociology that Professor Henderson presented.[55]

Henderson, a Baptist minister turned sociologist, was a man much in the image of Sutherland's father. It is noteworthy that the textbook that was used in the class, written by Henderson, contains material that Sutherland himself would echo more than thirty years later when setting forth his views about white-collar crime. Note, for instance, the following pronouncement:

> The social classes of the highest culture furnish few convicts, yet there are educated criminals. Advanced culture modifies the form of crime; tends to make it less coarse and violent, but more cunning; restricts it to quasi-legal forms. But education also opens up the way to new and colossal kinds of crime, as debauching of conventions, councils, legislatures, and bribery of the press and public officials. The egoistic impulses are masked and disguised in this way, the devil wearing the livery of heavenly charity for a cloak of wrong. Many of the "Napoleons" of trade are well named, for they are cold-blooded robbers and murderers, utterly indifferent to the inevitable misery which they must know will follow their contrivances and deals.[56]

From 1909 to 1911 Sutherland returned to Grand Island College to teach sociology and psychology; in 1911, he went back to Chicago for two years to finish his degree. Ultimately, Sutherland became disenchanted with the Chicago sociology department, whose members, he thought, were too intent upon constructing postulates about social existence without having become adequately immersed in the problems they were addressing.

In the end, Sutherland's intellectual commitment came to rest in the department of political economy. He signed up for a course with Thorstein Veblen, a man who had passed the biting judgment that the ideal captain of industry was like the ideal delinquent "in his unscrupulous conversion of goods and persons to his own ends, and a callous disregard of the feelings and wishes of others, and of the remoter effects of his ac-

55. Sutherland to Bernard, July 13, 1927.
56. Charles R. Henderson, *Introduction to the Study of Dependent, Defective, and Delinquent Classes,* 2d ed. (Boston: D. C. Heath, 1901), p. 250.

tions."[57] Veblen assuredly would have fueled whatever latent critical impulses about big business Sutherland held, but he left Chicago for Stanford before the semester began. Sutherland's closest intellectual and personal affiliation in political economy was formed with Robert Hoxie (1868–1916), a labor historian and Veblen protégé with a "suspicion of large and comfortable truths," a man who was said to have possessed "the keenest and most rigorous mind that has ever worked upon the problems of labor organizations."[58] Sutherland later would write that Hoxie "exerted more constructive influence in determining my thinking than did any of the sociologists."[59] What appealed to Sutherland about Hoxie was his "desire to understand" and his ability to "discover the truth and exhibit it so that it could not help but be recognized."[60]

Although Henderson was the adviser for Sutherland's Ph.D. work, it was Hoxie who primarily carried out the supervision since Henderson was in India at the time. Done in conjunction with the Chicago Commission on Unemployment, the dissertation was titled "Unemployment and Public Employment Agencies." Sutherland, at least in correspondence, dismissed it as "a very poor thing" and hoped that for the final examination "Henderson will not read it any more thoroughly than he reads the books he reviews."[61] His reservations notwithstanding, Sutherland was awarded his Ph.D. magna cum laude, with a major in both sociology and political economy.

Sutherland took a teaching position in the sociology department at William Jewell College in Liberty, Missouri, a Baptist institution, where he remained for six years, from 1913 to 1919. At William Jewell he occupied the John E. Franklin Chair, established by a St. Louis banker in 1913 to foster Christian socialism. The college president preferred an ecclesiastical sociologist to a socialist. Sutherland satisfied neither donor nor president. "I am going there," he wrote Luther Bernard, "to do work which the founder of the chair wants to make socialist, which the President wants to make political evangelism, and which I wish to use as a source of income and promotion."[62]

57. Thorstein Veblen, *The Theory of the Leisure Class* (New York: Macmillan, 1912), p. 237.
58. Carter Goodrich, "Robert Franklin Hoxie," *Encyclopedia of the Social Sciences*, 1937, pp. 524–25.
59. Sutherland to Bernard, July 13, 1927.
60. Sutherland to Bernard, July 11, 1916.
61. Sutherland to Bernard, May 17, 1913.
62. Sutherland to Bernard, Nov. 24, 1912.

In 1915 Sutherland wrote to Bernard along the same lines about some of his extracurricular activity at William Jewell:

I have been having a little publicity lately: I addressed the Kansas City ministers on unemployment, and the Kansas City Socialists on "Criticism of Marxism Theory of Class Conflict." I received the same treatment the ordinary church congregation would accord a person who stood up and attempted to convince them of the fallacy of belief in the virgin birth of Christ.[63]

Sutherland published only one article during his six years at William Jewell, "What Rural Health Surveys Have Revealed," in the June 1916 issue of the *Monthly Bulletin of the State Board of Charities and Corrections*. Perhaps much of his time was occupied with courtship. Sutherland married Myrtle Crews, his landlady's daughter, in May 1918. There was a substantial discrepancy in their education at the time, but Sutherland's wife later finished her bachelor degree with Phi Beta Kappa honors. The couple would have one child, Betty, who married Anthony B. Sand, a Rexall executive in Los Angeles, and in turn had a daughter, Laura.

After leaving William Jewell, Sutherland engaged in something of a Cook's tour of Big Ten universities. His first stop was the University of Illinois (1919–26). The Illinois chairman, E. C. Hayes ("too much of a clergyman," Sutherland's predecessor in the department said of him[64]), turned Sutherland's attention from labor problems to criminology. Hayes edited the sociology list for Lippincott, and he asked Sutherland to write a criminology textbook. That book, *Criminology*, published in 1924, came to dominate the field and is currently in its tenth edition (having been revised by Donald Cressey following Sutherland's death).

Minnesota, where Sutherland taught for the following three years (1926–29), was then regarded as the fourth leading sociology department in the country, behind Chicago, Columbia, and Wisconsin.[65] Sutherland, now a full professor, served as acting chair in 1926, when F. Stuart Chapin went on leave, and a department already rent by internal dissension deteriorated further under Sutherland's lightly held reins.[66]

63. Sutherland to Bernard, Mar. 8, 1915.
64. Personal interview, Colin Goff with Stuart Queen, San Diego, Nov. 8, 1980.
65. Don Martindale, *The Romance of a Profession* (St. Paul, Minn.: Windflower Publishing Co., 1976), p. 56.
66. Ibid., p. 62.

Sutherland's scholarly work at Minnesota largely emphasized the theme that scientific research must undergird treatment procedures for criminal offenders. A complete personality profile and a thorough determination of the circumstances that gave rise to the illegal behavior had to be accomplished before deciding what to do with a law violator. A general faith in the necessity and the efficacy of science for remedying social ills permeates Sutherland's writings of the period.[67]

There was thereafter a year (1929–30) of work for the Bureau of Social Hygiene in New York City. In the summer of 1930 Sutherland visited six prisons in England (as well as others in Western Europe and Scandinavia) for the bureau and provided a sketch of how the facilities looked and how they were run. He concluded that the differences between English and American prisons "are not nearly as great as the difference between the English public and the American public."[68]

That fall, Sutherland accepted an offer from the University of Chicago. His main assignment was to carry out funded research. In his early years at Chicago he worked on investigations of "The Fix" as a cause of crime, fining practices in Chicago, and the development of a library of case studies of delinquents. Thereafter, his work focused on topics which led to such publications as *The Professional Thief* and *Twenty Thousand Homeless Men.*

Sutherland left Chicago in 1935, enigmatically explaining his departure in a letter to a friend as the result of "certain distractions."[69] Indiana University, his next post, was to be his base for the following fifteen years, until his death. It was there that he carried out the research that led to *White Collar Crime.* Summer excursions were taken to teach at the University of Washington in 1942 and at San Diego State College in 1950. At Washington, in the midst of the Second World War, Sutherland had the courage to tell a reporter from the student newspaper that he believed the evacuation of the Japanese from the West Coast had "resulted more from race prejudice than from military needs."[70]

Sutherland was the first head of the Indiana sociology department,

67. See, e.g., "The Person Versus the Act in Criminology," *Cornell Law Quarterly,* 14 (1929), 162.
68. Edwin H. Sutherland, "Observations on European Prisons," unpublished manuscript in possession of Schuessler, 1930, p. 14.
69. Edwin H. Sutherland to C. Dunhey, May 7, 1935, Bureau of Social Hygiene, Rockefeller Foundation Archives, New York.
70. "Campus Impresses Sutherland," *The Daily,* University of Washington, Seattle, Aug. 6, 1942, 1.

which had been organized in 1935. He was regarded as something of an elder statesman, much beloved by a cadre of graduate students to whom he imparted an intense pleasure in learning. He was an outstanding seminar instructor; some of his seminar students remember particularly Sutherland's ruthless critiques of theoretical writings in criminology, including his own, as well as his ability to involve them intensely in a sense of intellectual discovery. Albert K. Cohen, himself later to become a preeminent sociologist, recalls his seminar experience with Sutherland:

It was not only that we felt that *Sutherland* was at the frontier; we felt that *we* were at the frontier. Although most of us were just beginning graduate students, we felt that we were participating in this work of pushing back the frontiers. I believe that any of Sutherland's students of those days will tell you that Sutherland, for all of his tenacity of views, was never overbearing, never didactic, never arrogant. He invariably treated his students with respect, never humiliated them, always made them feel that we were partners in a quest.[71]

Death came to Sutherland in the late morning of October 11, 1950, when he collapsed from a stroke suffered while he was walking to work. When he fell, his head struck a concrete pathway, causing severe injury. He died en route to the hospital.

Sutherland's monograph on white-collar crime was the publishing highlight of the 1940s in criminology. A survey completed in 1978 of the 100 most cited writers in the field indicated that Sutherland's book was regarded as "the most important contribution" made in that ten-year period.[72] The reviews of the book at the time of its appearance recognized its strength and uniqueness. Hermann Mannheim, a German emigré teaching at the University of London, called *White Collar Crime* "a milestone" and believed that it "should become the starting point of a new line of research." Mannheim lauded Sutherland's "ingenuity, persistence, and courage in studying and exposing [white-collar crime's] meaning, extent, and danger to society," adding that this "deserved every praise."[73] Selden Bacon, writing in the *American Sociological Re-*

71. Albert K. Cohen to Jon Snodgrass, Sept. 7, 1971.
72. Marvin E. Wolfgang, Robert M. Figlio, and Terence P. Thornberry, *Evaluating Criminology* (New York: Elsevier, 1978).
73. Hermann Mannheim, "White Collar Crime," *Annals of the American Academy of Political and Social Science*, 266 (1949), 244.

view, called the book "daring" in its challenge to the "arbiters of the alleged science of criminology."[74] In the *Harvard Law Review* Robert Sorenson, a law professor at the University of Nebraska, considered Sutherland's work "a deadly exposé of a way of life which society complacently accepts" and believed that the book deserved "excited promotion rather than mere reviewing."[75]

What have been some of the impacts of *White Collar Crime* since its initial appearance? Three major contributions might be noted: First, the swirling controversy about the proper definition of the subject matter, which helped refine the scientific boundaries of the realm of white-collar crime; second, the accumulation of scholarly work spurred by Sutherland's pioneering monograph; and third, the vigorous debate about the causes of crime, which was raised to a much higher level of sophistication by Sutherland's work.

The debate about a suitable definition of white-collar crime was highlighted in Sutherland's time by the views of Paul W. Tappan, a sociologist with extensive training in law. Tappan believed that white-collar crime studies would have to draw sharper distinctions between criminal and civil law and would have to determine whether white-collar crime was to be based upon the social class of the offender, the inherent wrongfulness of the act, the violation of law, the consequences of the behavior, or the motive for the violation.

Tappan had submitted an article, "Who is the Criminal?," to the *American Journal of Sociology* during the summer of 1946 outlining his views. The journal editor dispatched the paper to Sutherland for review. Sutherland deplored Tappan's idea that only convicted persons ought to be called "criminals" and studied as such, insisting that "conviction is important from the point of view of the authority of public agencies to administer punishment. It is not important as a definition of criminal behavior."[76] He thought that the article did not make a significant contribution, but he stressed that he was personally involved in the intellectual dispute it addressed and hoped that the editor would seek additional appraisals of the piece. Tappan's article was rejected by the *AJS* but gained publication in the *American Sociological Review.*[77]

74. Selden D. Bacon, "White Collar Crime," *American Sociological Review,* 15 (1950), 310.

75. Robert C. Sorenson, "White Collar Crime," *Harvard Law Review,* 41 (1950), 80.

76. Sutherland, "Is 'White-Collar Crime' Crime?"

77. Paul W. Tappan, "Who is the Criminal?," *American Sociological Review,* 12 (1947), 96–102.

Disputation over the proper definition of white-collar crime continues to surface in scholarly work on the subject. Some persons, particularly outside the United States, employ terms such as *economic crime* and *occupational crime* to cover behaviors equivalent to white-collar offenses. The United Nations uses the designation "abuse of power." But there is no gainsaying that by coining the phrase *white-collar crime* Sutherland created a label that now has become readily understood in a general sense, by both the public and politicians, and has established a rallying point for reform efforts directed at corruption, commercial exploitation, and the wide range of other acts examined in the present book.

Sutherland's *White Collar Crime,* as we have noted, also prompted a number of studies in its immediate wake, work that was carried out largely by his students and younger colleagues. Then, for a considerable period, there was a hiatus. The conservative tinge of the political climate may explain the absence of significant research on white-collar crime during this period. Another reason probably can be found in the priorities of sociology, the academic discipline under which criminology is subsumed. Sociology went through a long period in which highly quantitative, supposedly value-free empirical investigation was prized: white-collar crime studies do not readily lend themselves to the mathematical manipulations that mark articles in major sociological journals.

Nonetheless, the relative neglect of study of white-collar crime for so long a time remains puzzling, especially in light of the common belief that many persons are drawn to sociological research out of reformist zeal. Karl Schuessler has suggested that the affluence of American society undermined concern with white-collar crime, a hypothesis that merits scrutiny. Perhaps, having lain dormant for so long, the subject needed an economic downswing for the kind of strong revival that it now is experiencing. The increased personnel in social science research also may be related to the renewed focus on white-collar crime as scholars seek to cultivate intellectual fields that have not yet been adequately harvested. The prod of Marxist criminology assuredly also has given credence to a critical posture toward persons in powerful positions in the society and the arrangements that got and keep them there.[78] The work of Ralph Nader also has demonstrated the feasibility of gathering telling information about white-collar crimes.[79]

78. David M. Gordon, "Capitalism, Class, and Crime in America," *Crime and Delinquency,* 19 (1973), 163–86.

79. See, e.g., Ralph Nader and Mark Green, eds., *Corporate Power in America* (New York: Grossman, 1973).

It is difficult to determine the interaction between scholarly emphasis and public policy; but there is no questioning that there recently has been a change in priorities at the federal level toward increased concern with white-collar violations. Perhaps the surest sign was the decision by the Federal Bureau of Investigation to downgrade efforts to solve offenses such as bank robbery in order to concentrate more intensively on frauds, corruption, and the violations of federal statutes that are designed to control the behavior of members of the more "respectable" elements of society. The enforcement rankings established by the Department of Justice now give preeminence to acts such as "crimes against the government by public officials, including federal, state, and local corruption," and "crimes against consumers, including defrauding of consumers, antitrust violations, energy pricing violations, and related illegalities."[80]

In regard to theory, the introduction of the concept of white-collar crime into the study of criminal behavior revolutionized the thinking of the field by making it no longer possible to employ class-specific explanations to interpret such behavior. Through the years, sundry scholars in passing had, of course, had their say about the kinds of acts and the kinds of people Sutherland would denominate under the heading of white-collar crime. We have noted, for instance, the comments by Ross and Henderson. Albert Morris, a criminologist writing before Sutherland's work on white-collar crime, also had pointed the finger at the "criminals of the upperworld," persons "whose social position, intelligence, and criminal technique permit them to move among their fellow citizens virtually immune to recognition and prosecution as criminals."[81] Writers in other disciplines, such as law and economics, also were well aware of the depredations of the powerful.

Sutherland, however, brought these general views together into a single package and put forward a variety of interpretative ideas concerning the behaviors. Many of these ideas provide guidelines for further research and writing. Take, for instance, Sutherland's generalization that "the practice of politics is more honest than the conduct of business," with the corollary suggestion that "political graft almost always involves collusion between politicians and businessmen, but prosecutions are

80. U.S. Attorney General, *National Priorities for the Investigation and Prosecution of White Collar Crime: Report of the Attorney General* (Washington, D.C.: U.S. Government Printing Office, 1980).

81. Albert Morris, *Criminology* (New York: Longmans, Green, 1935), p. 153.

generally limited to the politicians."[82] More detailed work tied to many of Sutherland's postulations is only beginning to be carried out today: the press toward such work remains a major contribution of Sutherland's pathbreaking effort.

Broken homes, absent fathers, poor education, and similar presumptive factors could no longer, after *White Collar Crime,* be said to produce lawbreaking. It had always been known, of course, although rarely appreciated, that very many persons who suffered from such conditions lived law-abiding existences. Sutherland had added the fact that white-collar offenders, who are much less likely to suffer from such presumptive handicaps, themselves commit a goodly amount of crime. In Sutherland's time, unrestricted immigration was the whipping boy of criminologists. It was often claimed that the "flood" of aliens into America endangered the resident population. Sutherland's work on white-collar crime alerted people to the idea that danger lay equally as much with the resident population, particularly those in positions of power. Such individuals and their corporate employers were exploiting immigrants at the same time that they were denigrating them. Wages below permissible limits, unsafe working conditions, illegal union-breaking tactics—all these were crimes with consequences more severe than those street offenses which preoccupied public concern.

Sutherland's theoretical notions, and his illustrations of them from the realm of white-collar crime, tended to turn attention from such factors as poverty, often said to be directly causal of criminal conduct. It is sometimes maintained that an end to impoverishment and reduction of the unemployment rate would have a dramatic impact on the rate of crime. Sutherland would not have been so sanguine. These social goals ought to be pursued on their own merits, he undoubtedly would argue, but not in the expectation that they will significantly affect the amount of criminal activity. The root causes of crime, his white-collar investigations insist, lie within the values of the social system. Two persons who are ambitious and thwarted will respond differently: one will steal, the other will get an extra job or perhaps will do without. What such persons have learned from those with whom they associate (and more fundamentally from the culture of their society) will determine which of these paths they choose. Opportunity and possible consequences undoubtedly will play a part in determining their choice, but opportunity for crime

82. Sutherland, "The White-Collar Criminal," pp. 3–4.

often knocks, and the likelihood of apprehension and penalty rarely is very strong. In some societies, nonetheless, huge percentages of people will not consider violating the law, as regards either white-collar or street offenses; in others, equally large percentages will commit crimes whenever a reasonable occasion offers itself.

These are basic ideas that emerge from Sutherland's work on white-collar crime. They are not altogether popular, because they frustrate the social reformer; indeed, the implications of Sutherland's materials probably made their author uncomfortable, given his stress on social reform through sophisticated research. There is not much that can readily be done to alter the fundamental values of a social system, and even what can be done likely will produce only very gradual results at best.

For Sutherland, recent developments in regard to white-collar crime undoubtedly would have been a matter of personal satisfaction. Our review of Sutherland's background, as well as the panegyrics of his colleagues and former students, stresses his dedication to a search for truth and describes a man noted for his decency, integrity, and compassion. His work on white-collar crime—his very invention of the term—is deeply and strongly rooted in our intellectual soil. Mannheim, the distinguished British criminologist, has written that if there were a Nobel Prize in criminology, Sutherland undoubtedly would have been awarded it for his work on white-collar crime.[83] It is a well-earned tribute and a fitting introduction to the monograph that follows.

83. Hermann Mannheim, *Comparative Criminology* (London: Routledge & Kegan Paul, 1965), p. 470.

PART I

INTRODUCTION

1

THE PROBLEM OF WHITE COLLAR CRIME

Criminal statistics show unequivocally that crime, as popularly understood and officially measured, has a high incidence in the lower socioeconomic class and a low incidence in the upper socioeconomic class.
Crime, as thus understood, includes the ordinary violations of the penal
code, such as murder, assault, burglary, robbery, larceny, sex offenses,
and public intoxication, but does not include traffic violations. Persons
who are accused or convicted of these ordinary crimes are dealt with by
the police, juvenile or criminal courts, probation departments, and cor-
rectional institutions.

The concentration of crimes, as conventionally understood, in the
lower socioeconomic class has been demonstrated by two types of research studies. First, the analysis of case histories of offenders and of
their parents shows a high incidence of poverty in such cases. Sheldon
and Eleanor Glueck studied 1,000 juvenile delinquents who had appeared before the juvenile courts of Greater Boston, 500 young-adult
males who had been committed to the State Reformatory of Massachusetts, and 500 women who had been committed to the Massachusetts
Reformatory for Women. The economic status of the parents in these
three series of offenders is presented in Table 1. This shows that 76.3
percent of the offenders in one series and 91.3 percent in the series at
the other extreme were below the level of comfort, which was defined as
possession of sufficient surplus to enable a family to maintain itself for
four months of unemployment without going on relief. Other data in
these studies of the families of offenders show a high incidence of unemployment, of mothers engaged in remunerative occupations, of fathers
in unskilled and semiskilled occupations, and of parents who lacked formal education; they show, also, that a large proportion of the offenders
left school at an early age to engage in gainful occupations.[1]

The United States Bureau of the Census made an analysis of the eco-

3

Table 1. Percentage Distribution of Three Series of Offenders by
Economic Status of Parental Families

Economic status	1,000 juvenile delinquents	500 young-adult male delinquents	500 women delinquents
Dependent	8.1	14.8	13.3
Marginal	68.2	56.4	78.0
Comfortable	23.7	28.8	8.7
Total	100.0	100.0	100.0

nomic status and earnings of persons committed to state and federal prisons and reformatories in 1923. The usual weekly earnings of these prisoners prior to commitment are shown in Table 2. This indicates that 60.1 percent of the males and 92.1 percent of the females who were committed to prisons in 1923 had previous weekly earnings of less than $30.[2] Other evidence in this report, similarly, supports the conclusion that crimes are concentrated in the lower economic class.

The second method of demonstrating the concentration of crimes in the lower socioeconomic class is by statistical analysis of the residential areas of offenders; this is ordinarily called the "ecological distribution of offenders." Shaw and McKay have analyzed the data regarding residences of juvenile delinquents and adult criminals in twenty cities in the United States. In each of these cities the offenders are concentrated in areas of poverty. In Chicago the correlation between boy delinquency cases and families on relief by square mile areas is $+.89 \pm .01$. Boy delinquency is positively correlated by high coefficients with unemployment and buildings condemned as unsafe for residence, and negatively with rentals; also boy delinquency shows a high correlation with girl delinquency, with young-adult male delinquency, and with adult delinquency.[3]

The scholars who have stated general theories of criminal behavior

Table 2. Percentage Distribution of Persons
Committed to State and Federal Prisons in 1923 by
Sex of Offenders and by Usual Weekly Earnings

Weekly earnings ($)	Male	Female
Under 10	4.6	27.3
10–19	25.0	53.0
20–29	30.5	11.8
30 and over	39.9	7.9
Total	100.0	100.0

have used statistics such as those outlined above and individual case histories from which these statistics are compiled. Since these cases are concentrated in the lower socioeconomic class, the theories of criminal behavior have placed much emphasis on poverty as the cause of crime or on other social conditions and personal traits which are assumed to be associated with poverty. The assumption in these theories is that criminal behavior can be explained only by pathological factors, either social or personal. The social pathologies which have been emphasized are poverty and, related to it, poor housing, lack of organized recreations, lack of education, and disruptions in family life. The personal pathologies which have been suggested as explanations of criminal behavior were, at first, biological abnormalities; when research studies threw doubt on the validity of these biological explanations, the next explanation was intellectual inferiority, and more recently emotional instability. Some of these scholars believed that the personal pathologies were inherited and were the cause of the poverty as well as of the criminal behavior, while others believed that the personal pathologies were produced by poverty, and that this personal pathology contributed to the perpetuation of the poverty and of the related social pathologies.

The thesis of this book is that these social and personal pathologies are not an adequate explanation of criminal behavior. The general theories of criminal behavior which take their data from poverty and the conditions related to it are inadequate and invalid, first, because the theories do not consistently fit the data of criminal behavior; and, second, because the cases on which these theories are based are a biased sample of all criminal acts. These two defects are elaborated in the following paragraphs.

First, many of the facts regarding criminal behavior cannot be explained by poverty and its related pathologies. (a) The statistics of juvenile courts show at the present time that in the United States approximately 85 percent of the juveniles adjudged delinquent are boys and only 15 percent girls. The boys and girls of the United States are equally in poverty, come equally from homes with inadequate houses, are equally lacking in recreational facilities, are equal in intelligence tests and in emotional stability. With the approximate equality of the two sexes in these respects, poverty and its related pathologies obviously cannot explain the difference in the delinquency rates of the two sexes. (b) Many groups on the frontiers have been in extreme poverty but, nevertheless, have had low rates of juvenile delinquency and adult crime. (c) Many groups residing in slum areas of cities are in great poverty but have low rates of juvenile and adult delinquency, as illustrated by the Chinese colonies. (d) Certain immigrant groups have migrated from peasant communities in Europe, where they had high crime rates with perhaps less poverty than in their peasant communities.[4] (e) Studies of the relation between crime rates and the business cycle have shown no significant association or a very slight association between depressions and crime rates in general, and no significant association between depressions and the crimes against property.[5] These conclusions regarding crime and the business cycle, when considered in connection with the ecological studies, raise the question, Why does poverty, when distributed spatially by areas of a city, show a strikingly uniform and high association with crime, but when distributed chronologically in business cycles show a slight and inconsistent association with crime? The answer is that the causal factor is not poverty, in the sense of economic need, but the social and interpersonal relations which are associated sometimes with poverty and sometimes with wealth, and sometimes with both.

The second respect in which the conventional explanations of criminal behavior are invalid is their basis on biased statistics. This has two aspects: (a) Persons of the upper socioeconomic class are more powerful politically and financially and escape arrest and conviction to a greater extent than persons who lack such power. Wealthy persons can employ skilled attorneys and in other ways can influence the administration of justice in their own favor more effectively than can persons of the lower socioeconomic class. Even professional criminals, who have financial and political power, escape arrest and conviction more effectively than amateur and occasional criminals who have little financial or political power.[6] This bias, while indubitable, is not of great importance from the theoretical point of view.

(b) And much more important is the bias involved in administration of criminal justice under laws which apply exclusively to business and the professions and which therefore involve only the upper socioeconomic class. Persons who violate laws regarding restraint of trade, advertising, pure food and drugs, and similar business practices are not arrested by uniformed policemen, are not tried in criminal courts, and are not committed to prisons; their illegal behavior receives the attention of administrative commissions and of courts operating under civil or equity jurisdiction. For this reason such violations of law are not included in the criminal statistics nor are individual cases brought to the attention of the scholars who write the theories of criminal behavior. The sample of criminal behavior on which the theories are founded is biased as to socioeconomic status, since it excludes these business and professional men. The bias is quite as certain as it would be if the scholars selected only red-haired criminals for study and reached the conclusion that redness of hair was the cause of crime.

The thesis of this book, stated positively, is that persons of the upper socioeconomic class engage in much criminal behavior; that this criminal behavior differs from the criminal behavior of the lower socioeconomic class principally in the administrative procedures which are used in dealing with the offenders; and that variations in administrative procedures are not significant from the point of view of causation of crime. The causes of tuberculosis were not different when it was treated by poultices and bloodletting than when treated by streptomycin.

These violations of law by persons in the upper socioeconomic class are, for convenience, called "white collar crimes." This concept is not intended to be definitive, but merely to call attention to crimes which are not ordinarily included within the scope of criminology. White collar crime may be defined approximately as a crime committed by a person of respectability and high social status in the course of his occupation.[7] Consequently it excludes many crimes of the upper class such as most cases of murder, intoxication, or adultery, since these are not a part of the occupational procedures. Also, it excludes the confidence games of wealthy members of the underworld, since they are not persons of respectability and high social status.

The significant thing about white collar crime is that it is not associated with poverty or with social and personal pathologies which accompany poverty. If it can be shown that white collar crimes are frequent, a general theory that crime is due to poverty and its related pathologies is shown to be invalid. Furthermore, the study of white collar crime may assist in locating those factors which, being common to the crimes of the rich and the poor, are most significant for a general theory of criminal behavior.

A great deal of scattered and unorganized material indicates that white collar crimes are very prevalent. The "robber barons" of the last half of the nineteenth century were white collar criminals, as practically everyone now agrees. Their behavior was illustrated by such statements as the following. Colonel Vanderbilt asked, "You don't suppose you can run a railway in accordance with the statutes, do you?" A. B. Stickney, a railroad president, said to sixteen other railroad presidents in the home of J. P. Morgan in 1890, "I have the utmost respect for you gentlemen individually, but as railroad presidents, I wouldn't trust you with my watch out of my sight." Charles Francis Adams said, "One difficulty in railroad management . . . lies in the covetousness, want of good faith, low moral tone of railway managers, in the complete absence of any high standard of commercial honesty." James M. Beck said in regard to the period 1905–17, "Diogenes would have been hard put to it to find an honest man in the Wall Street which I knew as a corporation attorney."

The present-day white collar criminals are more suave and less forthright than the robber barons of the last century but not less criminal. Criminality has been demonstrated again and again in reports of investigations of land offices, railways, insurance, munitions, banking, public utilities, stock exchanges, the petroleum industry, the real estate industry, receiverships, bankruptcies, and politics. When the airmail contracts were canceled because of graft, Will Rogers said, "I hope they don't stop every industry where they find crookedness at the top," and Elmer Davis said, "If they are going to stop every industry where they find crookedness at the top they will have to stop them all." The Federal Trade Commission reported in 1920 that commercial bribery was a prevalent and common practice in many industries. In certain chain stores the net shortage in weight was sufficient to pay 3.4 percent on the investment, while no net shortage in weights was found in independent stores and cooperative stores. The Comptroller of the Currency reported in 1908 that violations of banking laws were found in 75 percent of the banks examined in a three-month period. Lie detector tests of all employees in certain Chicago banks, supported in almost all cases by subsequent confessions, showed that 20 percent of them had stolen bank property, and lie detector tests of a cross-section sample of the employees of a chain store showed approximately 75 percent had stolen money or merchandise from the store.[8] Investigators for the *Reader's Digest* in 1941 drove into a garage with a defect in the car, artificially produced for this experiment, for which a proper charge would be 25 cents, and learned that 75 percent of the garages misrepresented the defect and the work which was done; the average charge was $4 and some garages charged as much as $25. Similar frauds were found in the watch-repair and the typewriter-repair businesses.[9]

White collar crime in politics, which is popularly supposed to be very prevalent, has been used by some persons as a rough gauge by which to measure white collar crime in business. James A. Farley, who had experience both in business and in politics, said, "The standards of conduct are as high among office-holders and politicians as they are in commercial life." Cermak, mayor of Chicago and a businessman, said, "There is less graft in politics than in business." John Flynn wrote, "The average politician is the merest amateur in the gentle art of graft compared with his brother in the field of business." And Walter Lippmann wrote, "Poor as they are, the standards of public life are so much more social than those of business that financiers who enter politics regard themselves as philanthropists."

In the medical profession, which is used here as an example because it is probably less criminal than other professions, are found illegal sale of alcohol and narcotics, abortion, illegal services to underworld criminals, fraudulent reports and testimony in accident cases, extreme instances of unnecessary treatment and surgical operations, fake specialists, restriction of competition, and fee splitting. Fee splitting, for instance, is a violation of a specific law in many states and a violation of the conditions of admission to the profession in all states. The physician who participates in fee splitting tends to send his patients to the surgeon who will give the largest fee rather than to the surgeon who will do the best work. The report has been made that two-thirds of the surgeons in New York split fees and that more than half of the physicians in a central western state who answered a questionnaire on this point favored fee splitting.

The financial cost of white collar crime is probably several times as great as the financial cost of all the crimes which are customarily regarded as the "crime problem." An officer of a chain grocery store in one year embezzled $800,000, which was six times as much as the annual losses from 500 burglaries and robberies of the stores in that chain. Public enemies numbered one to six secured $130,000 by burglary and robbery in 1938, while the sum stolen by Krueger is estimated at $250 million, or nearly 2,000 times as much. The *New York Times* in 1931 reported four cases of embezzlement in the United States with a loss of more than $1 million each and a combined loss of $9 million. Although a million dollar burglar or robber is practically unheard of, the million dollar embezzler is a small-fry among white collar criminals. The estimated loss to investors in one investment trust from 1929 to 1935 was $580 million, due primarily to the fact that 75 percent of the values in the portfolio were in securities of affiliated companies, although the investment house advertised the importance of diversification in investments and its expert services in selecting safe investments. The claim was made in Chicago about 1930 that householders lost $54 million in two years during the administration of a city sealer who granted immunity from inspection to stores which provided Christmas baskets for his constituents. This financial loss from white collar crime, great as it is, is less important than the damage to social relations. White collar crimes violate trust and therefore create distrust, and this lowers social morale and produces social disorganization on a large scale. Ordinary crimes, on the other hand, produce little effect on social institutions or social organization.

Statements such as those made above do little more than provide a justification for further investigation. Obviously they are not precise. For that reason, a detailed investigation of violations of certain laws by a sample of the large corporations has been made and is reported in the following chapters.

PART II

RECORDS OF SEVENTY LARGE CORPORATIONS

2

THE STATISTICAL RECORD

In order to secure more definite information regarding the crimes of persons of the upper socioeconomic class, an attempt has been made to tabulate the decisions of courts and administrative commissions against the 70 largest manufacturing, mining, and mercantile corporations. The 70 largest corporations used in this analysis are, with two exceptions, included in each of two lists of the 200 largest nonfinancial corporations in the United States. One of these lists was prepared by Berle and Means in 1929 and the other by the Temporary National Economic Committee in 1938. From these lists were excluded the public utility corporations, including transportation and communications corporations, and also the petroleum corporations. This left 68 corporations common to both lists. To these were added two corporations which appeared in the list for 1938 but not in the list for 1929. One of these was Standard Brands, which was organized by the merger of preexisting corporations in 1929 and had grown to the dimensions of the other large corporations by 1938. The other was Gimbel Brothers, which was not far below the other corporations in 1929, and which was added to the present list in order to secure a larger representation of mercantile corporations. The list of 70 corporations is, therefore, unselected except as to size and type of specialization, with the two exceptions mentioned, and neither of these exceptions was selected with knowledge of its rank among large corporations as to violations of laws.

The present analysis covers the life careers of the 70 corporations. The average life of these corporations is approximately 45 years, but decisions as to the date of origin are arbitrary in a few cases. The analysis, also, includes the decisions against the subsidiaries of the 70 corporations, as listed in the standard manuals, for the period these subsidiaries have been under the control of the parent corporation.

The analysis is concerned with the following types of violations of laws: restraint of trade; misrepresentation in advertising; infringement of patent, trademarks, and copyrights; "unfair labor practices" as defined by the National Labor Relations Board and a few decisions under other labor laws; rebates; financial fraud and violation of trust; violations of war regulations; and some miscellaneous offenses. All of the cases included in the tabulation are defined as violations of law, most of them may properly be defined as crimes, and the others are closely allied to criminal behavior. The criminality of these violations of law will be discussed in chapter 4.

The sources of information regarding these violations of law are the decisions of the federal, state, and, in a few cases, municipal courts, as published in the *Federal Reporter* and the *American State Reports;* the published decisions of the Federal Trade Commission, the Interstate Commerce Commission, the Securities and Exchange Commission, the National Labor Relations Board, and, for the period 1934–37, of the Federal Pure Food and Drug Administration. These official reports have been supplemented, as to infringement, by the reports on infringement cases listed in the *Official Gazette* of the Patent Office, and as to violations of law in general by reports of decisions in newspapers. The *New York Times* has been used, especially, because its material has been indexed since 1913. The name of each of the 70 corporations and its subsidiaries was checked against the index of each of these series of reports and of the *New York Times.*

The enumeration of decisions as reported in these sources is certainly far short of the total number of decisions against these 70 corporations. First, many of the decisions of the lower courts are not published in the series of federal and state reports, and many of them are not published in the newspapers. Second, many suits are settled out of court and no outcome is reported in the series of reports or in newspapers. The number of suits initiated against the 70 corporations which dropped out of sight after preliminary motions and were presumably settled out of court is approximately 50 percent of the number included in the tabulation in this chapter. Presumably many of these involved violations of law and could have been tabulated as such if more complete information were available. Third, the Pure Food and Drug Administration has not published its decisions by names of offenders except during the years 1924–47. Fourth, many of the decisions are indexed under names such as "The John Doe Trade Association," or "John Doe et al." Consequently, many of the 70 corporations which have been defendants in those suits were not discovered because their names did not appear in the indexes, and often were not even mentioned in the published reports. Finally, many of the subsidiaries of these corporations are not listed in the financial manuals and could not be identified for the present study.

A decision against one of the 70 corporations is the unit in this tabulation. If a decision is made in one suit against 3 of the 70 corporations, that decision is counted three times, once against each of the 3 corporations. Also, if a criminal suit and an equity suit are initiated against one corporation for essentially the same overt behavior and a decision is made against the corporation in each of those suits, two decisions are counted. This, obviously, involves some duplication. On the other hand, one decision may contain scores of counts, each of which charges a specific violation of law and, also, may refer to a policy which has been in operation for a decade or longer. These are some of the reasons why these decisions are not an accurate index of the comparative amounts of illegal behavior by the several corporations.

The term "decision" is used here to include not only the formal decisions and orders of courts, but also the decisions of administrative commissions, stipulations accepted by courts and commissions, settlements ordered or approved by the court, confiscation of food as in violation of the Pure Food Law, and, in a few cases, which will be explained in the later chapters, opinion of courts that the defendant had violated the law at an earlier time even though the court then dismissed the suit.

The enumeration of the decisions which have been discovered is presented in Table 3. This shows that each of the 70 large corporations has 1 or more decisions against it, with a maximum of 50. The total number of decisions is 980, and the average per corporation is 14.0. Sixty corporations have decisions against them for restraint of trade, 53 for infringement, 44 for unfair labor practices, 43 for miscellaneous offenses, 28 for misrepresentation in advertising, and 26 for rebates.

Armour & Company and Swift & Company stand at the top of the list in the total number of adverse decisions, with 50 each. General Motors has third rank with 40, and Sears Roebuck ties with Montgomery Ward for fourth rank with 39 each. These five corporations are decidedly in excess of the other corporations in the number of decisions, for Loew's in sixth rank has only 31. These totals, however, are not a precise measure of the comparative amounts of illegal behavior by these corporations. Armour and Swift, for instance, are subject to the Pure Food and Drug

TABLE 3. Decisions by Courts and Commissions against 70 Large Corporations by Types of Laws Violated

Corporation	Restraint of trade	Misrepresentation in advertising	Infringement	Unfair labor practices	Rebates	Other	Total
Allied Chemical & Dye	7	1	—	5	—	—	13
Aluminum Co. of America	4	—	1	3	3	3	14
American Can	6	—	1	—	—	1	8
American Car & Foundry	1	—	6	2	—	1	10
Amer. Radiator & Stand. San.	—	—	—	2	—	—	2
American Rolling Mills	1	—	—	3	1	—	5
American Smelting & Refin.	2	—	1	4	2	5	14
American Sugar Refining	7	—	—	—	10	6	23
American Tobacco	19	—	2	—	2	2	25
American Woolen	1	1	1	—	—	—	3
Anaconda Copper	4	—	4	2	—	7	17
Armour & Company	12	6	2	11	6	13	50
Bethlehem Steel	3	—	2	5	4	—	14
Borden	7	2	1	—	1	1	12
Chrysler	1	3	1	1	1	2	9
Corn Products	3	4	1	—	1	1	10
Crane	3	—	1	1	1	—	6
Crown Zellerbach	5	—	—	—	—	—	5
Deere	—	—	2	2	—	—	4
DuPont	7	—	4	3	—	—	14
Eastman Kodak	5	—	3	—	—	—	8
Firestone	1	1	4	2	—	—	8
Ford	1	2	8	15	1	1	28
General Electric	13	2	9	—	—	1	25
General Motors	6	2	22	9	—	1	40
Gimbel	—	12	11	—	—	—	23
Glen Alden Coal	5	—	—	1	1	—	7
Goodrich	1	1	2	3	—	—	7

Company							
Goodyear	1	1	4	3	—	5	14
Great A & P	8	3	—	1	—	7	19
Inland Steel	1	—	—	3	1	3	8
International Harvester	11	—	3	2	3	—	19
International Paper	2	2	2	—	2	2	8
International Shoe	—	—	—	4	—	1	3
Jones & Laughlin	1	—	—	—	1	1	7
Kennecott Copper	2	—	1	2	—	—	5
Kresge	—	1	9	1	—	7	18
Liggett & Myers	1	—	—	—	—	1	2
Loew's	22	—	6	—	—	3	31
Macy & Company	—	5	13	—	—	—	18
Marshall Field	1	2	2	3	—	—	8
Montgomery Ward	1	12	15	5	—	6	39
National Biscuit	2	—	1	—	—	2	5
National Dairy Products	8	1	1	—	1	1	12
National Lead	3	—	3	5	—	1	12
National Steel	1	—	—	2	2	1	6
Paramount	21	—	4	9	—	—	25
Phelps Dodge	3	—	1	—	—	1	14
Philadelphia & Reading Coal	6	—	1	—	—	—	7
Pittsburgh Coal	1	—	—	—	—	—	1
Pittsburgh Plate Glass	6	—	3	3	4	1	17
Procter & Gamble	1	8	1	1	—	2	13
RCA	3	1	2	—	—	1	8
Republic Steel	3	—	—	7	1	—	11
Reynolds Tobacco	1	—	—	—	—	—	1
Sears Roebuck	—	18	20	1	—	—	39
Singer Mfg. Co.	—	—	5	2	—	—	7
Standard Brands	2	1	—	—	—	—	3
Swift & Company	12	1	1	10	5	21	50
Union Carbide & Carbon	—	—	5	—	—	2	7
United Fruit	3	—	1	1	—	1	5
United Shoe Machinery	1	—	3	3	—	2	6
U.S. Rubber	6	1	1	1	—	1	10

TABLE 3 (Continued)

Corporation	Restraint of trade	Misrepresentation in advertising	Infringement	Unfair labor practices	Rebates	Other	Total
U.S. Steel	9	2	5	2	5	3	26
Warner Bros.	21	—	3	—	—	1	25
Westinghouse Electric	10	1	5	2	—	1	19
Wheeling Steel	2	—	1	1	2	—	6
Wilson & Company	4	—	1	9	3	2	19
Woolworth	—	—	10	1	—	4	15
Youngstown	2	—	—	3	2	1	8
Total	307	97	222	158	66	130	980

Law, which does not apply to many other corporations. If the laws explicitly declared that any defects in shoes, electrical equipment, tobacco, films, or automobiles were misdemeanors, as they do in regard to foods, the number of decisions against the other corporations might be as high as the number against Swift and Armour. Table 3 shows, however, that Armour and Swift would be in the highest ranks even if decisions under the Pure Food Law were disregarded. General Motors, which stands in third rank, has more than half of the decisions against it on charges of infringements, while Sears Roebuck and Montgomery Ward have decisions concentrated in "misrepresentation in advertising" and "infringements."

The corporations in one industry frequently cluster in one part of the distribution and have ranks which are not far apart, considering the possible spread of 70 ranks. Three meat-packing corporations in the list of 70 corporations have ranks of 1, 2, and 17. The two mail order corporations tie for fourth rank. The two dairy corporations tie for 33rd rank. The ranks of the three motion picture corporations are: Loew's sixth, and Paramount and Warner tied for tenth position. On the other hand, the corporations in one industry are sometimes scattered more widely. The four rubber manufacturers have ranks as follows: Goodyear 25th, U.S. Rubber 35th, Firestone 43rd, and Goodrich 48th. The nine steel corporations range between ninth and 58th positions.

Table 4 presents an analysis of the 980 decisions by types of jurisdictions of the courts and commissions which rendered the decisions. This shows that 158 decisions were made against 41 of the 70 corporations by criminal courts, 296 decisions against 57 of the corporations by civil courts, and 129 decisions against 44 corporations by courts under equity jurisdiction. This gives a total of 583 decisions which were made by courts. The administrative commissions made 361 decisions, and approximately one-fourth of these were referred to courts and were sustained by the courts. The commissions, also, confiscated goods in 25 cases as in violation of the Pure Food law. Eleven cases are tabulated as "settlements," and all of these were civil suits in which the settlements were approved or ordered by the courts. In hundreds of other cases, settlements were reached outside of courts but these have not been included in the tabulation in this chapter.

This analysis shows that approximately 16 percent of the decisions were made by criminal courts. An analysis of the concept of "crime" from the point of view of these violations of law will be made in a subse-

TABLE 4. Decisions by Courts and Commissions against 70 Large Corporations for Violations of Specified Laws, by Jurisdictions and Procedures

Corporation	Court			Commission			Total
	Criminal	Civil	Equity	Order	Confiscation	Settlement	
Allied Chemical & Dye	3	—	1	9	—	—	13
Aluminum Co. of America	3	3	3	4	—	1	14
American Can	2	3	2	1	—	—	8
American Car & Foundry	—	6	1	3	—	—	10
Amer. Radiator & Stand. San.	—	—	—	2	—	—	2
Amer. Rolling Mills	1	—	—	4	—	—	5
American Smelting	3	1	4	6	—	—	14
American Sugar	12	3	7	—	—	1	23
American Tobacco	10	10	2	1	—	2	25
American Woolen	—	1	1	1	—	—	3
Anaconda	6	4	4	3	—	—	17
Armour	18	4	4	17	7	—	50
Bethlehem	3	2	1	8	—	—	14
Borden	6	1	—	5	—	—	12
Chrysler	2	2	—	5	—	—	9
Corn Products	2	1	3	4	—	—	10
Crane	1	1	1	3	—	—	6
Crown Zellerbach	3	—	1	1	—	—	5
Deere	—	2	—	2	—	—	4
DuPont	4	4	1	5	—	—	14
Eastman	—	4	2	2	—	—	8
Firestone	2	2	—	4	—	—	8
Ford	2	8	—	18	—	—	28
General Electric	4	9	5	6	—	1	25
General Motors	1	23	4	12	—	—	40
Gimbel	—	12	—	11	—	—	23
Glen Alden Coal	1	—	4	2	—	—	7

Company	1	2	3	4	5	6	7
Goodrich	—	2	—	5	—	—	7
Goodyear	2	5	—	5	2	2	14
Great A & P	7	4	—	6	—	—	19
Inland Steel	10	3	2	6	—	—	8
Intern. Harvester	3	4	1	5	—	—	19
Intern. Paper	—	1	1	—	—	—	8
Intern. Shoe	—	—	—	2	—	—	3
Jones & Laughlin	—	—	1	6	—	—	7
Kennecott	1	1	—	3	—	—	5
Kresge	2	9	5	2	—	—	18
Liggett & Myers	2	—	—	—	—	—	2
Loew's	—	15	13	3	—	—	31
Macy	—	13	—	5	—	—	18
Marshall Field	—	2	—	6	—	—	8
Montgomery Ward	—	18	2	19	—	1	39
National Biscuit	6	2	—	2	—	1	5
National Dairy Products	1	1	1	3	—	—	12
National Lead	—	5	1	5	—	—	12
National Steel	1	11	—	5	—	—	6
Paramount	1	1	10	4	—	—	25
Phelps Dodge	1	1	1	11	—	—	14
Phil. & Reading Coal	—	—	5	—	—	—	7
Pittsburgh Coal	—	—	—	1	—	—	1
Pittsburgh Plate	2	5	—	9	—	—	17
Procter & Gamble	1	1	1	9	1	—	13
RCA	—	3	1	3	1	—	8
Republic Steel	1	—	—	10	—	—	11
Reynolds Tobacco	1	—	—	—	—	—	1
Sears Roebuck	—	20	—	19	—	—	39
Singer	—	5	—	2	—	—	7
Standard Brands	18	—	—	3	—	13	3
Swift	—	3	6	10	—	—	50
Union Carbide & Carbon	—	6	—	1	—	—	7

TABLE 4 (Continued)

Corporatiom	Court			Commission			Total
	Criminal	Civil	Equity	Order	Confis-cation	Settle-ment	
United Fruit	—	3	1	—	1	—	5
United Shoe Mach.	—	5	1	—	—	—	6
U.S. Rubber	—	3	1	6	—	—	10
U.S. Steel	4	6	3	13	—	1	26
Warner Bros.	—	10	10	4	—	1	25
Westinghouse	3	6	3	6	—	1	19
Wheeling	—	1	1	4	—	—	6
Wilson	3	2	4	10	—	—	19
Woolworth	2	10	2	1	—	—	15
Youngstown	—	1	—	7	—	—	8
Total	158	296	129	361	25	11	980

quent chapter. Even if the present analysis were limited to these decisions by criminal courts, it would show that 60 percent of the 70 large corporations have been convicted in criminal courts and have an average of approximately four convictions each. In many states persons with four convictions are defined by statute to be "habitual criminals." The frequency of these convictions of large corporations might be sufficient to demonstrate the fallacy in the conventional theories that crime is due to poverty or to the personal and social pathologies connected with poverty.

One of the interesting aspects of these decisions is that they have been concentrated in the last decade. The distribution of the decisions in time is presented by types of offenses in Table 5. In this analysis the date of the first adverse decision in a particular suit was used. The case was not counted, of course, unless the final decision was against the corporation. Relatively few cases initiated after 1944 have been included in this study. Consequently, it is approximately correct to conclude that 60 percent of the adverse decisions were rendered in the 10-year period 1935–44, while only 40 percent were rendered in the 35-year period 1900–34.

One possible explanation of this concentration is that violations of laws by large corporations have increased and are much more prevalent in recent years than in earlier years. Since several other possible explanations may be equally significant, they are considered first.

First, the number of corporations has not remained constant during the period under consideration. Although the 70 corporations have had an average life of 45 years, only 63 of these corporations were in existence in 1920 and only 53 in 1910. This factor, however, seems to be relatively unimportant. A separate tabulation of the 53 corporations which originated prior to 1910 shows that 57.4 percent of the decisions were rendered in the period 1935–44, as contrasted with 59.7 percent for the entire list of 70 corporations.

Second, some of the laws which have been violated by these corporations were enacted during the last decade. The National Labor Relations Law was enacted in 1935, with a similar law under the National Industrial Recovery Act of 1934, and decisions under this law are necessarily concentrated almost entirely in the period 1935–44. If this law is disregarded, 52.5 percent of the decisions under the other laws were made in the ten-year period 1935–44. The enactment and amendment of other laws applying to corporations provide some explanation of this concen-

TABLE 5. Decisions against 70 Large Corporations by Five-Year Periods and by Types of Laws Violated

Dates	Restraint of trade	Misrepresentation in advertising	Infringement	Unfair labor practices	Rebates	Other	Total	Percentages
1940–date	102	34	52	102	7	43	340	34.7
1935–39	59	42	59	50	15	20	245	25.0
1930–34	27	8	36	4	7	10	92	9.4
1925–29	28	1	26	—	—	23	78	8.0
1920–24	18	3	12	—	—	9	42	4.3
1915–19	20	7	5	—	6	7	45	4.6
1910–14	29	1	13	—	14	7	64	6.5
1905–09	17	—	9	1	14	5	46	4.7
1900–04	5	1	6	1	3	1	17	1.7
1890–99	2	—	1	—	—	3	6	0.6
Prior to 1890	—	—	3	—	—	2	5	0.5
Totals	307	97	222	158	66	130	980	100.0

tration in the last decade. Although this influence cannot be measured with precision, it certainly accounts for a very small part of the concentration.

Third, vigorous prosecution of violations of law by corporations has been concentrated in the period since 1932. Budgets have been increased and additional assistants provided, so that violations were acted upon in the last decade which were neglected in the earlier decades. Probably both the enactment of laws and the enforcement of laws during this period are explained by the fact that businessmen lost much prestige in the depression which began in 1929. The increase in the number of decisions on restraint of trade and misrepresentation in advertising, especially, can be explained in this manner.

Fourth, businessmen are resorting to an increasing extent to "policies of social manipulation" in contrast with the earlier concentration on efficiency in production. With emphasis on advertising and salesmanship, as policies of social manipulation, have gone increased attention to lobbying and litigation. This is shown especially in the trend in decisions regarding infringements. Since these are civil suits, initiated by persons who regard their rights as infringed, they are not a direct reflection of governmental policies. They are, however, presumably affected somewhat by governmental policies in an indirect manner. The increase in the number of prosecutions on charges of restraint of trade, frequently involving patent manipulations, has given the general public and the owners of patents insight into the policies of these large corporations and has stimulated efforts of patent holders to protect their rights.

Of these possible explanations, the increased vigor of and facilities for prosecution are probably the most important. It is probable, also, that the frequency of violations of some of the laws has increased significantly, although this does not appear to be true of all laws.

Of the 70 corporations, 30 were either illegal in their origin or began illegal activities immediately after their origin, and 8 additional corporations were probably illegal in origin or in initial policies. Of the violations of law which appeared in these early activities, 27 were restraint of trade and 3 were patent infringements; of the 8 origins which were probably criminal, 5 involved restraint of trade, 2 patent infringements, and 1 fraud. The evidence for this appraisal of the origins of corporations consists in court decisions in 21 cases, and other historical evidence in the other cases.

3

THREE CASE HISTORIES

Three of the 70 corporations have been selected for connected accounts of their records. These three are American Smelting and Refining Company, which has 14 official decisions and is near the mid-point of the distribution; U.S. Rubber Company, which has 11 official decisions and is slightly below the mid-point; and Pittsburgh Coal Company, which has 1 official decision and is at the bottom of the list in the number of adverse decisions.

American Smelting and Refining Company

The American Smelting and Refining Company was organized in 1899 as a merger of 13 silver and lead refineries which had previously competed against each other. These included almost all of the refineries in these two branches. Several efforts had been made in earlier years to eliminate competition from this industry. The American Pig Lead Association was formed in 1878 with the policy of price fixing, but it was unable to hold its members to the prices which were fixed and soon disbanded. The Western Mining and Smelting Association was formed in 1883 to restrict production and reduce wages and railway rates. This association, also, was unable to achieve its purposes and soon passed out of existence. In 1894 the smelters at Leadville formed an association which undertook to fix the prices which smelters paid for ore; this also failed. Finally, in 1897 the smelters formed an association to act as a joint agency to buy ore from the mines for all of the smelters and thus eliminate competition. The Guggenheims, who had extensive interests in the smelter industry, joined this association but at the end of the first year they announced that they would not participate in the following year. The other smelters knew that the association would fail if the Guggenheims were on the outside, and they rushed to the mines to make individual contracts for the purchase of ore. To their chagrin they found that the Guggenheims had signed up practically all of the mine owners before they announced that they would not participate in the association in the following year.[1]

After these failures to reduce competition the smelters were interested in a merger of the smelters proposed by H. H. Rogers and his associates, who were regarded as representing the Rockefeller interests. The reduction of competition was the explicit objective of the merger. E. R. Chapman, a New York banker who was connected with the promotion of this merger, explained it in this manner:

> The evils of competition having been borne for years by the various smelting interests of the country had convinced the proprietors of these interests that some combinations should be effected with a view to reducing expenses and eliminating such competition.[2]

Another motive in the organization of this corporation was the promoters' profits. The smelters which were merged could have been constructed, according to estimates at that time, for $11½ million. The corporation was capitalized, however, for $65 million, half in common stock and half in 7 percent preferred stock. Thus approximately 80 percent of the capital was "water." The former owners of the smelters were paid $19 million in stock, and $8.1 million of the stock was appropriated by the promoters as reward for their efforts; the remainder was designed for the purpose of additional smelters. This group of promoters had made a reputation as looters of the corporations which they had promoted. In this case they organized and held privately the United Metals Selling Company. As directors of the American Smelting and Refining Company they made a contract with themselves, as owners of the United Metals Selling Company, that all products of the smelters designed for foreign trade would be sold through the United Metals Selling Company. This contract, obviously, increased their profits from this organization.

The promoters expected profits would be made by increasing the prices at which silver and lead were sold. The new corporation, however, was in a weak position because its capital was immensely inflated and also because the Guggenheims had refused to sell their smelters to the corporation or even name a price at which they would sell. On the contrary they were planning to ruin the new corporation and then take control of it. They paid higher prices for ore than the American Smelting and Refining Company was paying and thus forced up the expenses of that corporation. When the State of Colorado passed an eight-hour law, the American Smelting and Refining Company fought the law; as a result their employees struck. The Guggenheims, on the other hand, did not oppose the law and they continued to operate and make profits. Also, the Guggenheims bought lead mines in Missouri and dumped lead in the market to such an extent that the price slumped. Finally, they announced a plan to build more smelters. These tactics forced the American Smelting and Refining Company to surrender. It made an offer of $30 million for the Guggenheim smelters and voted to increase their capital to $100 million for this purpose. The cost of construction of the Guggenheim smelters was estimated by others to be about $5 million. The Guggenheims secured the higher price in part by misrepresentation of the earnings of their smelters. Although the directors had made an agreement to purchase, the stockholders had not voted on it. At this point the Guggenheims announced that foreign sales, thereafter, would be conducted through their own personal company. While Rogers and his associates had been forced into a bargain which was decidedly disadvantageous to the corporation, they were not willing to lose their private profits from the United Metals Selling Company. They began to fight the whole proposition. They dumped their stock on the market in the hope of ruining the American Smelting and Refining Company, but the Guggenheims bought this stock at a low price and are reported to have made profits of $8 million on these stock purchases. Rogers and his associates went to the courts for an injunction against the purchase of the Guggenheim properties, on the ground that the price to be paid was excessive. The court issued a temporary injunction and ordered a vote by the stockholders on the proposition. The vote was almost unanimously in favor of the purchase. The temporary injunction was then dissolved, but a higher court renewed the injunction against the purchase. Rogers then spread rumors that the Rockefeller interests were planning to form a new smelter trust. With this opposition, the Guggenheims decided it would be wise to compromise. They made an agreement that the foreign sales should be made through the United Metals Selling Company. Satisfied with this, Rogers and his associates withdrew their opposition and the injunction was dissolved. Thereafter the Guggenheims controlled the American Smelting and Refining Company.[3]

Many criticisms were made in subsequent years that the Guggenheims were using this corporation for their personal profit at the expense of the other stockholders. Moreover, in 1907 they sold most of their shares of this stock, although they continued to dominate the corporation because they were in the position of managers. In 1904 minority stockholders complained that the corporation was paying higher prices for ore purchased from the Guggenheim mines than for ore from other mines. The corporation began to expand in the copper industry. This began when they agreed to refinance the Utah Copper Company in return for a contract that the mine would sell all its copper to the American Smelting and Refining Company for 20 years. However, the Guggenheims soon secured control of the Utah Copper Company and, according to complaints, paid $3 a ton more to this mine for copper than to other mines. A new controversy and lawsuit developed between the corporation and the United Metals Selling Company, which at this time was controlled by John D. Ryan.

Nothing came of these complaints until 1920, when Karl Eilers started a suit against the corporation. Eilers had been owner of one of the smelters that went into the merger in 1899 and had remained as a director of the corporation. He was dismissed in 1920, when Dan Guggenheim was replaced as president by Simon Guggenheim. In his suit he charged that the Guggenheims had generally looted the corporation for their personal profit, although owning little of the stock. They had paid immense salaries to themselves as officers and not even the directors knew what these salaries were. They had taken off the most profitable properties for themselves and turned the poorer properties in to the corporation. A stockholders committee was organized, and after an investigation reported that although the Guggenheim management had been efficient as to earnings, they had received an excessive price for their properties, had transferred valuable properties from the corporation to their private companies, and in general had engaged in stock-jobbing for personal profit. The committee recommended that the representatives of the Guggenheims should not be included on the board of directors. A compromise was adopted by which 18 directors, not representing the Guggenheims, were added to the board.[4] These additional directors, together with the financial distress of the Guggenheims after 1929, resulted in their loss of control of this corporation. Thereafter it was dominated by Morgan interests.

The preceding description of this corporation for the first 20 years of its career has demonstrated that financial manipulations and violations of trust by the officers were present in its origin and development. The only additional decision as to such manipulations was the rejection by the Securities and Exchange Commission of a proposed security issue for about $15 million; the details of this proposal are not reported.[5]

The preceding description has demonstrated, also, that this corporation was violating the antitrust law in its origin and subsequent development. Complaints against it have been almost continuous. From the date of its origin it used the basing-point system of prices, which had the effect of standardizing prices and reducing competition.[6] A complaint was presented to the Federal Trade Commission that the purchase of the Federated Metals Corporation by American Smelting and Refining Company was a violation of the antitrust law, since the two corporations had been competing previously; this complaint was dismissed.[7] In 1943 the General Cable Company, a subsidiary, was convicted on a plea of nolo contendere of conspiring with other corporations to make identical bids on $50 million worth of cable for the U.S. Navy, and a fine of $10,000 was imposed on this corporation.[8] Also the Federal Trade Commission ordered the General Cable Company to cease making bids identical to those of other corporations on supplies for the Cramp Shipyards.[9]

Two fines were imposed on the Federated Metals Corporation, a subsidiary, for accepting rebates and for false billing.[10] The corporation was indicted in 1944 for soliciting concessions from railways but no decision on this case has been discovered.[11]

One decision has been made against the American Smelting and Refining Company on a charge of infringing a patent on the construction of the roof of an open hearth and reverberatory furnace, and damages of more than a million dollars have been awarded.[12]

Four decisions have been made against the American Smelting and Refining Company or its subsidiaries for violations of the National Labor Relations Law. A decision was made against the Revere Copper and Brass Company, a subsidiary, for maintaining a company union and interfering with the efforts of employees to organize a union of their own choice.[13] A decision was made against the Smelting Company for maintaining a company union in its plant in Omaha and for discriminating against members of the union; the corporation was ordered to desist from this illegal behavior and to compensate the employees against whom it had discriminated.[14] A decision was made, also, against this corporation for interference in its El Paso plant with the employees who were endeavoring to organize a union and for discriminations against union members; the corporation was ordered to desist from this illegal behavior and to compensate its employees.[15] Finally, General Cable Company was accused of organizing a company union and interfering with the employees who were organizing a union. The company stipulated that it would desist.[16]

The decisions under the National Labor Relations Law are consistent with the reputation this corporation had acquired prior to the enactment of the law as an antiunion company. It is reported that it cooperated with other employers in Colorado to maintain a central employment agency, through which union members were blacklisted.[17] It is reported also that they employed Waddell–Mahon guards in their labor conflicts and that many of the employees were murdered.[18] Finally, to a greater extent than the average of other large corporations they appealed decisions of state compensation commissions in the effort to avoid payment of compensation for industrial accidents. Four such appeals in which the courts sustained the compensation commissions have been discovered.[19]

Three decisions have been made against the American Smelting Company on charges that fumes from their plants were injuring farm crops in the vicinity. Damages of $3,000 were awarded in one case and injunctions issued in the two other cases.[20] One of these injunctions included an order that operations in the plant should be discontinued until the fumes could be controlled satisfactorily.

Hicks brought suit against the American Smelting and Refining Company, on the charge that ore had been stolen from his property by underground tunnels and was accepted by and in the possession of the American Smelting Company. Although this was a civil suit, with the effort to secure payment for the ore that had been stolen, the implicit charge was receiving stolen property.[21]

The copper and other nonferrous industries were accused of "profiteering" during the First World War. The Federal Trade Commission, which was ordered by Congress to investigate these charges, reported that the American Smelting and Refining Company had retained in its costs a payment for risks, that these risks were nonexistent in the war period, when the demand for copper was very great, and that this amounted to profiteering.[22]

Thus the American Smelting and Refining Company was illegitimate in origin, a persistent violator of laws in its early career, and has continued up to date to violate one law after another. It has engaged persistently in restraint of trade and in unfair labor practices through the first half of its career in looting corporate resources by officers and directors, and it has intermittent decisions of accepting rebates, infringing patents, profiteering in wartime, receiving stolen goods, and damaging community property by fumes from its plants.

United States Rubber Company

The United States Rubber Company was organized in 1892 as a merger of firms manufacturing rubber footwear. The preexisting firms had been competing against each other and the merger had the objective of reducing competition. It soon became known as "The Rubber Trust." At the same time, the same promoters organized the Mechanical Rubber Company, which was closely affiliated with the United States Rubber Company. By 1900 this combination controlled 80 percent of the rubber footwear business and 85 percent of the rubber mechanical goods. In 1899 the Mechanical Rubber Company combined with other companies to form the Rubber Goods Manufacturing Company. This company, at the turn of the century, carried on the manufacture of tires. By 1905 it had passed entirely under the control of the United States Rubber Company. The United States Rubber Company passed to the control of the DuPonts in 1928 because of financial difficulties and has remained a DuPont company since that date.

The prime mover in the organization of the merger which became known as the United States Rubber Company was Charles Ranlett Flint, who was known at the turn of the century as the "Father of Trusts." He was a member of the importing firm of W. R. Grace and Company. In that capacity he had been active in providing munitions to South American nations and thus became acquainted with the intrigues and manipulations of international diplomacy. Furthermore, the firm of W. R. Grace and Company, acting as the agent of the New York Trading Company, which kept its own activities secret, established a virtual monopoly on the importation of rubber to the United States. Flint, after an unsuccessful effort to merge firms in the electrical utility industry, returned to the rubber industry. He described the situation in the rubber industry as follows: First, the manufacturers were engaged in intense competition and were anxious to reduce this competition. Second, they held dinners and other conferences, in which all agreed that some method of reducing competition was desirable. Third, they did not know how to consolidate their activities so that competition might be reduced.

The specific difficulty was that they could not agree on the details of combination because of their antagonistic relations. Fourth, they finally agreed to disagree. Flint described the subsequent developments in this manner:

> At last in 1892 several of the rubber manufacturers interviewed me, and I conferred with them separately. I told them that, if they would leave me free to bring about the consolidation, I was satisfied that I could do so within sixty days, but that I would not attempt it unless they would agree not to discuss consolidation with one another. To this they consented . . . I was successful in bringing about the formation of the United States Rubber Company . . . I took options from the majority of the shareholders in each individual manufacturing company, in which options the other manufacturing companies which we expected would form part of that consolidation were not named. Instead, I provided that the options would not become operative unless the consolidation started with tangible assets to the amount of $12,000,000, so that the parties giving options fully understood that the consolidation must include important manufacturers, as tangible assets of this amount would not have been possible unless some of the large companies were included. Under this plan no manufacturing company was absolutely necessary, which materially facilitated the negotiations. No industrial consolidation including a considerable number of important manufacturers had been brought about up to that time, and pioneering in the securing of options was difficult.[23]

Three things were important, according to Flint's analysis, in his method of forming a consolidation: a disinterested intermediary who conducted the negotiations; a committee of financial leaders who appraised the assets of the several companies; and a board of directors composed of financial and industrial leaders. In addition, Flint frightened the manufacturers and thus drove them into the consolidation by announcing that the new company would control a ship line and would buy rubber at the sources at lower prices than others had been able to do. This technique of forming a consolidation had not been used previously and was essentially an invention. As soon as it became known it was adopted in other industries.

Not only was this corporation illegitimate in origin, but it persisted in illegal restraint of trade. Since it was not in its early history engaged in the manufacture of tires it did not participate directly in the patent pools which were maintaining a monopoly on tires. However, the Mechanical Rubber Company and the Rubber Goods Manufacturing Company, which were closely affiliated with U.S. Rubber and later merged with it, were the central figures in those patent pools, which were held by the courts to be illegal.

The subsequent decisions under the antitrust laws are described briefly.

In 1902 the Hood Rubber Company sued the U.S. Rubber Company and six others in Massachusetts under the antitrust law, claiming three-fold damages. It charged that the U.S. Rubber Co. in 1896 acquired control of ten corporations which manufactured and sold rubber footwear, and also made an agreement with all of the firms which made lasts for rubber foot-wear that they would not sell lasts to firms other than the U.S. Rubber Company. The Hood Rubber Company tried in vain to purchase lasts from each of the manufacturers. Although this declaration was filed in 1902, no court action appeared until 1916, when the demurrers by the U.S. Rubber Company were overruled. No further action is reported, and a settlement was probably made out of court.[24]

In 1919 the Mishawaka Woolen Manufacturing Company, a subsidiary of U.S. Rubber Company, was ordered by the Federal Trade Commission to cease and desist from resale price maintenance in rubber foot-wear. This company had signed agreements with dealers not to sell the products of this company below the price fixed by it. Moreover, Mishawaka Woolen Manufacturing Co. inspected the dealers and refused to sell to them if they violated the price agreements. The agreements at first were written, but later were made only in oral form.[25]

In 1930 and 1931 and in later years U.S. Rubber made arrangements with Montgomery Ward & Company to provide half of the tires needed by the latter at prices considerably lower than the same tires were sold to other dealers. This arrangement was similar to an agreement made earlier between Goodyear Rubber Company and Sears Roebuck. Because the Goodyear–Sears Roebuck case was before the Federal Trade Commission and the courts, nothing was done as to this illegal agreement for price discriminations by U.S. Rubber until 1939. At that time the Federal Trade Commission issued a desist order against discriminatory prices. This order included not only Montgomery Ward but also the Atlas Supply Company, the Western Auto Supply Company, and other dealers. The Commission found, also, that U.S. Rubber had given discounts of 7.5 per cent as commissions to operators of stations of Socony-Vacuum, American Oil Company, Pan-American Petroleum Company, Tidewater Associated Oil Company, including a total of 2,800 service stations, and that similar discounts were not available to other dealers with similar businesses.[26]

In 1935 the Federal Trade Commission issued a desist order against the Rubber Manufacturers Association, including the U.S. Rubber Products Company, on the charge that these companies had conspired to fix uniform prices on fire hose and chemical hose. They had entered into this conspiracy to fix prices at least as early as 1933, and also to maintain resale prices, and to quote higher prices to governmental departments than to commercial companies; moreover, they had arrangements to investigate any departures from uniform prices by the members of the Association and they refused to sell products to whole-sale or jobbing dealers who did not maintain the uniform prices.[27]

In 1936 the Federal Trade Commission issued a desist order against the National Electric Manufacturers Association, including the U.S. Rubber Products Co., on the charge that since 1929 the members of this association had conspired to suppress price competition on power cable and rubber-covered building wire which were sold to large industrial firms and to electric utilities. The members of this association quoted identical prices and conditions of sale. Three firms in the Association determined these prices and conditions of sale, and the other members followed these three. Moreover, the Association made inspections and investigations of departures from the uniform prices and refused to sell their products to wholesalers and jobbers who did not maintain the resale prices.[28]

In 1937 the Federal Trade Commission issued a desist order against the Golf Ball Manufacturers Association, and its individual members, including U.S. Rubber Co. This order included practically all the manufacturers of golf balls in the United States and also the Professional Golfers Association. The complaint charged that these firms and individuals had conspired to fix uniform prices on golf balls, to maintain resale prices, to coerce the manufacturers, wholesale dealers, and retail dealers to maintain uniform prices, and also that they had discriminated illegally by giving lower prices to members of the Professional Golfers Association than to other dealers.[29]

The U.S. government filed suit in 1939, as a person, against U.S. Rubber Products Co. and seventeen other rubber companies for damages of $1,053,474 due to a conspiracy of these companies to fix prices in violation of the antitrust law. This case was dismissed by the court on the ground that the U.S. government could not sue as a person.[30]

A criminal information was filed in 1947 against U.S. Rubber Company and others for a twelve-year policy of price-fixing and limitation of production. This case has not yet been tried, so far as discovered.[31]

The preceding cases show conclusively that the U.S. Rubber Company has had a consistent policy of restraint of trade, and that it has had this policy in association with other rubber manufacturing companies and with corporations in other industries.

Two decisions have been made against the U.S. Rubber Company on patent infringements. In 1908 the Metallic Rubber Wire Company sued the Hartford Rubber Works Company, subsidiary of U.S. Rubber, for infringing a patent on bicycle tires. The suit was dismissed in 1911, reversed on appeal in 1912, and an injunction and accounting ordered. A master reported nominal damages in 1915, but the court refused to accept this and remanded the matter for further consideration. A second report by a master was made in 1920, awarding damages of $183,383 plus interest since 1910. In the report it was pointed out that the Hartford Rubber Works Company had produced bicycle tires under license from the Metallic Rubber Wire Company for a time, then made slight modifications in the process and continued without a license. The court not only accepted the master's report but announced that the infringement was wanton and deliberate and made an additional punitive award. On appeal, the punitive award was eliminated.[32] In an infringement suit by Behrman against the U.S. Rubber Company, a consent order was issued.[33] Although damages were awarded in an infringement suit by ITS Rubber Company against U.S. Rubber Company, the decision was reversed on appeal.[34]

One decision has been made against the U.S. Rubber Company for misrepresentation in advertising. In 1936 the Federal Trade Commission ordered this corporation to desist from claiming in its advertisements that a majority of the automobile manufacturers equipped their cars with U.S. Rubber tires, and also from advertising a guarantee which gave an impression that it applied to all cars but on closer examination was found to apply only to passenger cars.[35] Shortly before this representatives of this corporation with representatives of other corporations in the rubber industry had drawn up an ethical code in which they pledged themselves to truth in advertising.

One decision was made against this corporation under the National Labor Relations Board. In 1935 this board decided that the Samson Tire and Rubber Corporation, subsidiary of U.S. Rubber, had refused to bargain collectively in their Los Angeles plant with the organization chosen by the employees, but instead bargained collectively with a company-controlled union which had been organized in 1933. The National Labor Relations Board states that unless the company within a specified time agreed to bargain collectively with the union chosen by the employees and refrained from bargaining collectively with the company union, the case would be referred to the NRA and other governmental agencies for appropriate action. In the next year an election was ordered in this plant and the AF of L union was clearly in the majority. It became clear, in this connection, that the employment policies of this plant were dominated by the New York office of the U.S. Rubber Company.[36] On the negative side, the *Reports* of the National Labor Relations Board do not show evidence that this corporation used the same brutality and coercion that some of the other rubber companies did.

Although U.S. Rubber Company has only one decision against it on financial manipulations, it has a number of questionable practices in its history. It was capitalized on its origin in 1892 at $50 million, which was much in excess of the capitalization of the constituent companies. Thereafter, it developed a sound financial structure and this was maintained until the decade of the twenties. At that time all of the rubber companies had difficult times, due to the reduction in the sale of automobiles, the increased length of service of the tires, and overexpansion of the industry. The U.S. Rubber Company became burdened with debt and was taken over before the end of that decade by the DuPonts, who were required to invest $18 million to keep the corporation out of bankruptcy.

Until 1934 this corporation had filed a consolidated federal income tax report for itself and all its subsidiaries, which numbered approximately one hundred. When these consolidated reports were prohibited by law in 1934, the U.S. Rubber Corporation reorganized. All of the manufacturing plants were turned over to the U.S. Rubber Products Company on a lease contract at 6 percent of the net book value of the property plus depreciation. U.S. Rubber Company then became a holding company, with all of the manufacturing and sales in the hands of U.S. Rubber Products Company. Dividends payable to U.S. Rubber are credited on the books of U.S. Rubber Products with interest at 5 percent. These two corporations, although separate legal entities, are merely fictions for the purpose of avoiding taxes, for they have the same officers and the same offices. Moreover, the various corporations within the system are pyramided, e.g., U.S. Rubber Company owns all the stock of the Meyer Rubber Company, which owns all the stock of the Samson Corporation, which owns 88 percent of the stock of Samson Tire and Rubber Company. This pyramiding of companies and juggling with corporate entities and finances is seldom found outside of the public utilities systems.

In 1896 the U.S. Rubber Company became a participant in the fraudulent bankruptcy of a corporation which was indebted to it. The C. H. Fargo Company owed $180,000 to the U.S. Rubber Company and was hopelessly insolvent. The Fargo Company issued judgment notes to U.S. Rubber Company for this amount and also for an additional loan of $50,000, which was used to pay the indebtedness of the company to its officers. These notes gave the U.S. Rubber Company a first claim on the assets of the Fargo Company and gave U.S. Rubber a preferential position when the Fargo Company became bankrupt. The circuit court of Illinois decided that this was fraudulent and the court prohibited preferential payments to U.S. Rubber. An appeal on this decision was dismissed, but a subsequent appeal resulted in the more severe decision that the assets of the Fargo Company were to be distributed among the other creditors first, and if a balance remained it could be used to meet the claims of the U.S. Rubber Company. The Supreme Court, however, reversed this decision and restored U.S. Rubber to a position of equality with other creditors.[37]

Several complaints of misapplication of funds of the corporation have been made. In 1913 Caroline De Wolf Theobald sued the U.S. Rubber Company to compel President Colt to return to the corporate treasury funds which had been illegally appropriated by him, involving nearly $1 million. A motion by the defendant to dismiss the suit was denied and no further action is reported in the published decision. The suit was probably settled out of court.[38] In 1928 J. H. McIntosh made public criticisms of the management of the company,[39] and in 1936 charges were made that the funds of the corporation were misapplied when stock options were given by the directors to two officers of the corporation.[40] In 1941 holders of preferred stock petitioned for an injunction against payment of dividends on common stock since no dividends had been paid on preferred stock from 1935 to 1937.[41] Finally in 1941 minority stockholders brought suit against the president and other officers of the U.S. Rubber Company, charging that the corporation was dominated by the DuPonts and managed in their interest and to the injury of the minority stockholders. The suit charged that 25,000 shares of stock had been given to the president, and nearly $3 million distributed among the officers on the managers' share plan, and also excess salaries of $2/3 million had been paid to two officers, unlawful dividends of $2½ million paid, and contributions made to the Tire Dealers Association, which was engaged in a conspiracy to violate the antitrust laws. This suit was dismissed.[42]

W. W. Ayer & Son won a suit against U.S. Rubber Company and were awarded damages of $178,600. This suit charged that U.S. Rubber Company had made a contract for advertising with W. W. Ayer & Son and refused to pay for the advertising until ordered by the court to do so.[43] Also, a breach of contract suit, involving fraud, was decided against the Fisk Tire Company in 1933, before it was taken over by the U.S. Rubber Company but when it was alleged to be closely affiliated with the U.S. Rubber Company.[44]

Thus the U.S. Rubber Company was illegitimate in origin and a persistent violator of laws since its origin. Particularly it has been a persistent violator of the antitrust laws, and this indicated that it is antagonistic toward the system of free competition and of free enterprise. Also, it has many complaints of financial manipulations both in its earlier and its later history, and occasional adverse decisions on infringements of patents, misrepresentation in advertising, and unfair labor practices.

The Pittsburgh Coal Company

The Pittsburgh Coal Company is described as an illustration of a corporation with the lowest number of adverse decisions of any of the 70 corporations. The evidence, although lacking the finality of official decisions, indicates that this corporation was not significantly different from the other corporations which have been described.

The one official decision against this corporation was directed at a subsidiary—the Pittsburgh Coal Company of Wisconsin. This subsidiary was a member of the Northwestern Coal Operators Association, which had been organized in 1914 by ten companies engaged in the purchase and transportation of coal to ports on Lake Superior. The association adopted a policy of uniform prices, with the purpose of eliminating price competition among these companies. It used coercion to force other coal companies to join the association and abide by the uniform prices. The Federal Trade Commission issued a desist order against the Pittsburgh Coal Company of Wisconsin and the other members of the association.[45] This decision, however, was only an incident in a long-continued policy of restraint of trade. The Pittsburgh Coal Company was organized in 1899, when many other mergers were being formed and when the Mellons had already secured a virtual monopoly in the aluminum industry. In that year the Mellon interests in Pittsburgh organized two coal companies, namely, the Pittsburgh Coal Company, which was a merger of more than 100 coal companies in the Pittsburgh district which shipped coal by rail, and the Monongahela River Consolidation Coal and Coke Company, which was a similar merger of coal mining companies which shipped coal by river. These two corporations were promoted by the same persons, had interlocking directorates, practical identity of stockholders, and agreements not to interfere with each other. They merged in 1911. One of the general conditions of the merger of 1899 was that the former owners of the coal companies which were being merged would not mine or ship coal within a specified time in this district. Shortly after the mergers were formed the price of coal in this district increased.[46]

At the end of the First World War, indictments were voted against the National Coal Operators' Association, of which the Pittsburgh Coal Company was said to be a member, and the United Mine Workers Union. They were charged with violation of the Sherman Antitrust Act and the war price regulations. The charge was that these two associations had entered into a conspiracy to increase the price of coal by staging fictitious labor difficulties with the design of frightening the public and inducing the public to buy coal at high prices and hoard it. The Federal Bureau of Investigation had secured documentary evidence of this conspiracy from the files of the two associations, and the assistant attorney general in charge of this prosecution claimed that this evidence was sufficient for a conviction. Attorney General Palmer, who was generally opposed to the prosecution of war frauds and who was himself later indicted, ordered D. W. Simms, special attorney in this case, not to use the documentary evidence in this trial. Simms promptly resigned and made public the Attorney General's order, with the explanation that this evidence was "the heart of the case." The suit was postponed again and again, until Daugherty, a new attorney general, appeared in person at the trial and moved for the dismissal of the indictment. While he castigated both associations, he explained that the collusion had been fostered by the Wilson administration as a method of preventing strikes during the war period.[47]

Several complaints have been made in regard to the financial policies of this corporation. The Industrial Commission, in its report in 1901, estimated that the value of the coal-mining companies which were merged was approximately half of the $64 million, at which the new corporation was capitalized, and that the other half was "water." The subsequent claims of this corporation that it was unable to pay adequate dividends should be interpreted in the light of this inflation of stock. At a later date, when the corporation was being reorganized, minority stockholders petitioned for an injunction against the proposed plan. The charge was that the holders of the 7 percent preferred stock would suffer a loss of approximately $7 million if the proposed plan were adopted. No decision on this question has been discovered.[48] Another illustration of the financial methods of this corporation occurred when the U.S. Steel Corporation was expected to buy the assets of the Pittsburgh Coal Company, and when the market value of the stock was increasing in value. The corporation, controlled by the Mellons, issued extra shares of treasury stock of the corporation to Richard B. Mellon at $35 a share, when the market value of these shares was $70. This amounted to a gift of $5 million.[49]

The Pittsburgh Coal Company, like other coal companies, was accused of violating the war regulations in both of the world wars. As soon as the First World War was under way the price of coal increased and continued to increase. Business and industrial firms made formal complaints, grand juries made investigations, and the Federal Trade Commission was ordered by Congress to make an investigation of these price increases. The commission reported that the increases were unreasonable, the Federal Administration fixed prices of coal, and a Fuel Administration was set up. The coal companies complained again and again that they could not mine coal at those prices and pressed for higher prices. Subsequently, McAdoo, who had been Secretary of the Treasury during the war, reported that the income tax reports of coal companies showed that they made profits of 200 to 300 percent on capital stock in many cases and even of 20,000 percent in one case. He urged that publicity be given to these income tax reports, but this proposal was strenuously resisted by the coal companies.[50] A study by the Coal Commission showed that the average profits on capital investments in certain districts was five times as high in the war years as in the prewar years.[51] During the Second World War, a suit for treble damages of $1,050,000 was initiated against the Pittsburgh Coal Company for violations of price ceilings on coal. No outcome of this suit has been discovered.[52]

The Pittsburgh Coal Company, like many other coal companies, has been in almost continuous conflict with organized labor. Its representatives have asserted again and again that they would have no dealings with the United Mine Workers. Through subsidiaries, it has purchased mines in some of the Kentucky counties in which the coal operators associations have conducted policies of terrorism. A few incidents in the labor relations of the Pittsburgh Coal Company will be described. This corporation signed a contract with the United Mine Workers in 1924, with the provision that it was to continue until March 31, 1927.

Following the example of the coal mining companies owned by the Standard Oil Company and the Bethlehem Steel Company, the Pittsburgh Coal Company in August 1925 canceled this contract, which was not to expire until March 1927. It posted notices that wages would be reduced approximately one-third. The union asserted that these cancellations of contracts were a part of a general campaign to destroy the union. An independent coal mine in the Pittsburgh District, which was heavily indebted to a Pittsburgh bank, was notified by the bank that its loans would be called if it made an agreement with the union, as it was inclined to do. Another independent mine in this district, which sold most of its output to General Motors, was notified by General Motors that no coal would be taken if the company signed an agreement with the union. Some railway companies refused to take coal from mines which signed the agreement with the union. The Pittsburgh Coal Company began to evict its employees from the company houses in its mining communities. In one community a court issued an injunction against these evictions. Employees of the corporation came to a house from which they had been unable to evict an employee and took the roof off the house, with the explanation that repairs were to be made. The house was left with no roof and with the occupants exposed to the weather. A Senate Committee was authorized to investigate this labor conflict. This committee printed, as part of its *Report*, the following letter, which was alleged to have been sent by the Pittsburgh Coal Company to the superintendents of its mines:

To all Mine Superintendents: The United States Senate Investigating Committee is now visiting the Pittsburgh District. Clear up all unsightly conditions. Keep our police in the background. Avoid all arrests. Instruct our men to keep out of trouble. If the Committee desires to question any of our employees, see to it that you present men you can trust and who can be depended upon to give the right kind of answers. If you are examined by the Committee, do not answer any questions you think might be harmful to our interests. The Company will protect you. The Company has mailed a spirited letter to each individual employee. If you know of any unsatisfactory condition in company camps or barracks, see that it is eliminated at once.

(Signed)   Pittsburgh Coal Co.

The Pittsburgh Coal Company asserts that this letter was not authorized and did not come from their office.

The Pittsburgh Coal police, operating under the direction of the Pittsburgh Coal Company in this labor controversy, have been convicted of two cases of felonious homicide. Two members of this police force beat a striker, John Barkoski, to death in the police barracks, continuing to beat him after they had been warned by a company doctor that it was dangerous to do so. These two members of the Coal Police were defended by the attorney for the Pittsburgh Coal Company, and were sentenced to relatively short terms of imprisonment. The Pittsburgh Coal Company paid the widow of the victim of this murder $13,500. Again, a member of the Pittsburgh Coal Police and the superintendent of one of the mines were convicted of felonious homicide when they shot John Philipovich as he was standing unarmed on the porch of his store, because he had expressed sympathy for the strikers.[53]

The U.S. Coal Commission developed a community scorecard and used this in scoring a total of 713 coal-mining communities. Of these 713 communities, only 66 scored as high as 75 on a scale of 100, and approximately the same number scored less than 50. The Pittsburgh Coal

Company's communities were in the lower extreme, with an average score of 40.4.[54]

The three detailed descriptions of corporations indicate that the number of official decisions against a corporation is not a good index of the extent to which it obeys the law. When other types of evidence are taken into consideration, these three corporations appear to differ in their violations of law to a very slight extent.

4

IS "WHITE COLLAR CRIME" CRIME?

It has been shown in an earlier chapter that 980 decisions have been made against the 70 largest industrial and mercantile corporations, with an average of 14.0 decisions per corporation. Although all of these are decisions that the corporations have acted unlawfully, only 158, or 16 percent, of them were made by criminal courts and were ipso facto decisions that the behavior was criminal. Since not all unlawful behavior is criminal behavior, these decisions can be used as a measure of criminal behavior only insofar as the other 822 decisions can be shown to be decisions that the behavior was criminal as well as unlawful.

This is a problem in the definition of crime and involves two types of questions: First, may the word "crime" be applied to the behavior regarding which these decisions were made? Second, if so, why is it not generally applied and why have not criminologists regarded white collar crime as cognate with other crime? The first question involves semantics, the second explanation or interpretation. The following analysis will be limited almost entirely to the laws regarding restraint of trade, misrepresentation in advertising, infringements of patents and analogous rights, and unfair labor practices in violation of the National Labor Relations Law. Little attention is devoted to the other laws, in part because some of the other laws are explicit criminal laws, such as those relating to rebates or adulteration of foods and drugs, and in part because so many different laws are involved in the miscellaneous group of offenses that the analysis would be unduly extended if each of those laws was given specific attention.

The definition of crime, from the point of view of the present analysis, is important only as a means of determining whether the behavior should be included within the scope of a theory of criminal behavior. More specifically, the problem is: From the point of view of a theory of criminal behavior, are the illegal acts of corporations which have been tabulated above cognate with the burglaries, robberies, and other crimes which are customarily included within the scope of theories of criminal behavior? Some writers have argued that an act is criminal only if a criminal court has officially determined that the person accused of that act has committed a crime. This limitation in the definition of crime may be made properly if a writer is interested primarily in administrative questions. The warden of a prison would not be justified in receiving an offender in the penal institution unless that offender had been officially convicted and sentenced to serve a term of imprisonment in that institution. Similarly, public authorities would not be justified in denying civil rights to offenders who had not been convicted of crimes. In contrast, the criminologist who is interested in a theory of criminal behavior needs to know only that a certain class of acts is legally defined as crime and that a particular person has committed an act of this class. The criminologist needs to have certain knowledge on both of these points, but for this purpose a decision of a court is no more essential than it is for certain knowledge in chemistry or biology. However, in the tabulations in this book decisions of courts and commissions have been used as proof that prohibited acts have been committed.

The essential characteristic of crime is that it is behavior which is prohibited by the State as an injury to the State and against which the State may react, at least as a last resort, by punishment. The two abstract criteria generally regarded by legal scholars as necessary elements in a definition of crime are legal description of an act as socially harmful and legal provision of a penalty for the act.[1]

The first of these criteria—legal definition of a social harm—applies to all of the classes of acts which are included in the 980 decisions tabulated above. This can be readily determined by the words in the statutes—"crime" or "misdemeanor" in some, and "unfair," "discrimination," or "infringement" in all the others. The persons injured may be divided into two groups: first, a relatively small number of persons engaged in the same occupation as the offenders or in related occupations, and second, the general public either as consumers or as constituents of the general social institutions which are affected by the violations of the laws.

The antitrust laws are designed to protect competitors and also to protect the institution of free competition as the regulator of the economic system and thereby to protect consumers against arbitrary prices, and to protect the institution of democracy against the dangers of great concentration of wealth in the hands of monopolies. Laws against false advertising are designed to protect competitors against unfair competition and also to protect consumers against fraud. The National Labor Relations Law is designed to protect employees against coercion by employers and also to protect the general public against interferences with commerce due to strikes and lockouts. The laws against infringements are designed to protect the owners of patents, copyrights, and trademarks against deprivation of their property and against unfair competition, and also to protect the institution of patents and copyrights which was established in order to "promote the progress of science and the useful arts." Violations of these laws are legally defined as injuries to the parties specified.

Each of these laws has a logical basis in the common law and is an adaptation of the common law to modern social organization. False advertising is related to common law fraud, and infringement to larceny. The National Labor Relations Law, as an attempt to prevent coercion, is related to the common law prohibition of restrictions on freedom in the form of assault, false imprisonment, and extortion. For at least two centuries prior to the enactment of the modern antitrust laws the common law was moving against restraint of trade, monopoly, and unfair competition.

Each of the four types of laws under consideration, with the possible exception of the laws regarding infringements, grew primarily out of considerations of the welfare of the organized society. In this respect, they are analogous to the laws of the earliest societies, where crimes were largely limited to injuries such as treason, in which the organized society was the victim and particular persons suffered only as they were members of the organized society. Subsequent criminal laws have been concerned principally with person-to-person injuries, as in larceny, and the State has taken jurisdiction over the procedures principally in order to bring private vengeance under public control. The interest of the State in such behavior is secondary or derivative. In this sense, the four laws under consideration may properly be regarded as criminal laws in a more fundamental sense than the laws regarding larceny.

Each of the four laws provides a penal sanction and thus meets the second criterion in the definition of crime, and each of the adverse decisions under these four laws, except certain decisions under the infringement laws to be discussed later, is a decision that a crime was committed. This conclusion will be made more specific by analysis of the penal sanctions provided in the four laws.

The Sherman Antitrust Act states explicitly that a violation of the law is a misdemeanor. Three methods of enforcement of this law are provided, each of them involving procedures regarding misdemeanors. First, it may be enforced by the usual criminal prosecution, resulting in the imposition of fine or imprisonment. Second, the attorney general of the United States and the several district attorneys are given the "duty" of "repressing and preventing" violations of the law by petitions for injunctions, and violations of the injunctions are punishable as contempt of court. This method of enforcing a criminal law was an invention and, as will be described later, is the key to the interpretation of the differential implementation of the criminal law as applied to white collar criminals. Third, parties who are injured by violations of the law are authorized to sue for damages, with a mandatory provision that the damages awarded be three times the injuries suffered. These damages in excess of reparation are penalties for violation of the law. They are payable to the injured party in order to induce him to take the initiative in the enforcement of the criminal law and in this respect are similar to the earlier methods of private prosecutions under the criminal law. All three of these methods of enforcement are based on decisions that a criminal law was violated and therefore that a crime was committed; the decisions of a civil court or a court of equity as to these violations are as good evidence of criminal behavior as is the decision of a criminal court.

Judge Carpenter stated in regard to the injunctions under the antitrust law, "The Supreme Court in upholding them necessarily has determined that the things which were enjoined were crimes, as defined by one at least of the first three sections of the Act."[2]

The Sherman Antitrust Act has been supplemented by the Federal Trade Commission Law, the Clayton Law, and several other laws. Some of these supplementary laws define violations as crimes and provide the conventional penalties, but most of them do not make the criminality explicit. A large proportion of the cases which are dealt with under these supplementary laws could be dealt with, instead, under the original Sherman Act, which is explicitly a criminal law, or under the antitrust laws of the several states, which also are explicit criminal laws. In practice, the supplementary laws are generally under the jurisdiction of the Federal Trade Commission, which has authority to make official decisions as to violations. The commission has two principal sanctions under its control, namely: the stipulation and the cease and desist order. The commission may, after the violation of the law has been proved, accept a stipulation from the corporation that it will not violate the law in the future. Such stipulations are customarily restricted to the minor or technical violations. If a stipulation is violated or if no stipulation is accepted, the commission may issue a cease and desist order; this is equivalent to a court's injunction except that violation is not punishable as contempt. If the commission's desist order is violated, the commission may apply to the court for an injunction, the violation of which is punishable as contempt. By an amendment to the Federal Trade Commission Law in the Wheeler–Lea Act of 1938 an order of the commission becomes "final" if not officially questioned within a specified time and thereafter its violation is punishable by a civil fine. Thus, although certain interim procedures may be used in the enforcement of the laws supplementary to the Sherman Antitrust Act, fines or imprisonment for contempt is available if the interim procedures fail. In this respect the interim procedures are similar to probation in ordinary criminal cases. An unlawful act is not defined as criminal by the fact that it is punished, but by the fact that it is punishable. Larceny is as truly a crime when the thief is placed on probation as when he is committed to prison. The argument may be made that punishment for contempt of court is not punishment for violation of the original law and that, therefore, the original law does not contain a penal sanction. This reasoning is specious since the original law provides the injunction with its penalty as a part of the procedure for enforcement. Consequently all of the decisions made under the amendments to the antitrust law are decisions that the corporations committed crimes.[3]

The laws regarding false advertising, as included in the decisions under consideration, are of two types. First, false advertising in the form of false labels is defined in the Pure Food and Drug Law as a misdemeanor and is punishable by a fine. Second, false advertising generally is defined in the Federal Trade Commission Act as unfair competition. Cases of the second type are under the jurisdiction of the Federal Trade Commission, which uses the same procedures as in antitrust cases. Penal sanctions are available in antitrust cases, as previously described, and are similarly available in these cases of false advertising. Thus, all of the decisions in false advertising cases are decisions that the corporations committed crimes.

The National Labor Relations Law of 1935 defines a violation as "unfair labor practice." The National Labor Relations Board is authorized to make official decisions as to violations of the law and, in case of violation, to issue desist orders and also to make certain remedial orders, such as

reimbursement of employees who had been dismissed or demoted because of activities in collective bargaining. If an order is violated, the
board may apply to the court for enforcement and a violation of the order
of the court is punishable as contempt. Thus, all of the decisions under
this law, which is enforceable by penal sanctions, are decisions that
crimes were committed.[4]

The laws regarding infringements are more complex than those previously described. Infringements of a copyright or of a patented design
are defined in the federal statutes as misdemeanors, punishable by
fines. Decisions against the 70 corporations have been made in 7 cases
under the copyright laws and in no cases, so far as discovered, on
charges of infringement of patented designs. Other infringements are
not explicitly defined in the federal statutes on patents and trademarks
as crimes, although many states have so defined infringements of trademarks.[5] Nevertheless, these infringements may be criminal acts under
federal statutes in either of two respects. First, the statutes provide that
damages awarded to injured owners of patents or trademarks may be
greater than the injuries actually suffered. These are punitive damages
and constitute one form of punishment. Although these punitive damages are not mandatory under the Sherman Antitrust Act, they are not
explicitly limited to wanton and malicious infringements. Also, the rule
in federal trademark cases is that an account of profits is taken only
when the infringement involves wrongful intent to defraud the original
owner or deceive the public. These decisions, therefore, are equivalent
to convictions in criminal trials. On these principles 3 of the decisions
against the 70 corporations in patent cases and 6 in trademark cases are
classified as criminal convictions. Second, agents of the Federal Trade
Commission may initiate actions against infringers as unfair competition.
Infringements proceeded against in this manner may be punished in
the same sense as violation of the antitrust law, namely, by stipulations,
desist orders, and fines or imprisonment for violation of desist orders.
Five decisions in infringement cases against the 70 corporations are
classified as criminal actions in this sense. This gives a total of 21 decisions in infringement cases which may be classified as evidence of criminal behavior of the 70 corporations. Of the 222 decisions, 201 are left
unaccounted for in terms of criminality. The evidence in some of these
cases and in the descriptions of general practices regarding patents and
trademarks justifies an estimate that a large proportion of the 201
cases—perhaps half—involved willful appropriation of the property of

others and might have resulted in penalties under state or federal laws if the injured parties had approached the behavior from the point of view of crime. In spite of this estimate, the 201 decisions are not included as evidence of criminal behavior.

The laws in regard to financial manipulations, such as violations of trust, stock market manipulations, stock watering, misrepresentation in the sale of securities, are generally based on the laws of fraud or violation of trust. A poor man was recently sentenced in Indiana to serve from one to seven years in the state prison on conviction of false pretenses; he had listed with a finance company household goods which he did not own as a means of securing a loan. The same law applies to corporations but it is seldom used when corporations misrepresent their assets. The judicial decisions have tended toward higher standards of protection of stockholders and the public, and the Securities and Exchange Commission has been organized to implement these laws. Most of the regulations imposed by this commission during the last decade and a half were in accordance with some of the earlier decisions of courts.[6]

The penalties presented in the preceding section as definitive of crime were limited to fines, imprisonment, and punitive damages. In addition, the stipulation, the desist order, and the injunction without reference to penalty for contempt have the attributes of punishment. This is evident both in the fact that they result in some suffering on the part of the corporation against which they are issued, and also in the fact that they were designed by legislators and administrators to produce suffering. The suffering takes the form of public shame, which is an important aspect of all penalties. This was illustrated in extreme form in the colonial penalty of sewing the letter "T" on the clothing of a thief. In England the Bread Act of 1836 and the Adulteration of Seeds Act in 1869 provided the penalty of publication in the newspaper of the details regarding the crimes of adulteration of these products; the Public Health Act of 1891 authorized the court to order a person twice convicted of selling meat unfit for human consumption to fix a sign on his place of business of a size to be specified by the court, stating that he had been convicted twice of violating this law. Stipulations, desist orders, and injunctions to some extent resemble these publicity penalties of England. That the publication of the stipulation in Federal Trade Commission cases is a punishment is attested by Lowell B. Mason, a member of the commission.[7]

That this suffering is designed is apparent from the sequence of sanctions used by the Federal Trade Commission. The stipulation involves the least publicity and is used for minor and technical violations. The desist order is used if the stipulation is violated and also if the violation of the law is appraised by the commission as willful and major. The desist order involves more public shame than the stipulation. The shame resulting from the stipulation and the desist order is somewhat mitigated by the argument made by corporations, in exculpation, that such orders are merely the acts of bureaucrats. Still more shameful to the corporation is an injunction issued by a court. The shame resulting from an injunction is sometimes mitigated and the corporation's face is saved by taking a consent decree, or making a plea of nolo contendere. The corporation may insist that the consent decree is not an admission that it violated the law. For instance, the meat packers took a consent decree in an antitrust case in 1921, with the explanation that they had not knowingly violated any law and were consenting to the decree without attempting to defend themselves because they wished to cooperate with the government in every possible way. This patriotic motivation appeared questionable, however, after the packers fought during the next decade and a half for a modification of the decree. The plea of nolo contendere was first used in antitrust cases in 1910 but has been used in hundreds of cases since that date. This plea at the same time saves the face of the corporation and protects the corporation against suits for damages, since the decision in a case in which the plea is nolo contendere may not be used as evidence in other cases.[8] The sequence of stipulation, desist order, and injunction indicates that the variations in public shame are designed; also, the arguments and tactics used by corporations to protect themselves against public shame in connection with these orders indicate that the corporations recognize them as punishments.

The conclusion in this semantic portion of the analysis is that 779 of the 980 decisions against the 70 large corporations are decisions that crimes were committed.

This conclusion may be questioned on the ground that the rules of proof and evidence used in reaching many of these decisions were not the same as the rules used in criminal courts. This involves, especially, the proof of criminal intent and the presumption of innocence. These rules of criminal intent and presumption of innocence, however, are not required in all prosecution in criminal courts and the number of exceptions authorized by statutes is increasing. In many states a person may be committed to prison without protection of one or both of these rules on charges of statutory rape, bigamy, adultery, passing bad checks, selling mortgaged property, defrauding a hotel keeper, and other offenses.[9] Jerome Hall and others who include *mens rea* or criminal intent as one of the essential and universal criteria of crime, justify this inclusion by the argument that exceptions such as those just listed are "bad law."[10] The important consideration here is that the criteria which have been used in defining white collar crimes are not categorically different from the criteria used in defining some other crimes. The proportion of decisions rendered against corporations without the protection of the rules of criminal intent and presumption of innocence is probably greater than the proportion rendered against other criminals, but a difference in proportions does not make the violations of law by corporations categorically different from the violations of laws by other criminals. Moreover, the difference in proportion, as the procedures actually operate, is not great. On the one hand, many of the defendants in usual criminal cases, being in relative poverty, do not get good defense and consequently secure little benefit from these rules; on the other hand, the commissions come close to observing these rules of proof and evidence although they are not required to do so. This is illustrated by the procedure of the Federal Trade Commission in regard to advertisements. Each year it examines several hundred thousand advertisements and appraises about 50,000 of them as probably false. From the 50,000 it selects about 1,500 as patently false. For instance, an advertisement of gumwood furniture as "mahogany" would seldom be an accidental error and would generally result from a state of mind which deviated from honesty by more than the natural tendency of human beings to feel proud of their handiwork.

The preceding discussion has shown that these 70 corporations committed crimes according to 779 adverse decisions, and also has shown that the criminality of their behavior was not made obvious by the conventional procedures of the criminal law but was blurred and concealed by special procedures. This differential implementation of the law as applied to the crimes of corporations eliminates or at least minimizes the stigma of crime. This differential implementation of the law began with the Sherman Antitrust Act of 1890. As previously described, this law is explicitly a criminal law and a violation of the law is a misdemeanor no matter what procedure is used. The customary policy would have been to rely entirely on criminal prosecution as the method of enforcement.

But a clever invention was made in the provision of an injunction to enforce a criminal law; this was an invention in that it was a direct reversal
of previous case law. Also, private parties were encouraged by treble
damages to enforce a criminal law by suits in civil courts. In either case,
the defendant did not appear in the criminal court and the fact that he
had committed a crime did not appear on the face of the proceedings.

The Sherman Antitrust Act, in this respect, became the model in
practically all the subsequent procedures authorized to deal with the
crimes of corporations. When the Federal Trade Commission bill and
the Clayton bill were introduced in Congress, they contained the conventional criminal procedures; these were eliminated in committee discussions, and other procedures which did not carry the external symbols
of criminal process were substituted. The violations of these laws are
crimes, as has been shown above, but they are treated as though they
were not crimes, with the effect and probably the intention of eliminating the stigma of crime.

This policy of eliminating the stigma of crime is illustrated in the following statement by Wendell Berge, at the time assistant to the head of
the antitrust division of the Department of Justice, in a plea for abandonment of the criminal prosecution under the Sherman Antitrust Act
and the authorization of civil procedures with civil fines as a substitute.

> While civil penalties may be as severe in their financial effects as
> criminal penalties, yet they do not involve the stigma that attends
> indictment and conviction. Most of the defendants in antitrust
> cases are not criminals in the usual sense. There is no inherent rea-
> son why antitrust enforcement requires branding them as such.[11]

If a civil fine were substituted for a criminal fine, a violation of the antitrust law would be as truly a crime as it is now. The thing which would
be eliminated is the stigma of crime. Consequently, the stigma of crime
has become a penalty in itself, which may be imposed in connection
with other penalties or withheld, just as it is possible to combine imprisonment with a fine or have a fine without imprisonment. A civil fine is a
financial penalty without the additional penalty of stigma, while a criminal fine is a financial penalty with the additional penalty of stigma.

When the stigma of crime is imposed as a penalty, it places the defendant within the popular stereotype of "the criminal." In primitive society "the criminal" was substantially the same as "the stranger,"[12]
while in modern society the stereotype is limited largely to the lower so-

cioeconomic class. Seventy-five percent of the persons committed to state prisons are probably not, aside from their unesteemed cultural attainments, "criminals in the usual sense of the word." It may be excellent policy to eliminate the stigma of crime from violations of law by both the upper and the lower classes, but we are not here concerned with policy.

White collar crime is similar to juvenile delinquency in respect to the stigma. In both cases the procedures of the criminal law are modified so that the stigma of crime will not attach to the offenders. The stigma of crime has been less completely eliminated from juvenile delinquency than from white collar crimes because the procedures for the former are a less complete departure from conventional criminal procedures, because most juvenile delinquents come from the lower class, and because the juveniles are not organized to protect their good names. Because these juvenile delinquents have not been successfully freed from the stigma of crime, they have been generally held to be within the scope of the theories of criminal behavior and in fact provide a large part of the data for criminology. Because the external symbols have been more completely eliminated from white collar crimes, white collar crimes have not generally been included within the scope of criminology. These procedural symbols, however, are not the essential elements in criminality and white collar crimes belong logically within the scope of criminology, just as do juvenile delinquencies.

Those who insist that moral culpability is a necessary element in crime may argue that criminality is lacking in the violations of laws which have eliminated the stigma from crime. This involves the general question of the relation of criminal law to the mores. The laws with which we are here concerned are not arbitrary, as is the regulation that one must drive on the right side of the street. The Sherman Antitrust Act, for instance, represents a settled tradition in favor of free competition and free enterprise. This ideology is obvious in the resentment against communism. A violation of the antitrust laws is a violation of strongly entrenched moral sentiments. The value of these laws is questioned principally by persons who believe in a more collectivistic economic system, and these persons are limited to two principal groups, namely, socialists and the leaders of Big Business. When the leaders of business, through corporate activities, violate the antitrust law, they are violating the moral sentiments of practically all parts of the American public except the socialists.

The other laws for the regulation of business are similarly rooted in moral sentiments. Violations of these laws, to be sure, do not call forth as much resentment as do murder and rape, but not all laws in the penal code involve equal resentments by the public. We divide crimes into felonies, which elicit more resentment, and misdemeanors, which elicit less resentment. Within each of these classes, again, the several statutes may be arranged in order of the degree of atrocity. White collar crimes, presumably, would be in the lower part of the range, in this respect, but not entirely out of the range. Moreover, very few of the ordinary crimes arouse much resentment in the ordinary citizen, unless the crimes are very spectacular or unless he or his immediate friends are affected. The average citizen, reading in the morning newspaper that the home of an unknown person has been burglarized by another unknown person, has no appreciable increase in blood pressure. Fear and resentment develop in the modern city principally as the result of an accumulation of crimes, as depicted in crime rates or in general descriptions. Such resentment develops under those circumstances both as to white collar crimes and other crimes. Finally, not all parts of the society react in the same manner against the violation of a particular law. It is true that one's business associates do not regard a violation of a business regulation as atrocious. It is true, also, that people in certain city slum areas do not regard larceny by their neighbors as atrocious, for they will ordinarily give assistance to these neighbors who are being pursued by the agents of criminal justice.

The differential implementation of the law as it applies to large corporations may be explained by three factors, namely, the status of the businessman, the trend away from punishment, and the relatively unorganized resentment of the public against white collar crimes. Each of these will be described.

First, the methods used in the enforcement of any law are an adaptation to the characteristics of the prospective violators of the law, as appraised by the legislators and the judicial and administrative personnel. The appraisals regarding businessmen, who are the prospective violators of the laws which are now under consideration, include a combination of fear and admiration. Those who are responsible for the system of criminal justice are afraid to antagonize businessmen; among other consequences, such antagonism may result in a reduction in contributions to the campaign funds needed to win the next election. The amendment to the Pure Food and Drug Law of 1938 explicitly excludes from the penal provisions of that law the advertising agencies and media (that is, principally, newspapers and journals) which participate in the misrepresentation. Accessories to crimes are customarily included within the scope of the criminal law, but these accessories are very powerful and influential in the determination of public opinion and they are made immune. Probably much more important than fear, however, is the cultural homogeneity of legislators, judges, and administrators with businessmen. Legislators admire and respect businessmen and cannot conceive of them as criminals; businessmen do not conform to the popular stereotype of "the criminal." The legislators are confident that these respectable gentlemen will conform to the law as the result of very mild pressures. The most powerful group in medieval society secured relative immunity by "benefit of clergy," and now our most powerful group secures relative immunity by "benefit of business," or more generally "high social status." The statement of Daniel Drew, a pious old fraud, describes the working of the criminal law with accuracy, "Law is like a cobweb: it's made for flies and the smaller kind of insects, so to speak, but lets the big bumblebee break through. When technicalities of the law stood in my way, I have always been able to brush them aside easy as anything."

This interpretation meets with considerable opposition from persons who insist that this is an egalitarian society in which all men are equal in the eyes of the law. It is not possible to give a complete demonstration of the validity of this interpretation but four types of evidence are presented in the following paragraphs as partial demonstration.

The Department of Justice is authorized to use both criminal prosecutions and petitions in equity to enforce the Sherman Antitrust Act. The department has selected the method of criminal prosecution in a larger proportion of cases against trade unions than of cases against corporations, although the law was enacted primarily because of fear of the corporations. From 1890 to 1929 the Department of Justice initiated 438 actions under this law with decisions favorable to the United States. Of the actions against business firms, 27 percent were criminal prosecutions, while of the actions against trade unions 71 percent were criminal prosecutions.[13] This shows that the Department of Justice has been comparatively reluctant to use a method against business firms which carries with it the stigma of crime.

The method of criminal prosecution in enforcement of the Sherman Antitrust Act has varied from one presidential administration to another.

It was seldom used in the administrations of the presidents who were popularly appraised as friendly toward business, namely, McKinley, Harding, Coolidge, and Hoover.

Businessmen suffered their greatest loss of prestige in the depression which began in 1929. It was precisely in this period of low status of businessmen that the most strenuous efforts were made to enforce the old laws and enact new laws for the regulation of businessmen. The appropriations for this purpose were multiplied several times and persons were selected for their vigor in administration of the law, with the result that the number of decisions against the 70 corporations was quadrupled in the next decade.

The Federal Trade Commission Law states that a violation of the law by a corporation shall be deemed to be also a violation by the officers and directors of the corporation. Businessmen, however, are seldom convicted in criminal courts, and several cases have been reported, like the 6 percent case of the automobile industry, in which corporations were convicted and the persons who directed the corporation were all acquitted. Executives of corporations are convicted in criminal courts principally when they use methods of crime similar to the methods of the lower socioeconomic class.

A second factor in the explanation of the differential implementation of the law as applied to white collar criminals is the trend away from penal methods. This trend advanced more rapidly in the area of white collar crimes than of other crimes. The trend is seen in general in the almost complete abandonment of the extreme penalties of death and physical torture; in the supplanting of conventional penal methods by nonpenal methods such as probation and the case work methods which accompany probation; and in the supplementing of penal methods by nonpenal methods, as in the development of case work and educational policies in prisons. These decreases in penal methods are explained by a series of social changes: the increased power of the lower socioeconomic class upon which previously most of the penalties were inflicted; the inclusion within the scope of the penal laws of a large part of the upper socioeconomic class as illustrated by traffic regulations; the increased social interaction among the classes, which has resulted in increased understanding and sympathy; the failure of penal methods to make substantial reductions in crime rates; and the weakening hold on the legal profession and others of the individualistic and hedonistic psychology which had placed great emphasis on pain in the control of behavior. To some extent overlapping those just mentioned is the fact that punishment, which was previously the chief reliance for control in the home, the school, and the church, has tended to disappear from those institutions, leaving the State without cultural support for its own penal methods.[14]

The third factor in the differential implementation of the law in the area of white collar crime is the relatively unorganized resentment of the public toward white collar crimes. Three reasons for the different relation between law and mores in this area may be given. (a) The violations of law by businessmen are complex and their effects diffused. They are not simple and direct attack by one person on another person, as is assault and battery. Many of the white collar crimes can be appreciated only by persons who are experts in the occupations in which they occur. A corporation often violates a law for a decade or longer before the administrative agencies or the public becomes aware of the violation. The effects of these crimes may be diffused over a long period of time and perhaps millions of people, with no particular person suffering much at a particular time. (b) The public agencies of communication do not express the organized moral sentiments of the community as to white collar crimes, in part because the crimes are complicated and not easily presented as news, but probably in greater part because these agencies of communication are owned or controlled by businessmen and because these agencies are themselves involved in the violations of many of these laws. Public opinion in regard to picking pockets would not be well organized if most of the information regarding this crime came to the public directly from the pickpockets themselves. This failure of the public agencies of communication may be illustrated by the almost complete lack of attention by newspapers to the evidence presented in the trial of A. B. Dick and other mimeographing companies that these companies maintained a sabotage school in Chicago in which their employees were trained to sabotage the machines of rival companies, and even their own machines if the supplies of rival companies are being used.[15]

Analogous behavior of trade unions, with features as spectacular as in this case, would have been described in hundreds of newspapers with large headlines on the front page, while many newspapers did not even mention this decision, and those which did mention it placed a brief paragraph on an inner page. (c) These laws for the regulation of business belong to a relatively new and specialized part of the statutes. The old common law crimes, as continued in the regular penal codes, were generally limited to person-to-person attacks, which might be committed by an person in any society. In the more complex society of the present day, legislatures have felt compelled to regulate many special occupations and other special groups. The penal code of California, for instance, contains an index of penal provisions in the statutes outside of the penal code, which are designed to regulate barbers, plumbers, farmers, corporations, and many other special groups. This index occupies 46 pages, and the complete statutes to which reference is made in the index would occupy many hundreds of pages. This illustrates the great expansion of penal provisions beyond the simple requirements of the earlier societies. The teachers of criminal law, who generally confine their attention to the old penal code, are missing the larger part of the penal law of the modern state. Similarly, the general public is not generally aware of many of these specialized provisions and the resentment of the public is not organized.

For the three reasons which have been presented, the public does not have the same organized resentment toward white collar crimes as toward certain of the serious felonies. The relation between the law and mores, finally, tends to be circular. The laws, to a considerable extent, are crystallizations of the mores, and each act of enforcement of the laws tends to reenforce the mores. The laws regarding white collar crimes, which conceal the criminality of the behavior, have been less effective than other criminal laws in reenforcing the mores.

The answers to the questions posed at the beginning of this chapter may be given in the following propositions: First, the white collar crimes which are discussed in this book have the general criteria of criminal behavior, namely, legal definition of social injuries and penal sanctions, and are therefore cognate with other crimes. Second, these white collar crimes have generally not been regarded by criminologists as cognate with other crimes and as within the scope of theories of criminal behavior because the administrative and judicial procedures have been different for these violations of criminal law than for other violations of criminal law. Third, this differential implementation of the criminal law as applied to businessmen is explained by the status of the businessman, the trend away from reliance on punitive methods, and the relatively unorganized resentment of the public toward white collar crimes.

Since this analysis is concerned with violations of laws by corporations, a brief description of the relation of the corporation to the criminal law is necessary. Three or four generations ago the courts with unanimity decided that corporations could not commit crimes. These decisions were based on one or more of the following principles. First, since the corporation is a legislative artifact and does not have a mind or soul, it cannot have criminal intent and therefore cannot commit a crime. Second, since a corporation is not authorized to do unlawful acts, the agents of a corporation are not authorized to do unlawful acts. If those agents commit unlawful acts, they do so in their personal capacity and not in their capacity as agents. They may be punished, therefore, as persons but not as agents. Third, with a few exceptions the only penalties that can be imposed on corporations, if found guilty of crimes, are fines. These fines are injurious to stockholders, and consequently, as a matter of policy, should not be imposed.

These principles have now been reversed by the courts and corporations are now frequently convicted of crimes. Corporations have been convicted of larceny, manslaughter, keeping disorderly houses, breaking the Sabbath, destruction of property and a great variety of other crimes.[16] Such decisions involved reversal of the three principles on which the earlier decisions were based. First, the corporation is not merely a legislative artifact. Associations of persons existed prior to the law and some of these associations have been recognized as entities by legislatures. These corporations and other associations are instrumental in influencing legislation. Consequently legislation is in part an artifact of corporations, just as corporations are in part an artifact of legislatures.[17] Second, the requirement that criminal intent be demonstrated has been eliminated from an increasing number of criminal laws, as was described above. Third, the location of responsibility has been extremely difficult in many parts of modern society, and responsibility is certainly a much more complicated concept than is ordinarily believed. The old employers' liability laws, which were based on the principle of individual responsibility, broke down because responsibility for industrial accidents could not be located. Workmen's compensation laws were substituted, with their principle that the industrial establishment should bear the cost of industrial accidents. Some attention has been given to the location of responsibility for decisions in the large corporations.[18] Although responsibility for actions of particular types may be located, power to modify such actions lies also at various other points. Due largely to the complexity of this concept, the question of individual responsibility is frequently waived and penalties are imposed on corporations. This does, to be sure, affect the stockholder who may have almost no power in making decisions as to policy, but the same thing is true of other penalties which have been suggested as substitutes for fines on corporations, namely, dissolution of the corporation, suspension of business for a specified period, restriction of sphere of action of the corporation, confiscation of goods, publicity, surety for good behavior, and supervision by the court.

Two questions may be raised regarding the responsibility of corporations from the point of view of the statistical tabulation of violations of law. The first is whether a corporation should be held responsible for the action of a special department of the corporation. The advertising department, for instance, may prepare and distribute advertising copy which violates the law. The customary plea of the executives of the corporation is that they were ignorant of and not responsible for the action of the special department. This plea is akin to the alibi of the ordinary criminal and need not to be taken seriously. The departments of a corporation know that their recognition by the executives of the corporation depends on results and that few questions will be asked if results are achieved. In the rare case in which the executives are not only unaware of but sincerely opposed to the policy of a particular department, the corporation is customarily held responsible by the court. That is the only question of interest in the present connection. Consequently, an illegal act is reported as the act of the corporation, without consideration of the location of responsibility within the corporation.

The second question is concerned with the relation between the parent corporation and the subsidiaries. This relationship varies widely from one corporation to another and even within one corporate system. When subsidiaries are prosecuted for violations of law, the parent company generally pleads ignorance of the methods which have been used. This, again, is customarily an alibi, although it may be true in some cases. For instance, the automobile corporations generally insist that the labor policy of each subsidiary is determined by that subsidiary and is not within the control of the parent company. However, when a labor controversy arose in a plant in Texas and a settlement was proposed by the labor leaders, the personnel department of that plant replied, "We must consult Detroit." They reported the following morning, "Detroit says 'No.' " For the present purpose, the corporation and its subsidiaries are treated as a unit, without regard to the location of responsibility within that unit.

5

RESTRAINT OF TRADE

Number of Violations

Businessmen by restraint of trade have committed many crimes against other businessmen and against consumers. The prevalence of illegal restraint of trade is shown in Table 6, which presents the official decisions on this offense against the 70 large industrial and mercantile corporations during their life careers. A total of 307 decisions have been made against 60 of the 70 corporations.[1] All of these are decisions of federal courts or commissions except 23, which were state suits; of the 23 state suits, 16 resulted in convictions in criminal courts and 7 in decisions under equity jurisdiction.

In addition, 157 cases which are not complete or definite enough to include in the tabulation provide further evidence of the prevalence of illegal restraint of trade. These cases are as follows: 23 of the corporations were named in 33 suits as coconspirators although the decisions were not directed against them; 10 were private suits for damages which were settled out of court by payment of damages; 39 were private suits for damages which did not reach a decision in court and which were perhaps settled out of court by payment of damages; 5 were government suits which were dismissed prior to a decision when the corporations took the action requested by the Department of Justice; 41 were suits initiated in 1944 or earlier which were postponed on account of the war and which have not yet been decided; and 31 were complaints initiated since the end of 1944, which is the limit set in this study for the inclusion of cases of restraint of trade.

A decision that a corporation has engaged in illegal restraint of trade refers in most cases to a policy which has been continued for many years. Decisions generally include evidence as to the duration of the policy which is held to be illegal and additional evidence is available in reports of official investigating commissions. This evidence indicates that at least 48 of the 60 large corporations with adverse records have en-

TABLE 6. Decisions against 70 Large Corporations on Restraint of Trade

Corporation	Total	Federal and state criminal suits	Federal and state equity suits	Private suits	Administrative desist orders
Allied Chem. & Dye	7	3	1	—	3
Aluminum Co. of America	4	1	3	—	—
American Can	6	—	1	3	2
American Car & Foundry	1	—	—	—	1
American Rolling Mills	1	1	—	—	—
American Smelting	2	1	—	—	1
American Sugar	7	—	4	3	—
American Tobacco	19	9	2	8	—
American Woolen	1	—	1	—	—
Anaconda	4	1	1	—	2
Armour	12	6	1	—	5
Bethlehem	3	1	—	2	—
Borden	7	5	—	—	2
Chrysler	1	1	—	—	—
Corn Products	3	—	2	—	1
Crane	3	1	1	—	1
Crown Zellerbach	5	3	1	—	1
DuPont	7	3	2	—	2
Eastman	5	—	1	2	2
Firestone	1	—	—	—	1
Ford	1	1	—	—	—
General Electric	13	4	3	2	4
General Motors	6	1	3	1	1
Glen Alden Coal	5	1	4	—	—
Goodrich	1	—	—	—	1
Goodyear	1	—	—	—	1
Great A & P	8	3	—	—	5
Inland	1	—	—	—	1
Intern. Harvester	11	10	1	—	—
Intern. Paper	2	1	1	—	—
Jones & Laughlin	1	—	—	—	1
Kennecott	2	1	—	—	1
Liggett & Myers	1	1	—	—	—
Loew's	22	—	11	7	4
Marshall Field	1	—	—	—	1
Montgomery Ward	1	—	—	—	1
National Biscuit	2	—	—	—	2
National Dairy	8	5	1	—	2
National Lead	3	1	2	—	—
National Steel	1	—	—	—	1
Paramount	21	—	10	7	4
Phelps Dodge	3	1	—	—	2
Phil. & Reading Coal	6	1	5	—	—
Pittsburgh Coal	1	—	—	—	1
Pittsburgh Plate	6	1	1	—	4
Procter & Gamble	1	1	—	—	—
RCA	3	—	1	1	1

TABLE 6 (Continued)

Corporations	Total	Federal and state criminal suits	Federal and state equity suits	Private suits	Administrative desist orders
Republic Steel	3	1	—	—	2
Reynolds Tobacco	1	1	—	—	—
Standard Brands	2	—	—	—	2
Swift	12	7	4	—	1
United Fruit	3	—	1	2	—
United Shoe Mach.	1	—	1	—	—
U.S. Rubber	6	—	—	1	5
U.S. Steel	9	3	1	—	5
Warner Bros.	21	—	10	7	4
Westinghouse	10	3	3	1	3
Wheeling	2	—	—	—	2
Wilson	4	—	3	—	1
Youngstown	2	—	—	—	2
Total	307	84	87	47	89

Note: No adverse decisions on restraint of trade against the following 10 corporations in the list of 70: American Radiator & Standard Sanitary, Deere, Gimbel, International Shoe, Kresge, Macy, Sears Roebuck, Singer, Union Carbide & Carbon, Woolworth.

gaged in illegal restraint of trade almost continuously from their organization to the end of the year 1944.

Among the large corporations which engage in illegal restraint of trade as shown in Table 6, the three motion picture corporations—Loew's, Paramount, and Warner—stand at the top of the list, with 22, 21, and 21 decisions, respectively. The American Tobacco Company is near the same level, with 19 adverse decisions. Following them come General Electric with 13, Armour and Swift with 12 each, International Harvester with 11, Westinghouse Electric with 10, U.S. Steel with 9, and Great A & P with 8. Thus, 86 percent of the 70 large corporations have official records as violators of the antitrust laws, and 73 percent of the corporations with such records are recidivists.

The record of the American Tobacco Company is presented as an illustration of the corporations with many adverse decisions. In this record are included not only the definite decisions but also the suits dismissed and the reports of the official investigating commissions.

1. Suits in 1890–97 under state antitrust laws in Illinois, New Jersey, New York, and Texas, with dismissal in New Jersey and final decisions not discovered in the other three states.[2]

2. Indictment of James B. Duke and other executives of the American Tobacco Co. in New York; dismissed.[3]
3. Report of the U.S. Industrial Commission in 1901, charging that the American Tobacco Company was a combination in restraint of trade, with detailed evidence.[4]
4. Suit under the Missouri antitrust law against Continental Tobacco Co., a subsidiary, dismissed in 1903.[5]
5. Injunction against the Continental Tobacco Co. under Massachusetts antitrust law in 1905.[6]
6. Conviction of two subsidiaries—McAndrews & Forbes and J. S. Young—for restraint of trade in licorice paste.[7]
7. Report of Commissioner of Corporations in 1909, charging monopoly of the tobacco industry by the American Tobacco Co., with detailed evidence.[8]
8. Three criminal suits under the Kentucky state antitrust law, in which demurrers had been sustained, reversed in 1909, and three criminal suits, in which demurrers had been sustained, reversed in 1915.[9]
9. Decree of dissolution of the American Tobacco Co. in 1911 on complaint that this corporation had engaged in restraint of trade since 1890.[10]
10. Seven private suits for damages under the federal antitrust law decided against the American Tobacco Co.,—four in 1908, and one each in 1910, 1912, and 1913—with many other private suits at this time dismissed.[11]
11. Report of the Commissioner of Corporations in 1915, asserting that the decree of dissolution in 1911 had been futile and that restraint of trade in the tobacco industry remained unabated.
12. Complaint by the Federal Trade Commission in 1918 that the American Tobacco Co. was engaged in resale price maintenance in violation of the antitrust law; dismissed by the commission.[12]
13. Report of the Federal Trade Commission in 1920 that the decree of dissolution in 1911 had not restored competition in the tobacco industry and that the decree should be modified.[13]
14. Report of the Federal Trade Commission in 1922 that the American Tobacco Co. had conspired with other tobacco companies and with regional associations of jobbers to prevent price cutting and to discipline those who engaged in price cutting.[14]
15. Desist orders by the Federal Trade Commission in 1923–24 against

the American Tobacco Co., other tobacco companies, and several regional associations of jobbers for conspiring to prevent price cutting; some of the complaints were dismissed on stipulation by the companies that these practices had ceased two years prior to the hearings and would not be resumed. In a test case, which was appealed to the court, the order of the commission was set aside, in part on the ground that the practices had already ceased.[15]

16. Desist order by the Federal Trade Commission against the American Snuff Co., subsidiary, reversed by the court in 1927.[16]

17. Injunction against American Tobacco Company on petition of the Porto Rican American Tobacco Co., on complaint of price discriminations.[17]

18. Conviction in 1940 under criminal process with other tobacco companies for restraint of trade both in the purchase and sale of tobacco, affirmed by U.S. Supreme Court in 1946.[18]

The record of General Motors illustrates a long-time policy of violation of the antitrust laws in the field of parts and accessories. The price-cutting practices of Henry Ford, at least until the late twenties, prevented restraint of trade in the sale of automobiles.

1. General Motors was organized in 1908 by Durant with the stated objective of merging the principal corporations in the automobile industry. Demands were made in Congress that the Department of Justice prosecute this corporation as a monopoly, but no action was taken, presumably because Durant was unable to carry out his plan.

2. An injunction was issued in 1925 against General Leathers Co., subsidiary to General Motors, and other leather companies for price fixing; with consent decree.[19]

3. (a) The Federal Trade Commission made complaint in 1924, amended in 1928, against General Electric, Westinghouse, RCA, General Motors, and United Fruit Co. for restraint of trade in radio apparatus and broadcasting. This complaint was dismissed by the commission.[20] (b) De Forest sued these corporations (not including General Motors) for damages due to restraint of trade on radio apparatus resulting in an injunction.[21] (c) The Department of Justice initiated a suit against the firms named above for restraint of trade on radio apparatus and broadcasting; before this petition came to a hearing General Motors and United Fruit withdrew from the

combination, and the petition was amended to exclude them; the other corporations named took a consent decree in 1932.[22]

4. The air-mail contracts of aviation companies, some of which were owned in part by General Motors, were canceled in 1930 on charges of restraint of trade and fraud.[23]

5. Pick Manufacturing Co. sued General Motors for damages under the antitrust law, dismissed in 1934.[24]

6. The Federal Trade Commission made complaints in 1935 against the A. C. Spark Plug Co., subsidiary of General Motors, and other members of the Standard Parts Association, charging conspiracy made in 1926 to fix prices on parts and accessories; the policy of the association was changed subsequent to the complaint and the proceedings against them were discontinued.[25]

7. The Federal Trade Commission issued a desist order in 1937 on the 6 percent installment policies, with an order to General Motors to divest itself of its affiliated finance corporation as in restraint of trade. Several subsidiaries of General Motors stipulated that they would obey the law in the future, but General Motors appealed the order.[26]

8. An indictment in Milwaukee in 1937 on the 6 percent policy of General Motors was dismissed by the court on the ground that the Department of Justice had attempted to make a bargain with the defendants as to the penalty.[27]

9. General Motors was convicted in South Bend in 1941 on the 6 percent installment purchase policy, involving restraint of trade through affiliated finance companies.[28]

10. An injunction was issued in 1939 against the Ethyl Gasoline Corporation, owned half by General Motors and half by Standard Oil, on the charge that the licenses to jobbers to handle ethyl were used to control prices and policies of jobbers.[29]

11. Report by the Federal Trade Commission in 1939, charging concentration of the automobile industry in a few firms, limitation on competition by exclusive-handling contracts, price fixing on new and used cars, coercions of dealers through a general system of regimentation. Some of these policies were modified during the investigation.[30]

12. Report of the Temporary National Economic Committee in 1939, charging coercion of dealers by General Motors and asserting that price competition on automobiles had been generally lacking since Ford ceased cutting prices in 1929.[31]

13. Desist order of the Federal Trade Commission in 1941, charging coercion of dealers by General Motors as to prices on parts and accessories and exclusive-handling contracts; General Motors appealed this order but withdrew the appeal before a hearing.[32]

14. Four private suits were initiated against Ethyl Gasoline Corporation for damages under the antitrust law; the preliminary motions for dismissal made by the corporation were denied and no further action was reported.[33]

15. An equity suit was initiated in 1940 to compel General Motors to separate from its finance corporation, with no final decision reported.[34]

16. Suit for damages on the complaint that General Motors restrained trade through an affiliated finance corporation; no final decision reported.[35]

17. General Motors and other corporations were convicted in 1946 on plea of nolo contendere and fined for conspiracy to monopolize ball bearings.[36]

18. General Motors and others were indicted in 1947 for conspiracy to monopolize brake linings; not tried.[37]

19. The Bendix Aviation Corporation, partially owned by General Motors, was indicted in 1942 for participating in a cartel to restrain trade on aviation instruments, and in 1947 for participating in a conspiracy to monopolize brake linings; neither case has been decided so far as available evidence discloses.[38]

Although no official decisions have been made against 10 of the 70 large corporations, these 10 corporations are not clearly different from other large corporations in their policies. Five of these 10 corporations are manufacturing corporations, and 5 are mercantile corporations. A brief summary of the evidence which is less conclusive than the judicial decisions will be presented regarding these 10 corporations. The American Radiator and Standard Sanitary Manufacturing Company has no adverse decisions under the antitrust laws since it was organized in 1929 as a merger of the American Radiator Company and the Standard Sanitary Manufacturing Company. Prior to that merger each of the constituent companies had official records or adverse reports of investigating commissions. The Standard Sanitary Manufacturing Company was organized in 1899 as a merger of the principal firms in its industry and it became known as the "Bathtub Trust." In 1910 an injunction was issued against this corporation and 15 other members of the Sanitary

Enameled Ware Association on complaint of price fixing, limitation of production, and agreements that the jobbers would not purchase products of competing manufacturers. In the same year these firms were convicted and fined for monopolizing this industry. Similarly, the American Radiator Company was organized in 1899 as a merger of nearly all the heating-apparatus firms in the United States. A complaint by the Federal Trade Commission against this corporation for price discriminations in favor of dealers who refused to handle competing products was dismissed in 1920. The Federal Trade Commission in an investigation of the House Furnishings Industries reported in 1924 that the American Radiator Company was a charter member of the Vacuum Cleaner Manufacturers Association, which was described as an organization formed for the purpose of pooling patents and restricting competition. Subsequent to the merger of the two firms in 1920, the corporation was indicted in 1940 in several cities with other manufacturers, jobbers, contractors, and trade unions for conspiring to monopolize the plumbing industry. One of these indictments was dismissed, while others, according to reports, were·postponed until the end of the war.

Union Carbide & Carbon Company was organized in 1917 as a merger of corporations. The Union Carbide Company, which was the principal constituent, had been organized in 1898 as a merger of competing firms, and this policy had been used also in the organization of other constituent companies. The final merger in 1917 was in general a merger of the vertical type, in which the firms supplemented each other rather than competed against each other. A Federal Trade Commission complaint against Prest-O-Lite Company, one of the subsidiaries, for price discrimination was dismissed in 1920, and three complaints against this company for resale price maintenance policies were dismissed in 1921, 1922, and 1923. A suit by Alexander Milburn Company for damages due to violation of the antitrust law was dismissed in 1926 as not proved, although the court expressed the opinion that the evidence indicated that Union Carbide & Carbon had used unfair methods of competition. A Federal Trade Commission complaint against Carbide and Carbon Chemical Corporation for exclusive and typing contracts regarding liquefied hydrocarbon was dismissed in 1928. A suit by the Empire State Theatre Supply Company in 1936 on charge of price discrimination has not been officially decided so far as published records show and may have been settled out of court. The Temporary National Economic Committee reported in 1939 that this corporation shared with one other corporation nine-tenths of the business in compressed oxygen and acetylene, with contractual arrangements which made it practically impossible for new companies to enter the industry, and that prices were high in relation to the cost of production and were relatively inflexible. It was indicted with others in 1946 for a conspiracy to monopolize vanadium, and this case has not yet been decided.

A complaint against the International Shoe Company was dismissed with a divided opinion, and a suit is pending against a subsidiary of that corporation. The Deere Company, according to an investigation by the Federal Trade Commission, participated in the policies of the farm machinery associations, which were obviously in violation of the antitrust law. The Singer Sewing Machine Company secured a virtual monopoly in its industry prior to the enactment of the Sherman Antitrust Act by methods which would certainly have been in violation of that law, if the law had been applicable at the time, and which were probably in violation of the common law prohibition against restraint of trade, which was applicable.

No adverse decisions on restraint of trade have been made against Gimbel, Macy, Kresge, Sears Roebuck, and Woolworth. These five department stores, chain stores, and mail order corporations, however, are not entirely clear of suspicion, as illustrated by the record of Sears Roebuck.

1. Sears Roebuck sued the Winchester Repeating Arms Co. for a rebate on guns purchased in 1904 under a contract which provided for resale price maintenance, which contract was in violation of the antitrust law.[39]
2. The Federal Trade Commission issued a desist order against Sears Roebuck for misrepresentation in advertising sugar in 1918; this complaint could have been stated as price discrimination, which would have been restraint of trade.[40]
3. Sears Roebuck, as owner of the King Sewing Machine Co., was a member of the Sewing Machine Manufacturers Association in 1917–21, and according to the Report of the Federal Trade Commission this association held discussions on uniform cost accounting and uniform discounts, which were generally associated with price-fixing policies.[41]
4. Sears Roebuck agreed under pressure from the National Association of Hardware Dealers not to cut prices on certain items in its catalogue for 1921.[42]
5. Sears Roebuck entered into contracts in 1926–33 to receive dis-

criminatory prices on automobile tires from the Goodyear Company. A desist order by the Federal Trade Commission was reversed by the court, partially on the ground that the contract had been canceled.[43]

6. Sears Roebuck are reported to have received discriminatory prices from a drug and cigar chain.[44]

7. Sears Roebuck was named in a report to the Department of Justice as making bids on tires for the government identical to the bids of other manufacturers in 1937. No action was taken on this complaint, so far as Sears Roebuck was concerned.

Thus, no one of the 70 large corporations is a good illustration of corporations which do not engage in restraint of trade.

The most obvious distinction among large corporations as to restraint of trade is that between the manufacturing corporations and the mercantile corporations. Of the 62 manufacturing corporations, 57, or 94 percent, have adverse decisions under the antitrust laws, with an average of six, while of the 8 mercantile corporations only 3, or fewer than 40 percent, have such adverse decisions, and of these 3, 2 have only one decision each.

These decisions under the antitrust law do not in general differentiate clearly between the more persistent and the less persistent offenders. The Aluminum Company of America, which has probably achieved the most complete monopoly of any American corporation, has only four adverse decisions, while 21 of the 70 corporations with a smaller degree of monopoly have larger numbers of adverse decisions. The United Shoe Machinery Company probably ranks next to the Aluminum Company of America in the completeness of its monopoly and has only one adverse decision. The U.S. Steel Corporation has nine adverse decisions while the "Little Steel" companies which use the same policies as U.S. Steel have from one to three decisions each under the antitrust laws.

Restraint of trade has probably been increasing in prevalence. This is demonstrated, first, by the increasing frequency of decisions against the 70 corporations on charges of restraint of trade. Of the 307 adverse decisions, 35 percent were made after January 1, 1940, and 60 percent after January 1, 1930. That is, approximately 60 percent of these adverse decisions were made in the last 15 years and only 40 percent in the preceding 40 years. These decisions, however, are not an accurate index of the prevalence of restraint of trade, since administrative and judicial policies vary independently of the prevalence of the offense. For instance, both the Department of Justice and the Federal Trade Commission were more reluctant during the decade of the twenties to prosecute large corporations than they had been under preceding administrations and have been subsequently. Second, the general studies of the economic system by economists and official investigating commissions have shown that the economic system has become progressively concentrated and that prices have become increasingly rigid, which has been taken as an index of the lack of competition. Finally, the leaders of industry have become more open and explicit in their demands for modification of the antitrust law so that "industry may be stabilized" and "cut-throat competition may be eliminated." This means that businessmen have a developing consensus that restraint of trade is desirable.

The preceding analysis has demonstrated that practically all large corporations engage in illegal restraint of trade and that from half to three-fourths of them engage in such practice so continuously that they may properly be called "habitual criminals." While some corporations engage in restraint of trade in their principal purchases and sales, others engage in restraint of trade only on selected commodities. Walter Lippmann summarized the available evidence accurately in the statement: "Competition has survived only where men have been unable to abolish it." Not law, but expediency and practicability have determined the limits of restraint of trade. Some businessmen claim that their industries are highly competitive. One of the leaders in the tin industry presented the following self-contradictory statements before the Temporary National Economic Committee: first, competition in the tin industry is very active; second, prices of tin sheets are fixed for the season by negotiations between the Carnegie-Illinois Steel Company (subsidiary to U.S. Steel) and the American Can Company, and the other tin-plate manufacturing companies and can-manufacturing companies accept these prices for the season; the tin cans are then sold to customers at a specified percentage above the price of tin sheets.[45] This arrangement, obviously, eliminated all price competition among the can manufacturers and also among the tin-plate manufacturers. On the other hand, some industrial leaders are forthright, at least in their secret correspondence. A prominent cement manufacturer, in writing an officer of his trade association, characterized as "sheer bunk and hypocrisy" the contention that the system is an expression of free competition. He stated that the cement industry "must systematically restrain competition or be ruined."[46]

Methods of Restraint of Trade

The simplest method of eliminating competitors is by consolidating them through mergers or holding companies. When the number of firms in an industry is reduced to a small number by such consolidations, agreements regarding prices are facilitated and also price discriminations. The following analysis of the methods used in restraint of trade will consider three procedures used by large corporations: consolidations, price uniformity, and price discriminations.

The Sherman Antitrust Act was instituted as a reaction against the huge establishments which were developing during the decades of the seventies and eighties. This statute, with the supplementary statutes enacted in later decades, failed to stop the trend toward concentration of ownership. This concentration was pointed out to the public in the report of the Industrial Commission in 1901, in reports of the Commissioner of Corporations from 1905 to 1915, in reports of the Federal Trade Commission from 1915 to date, in the report of the Temporary National Economic Committee in 1939, and in the report of the Smaller War Plants Corporation in 1947. The trend may be seen, likewise, in the history of the 70 large industrial and mercantile corporations.

Twenty-one of these 70 large corporations began their existence in 1802–89 as small establishments owned by individuals or partnerships. Although some of them had, prior to 1890, expanded by purchasing the assets of competitors, only one of them had participated in a major consolidation. The consolidation of these firms occurred almost entirely after the establishment of the Sherman Antitrust Act in 1890, although this law was designed to prevent such consolidations. Eight of the 70 large corporations originated in 1890–97, 23 in 1898–1902, 18 in 1903–29, and practically all of these were consolidations of firms which had previously competed against each other.

The two periods of greatest importance in this trend toward concentrated ownership were 1898–1902, and 1918–29. These two spurts in the development of huge corporations were based, in part, on three court decisions under the antitrust law. In 1895 the Supreme Court decided that the purchase of competing refineries by the American Sugar Refining Company was not a violation of the Sherman Antitrust Act, which prohibited restraint of trade in interstate commerce, since these establishments were manufacturing establishments, and manufacturing, as such, is not interstate commerce.[47] This specious argument was later reversed by the Supreme Court, but in the interim the doors were opened to consolidations and businessmen flocked through the doors. One-third of the corporations which are today the largest corporations in the United States originated within a few years after that decision. The second surge of consolidations occurred in the decade after the First World War, and was the result, in part, of the huge surpluses accumulated by profiteering during the war, in part of two court decisions on the antitrust law. The first of these was the decision in the suit against U.S. Steel that "size as such is no violation of the antitrust law," and the second was the decision that the antitrust law did not prohibit the purchase of assets of a competitor, although it did prohibit the purchase of the stocks of a competitor. These decisions, likewise, opened the doors for further concentration of ownership. In consequence, 7,000 manufacturing establishments were swallowed up in 1,268 mergers during the decade ended 1929; only 60 of these mergers were questioned by the federal authorities and only 11 were prevented.[48]

The major consolidations, especially as they developed at the turn of the century, may be illustrated by the American Can Company. Prices in the can-manufacturing industry had been regulated for short periods in the eighties and nineties by gentlemen's agreements. Sharp price wars ensued when these agreements were not kept. Immediately after such a price war in 1898, five persons, four of whom had been active in forming mergers in the steel industry and only one of whom had been connected with the can industry, secured options on plants conditional on the merger of a large proportion of the can-manufacturing establishments. This merger was consummated in 1901, and included about 100 firms which had previously competed against each other except in the periods in which illegal agreements were in force. The firms which were merged had been producing from 90 to 100 percent of the commercial cans in the United States. The establishments were willing to enter this merger for the following reasons: First, they had suffered severely in the price wars. Second, explicit threats were made by the promoters, or were implicit in the behavior of the promoters, that the several establishments would be ruined if they did not enter the merger. It was generally known that these promoters were also promoting the American Sheet and Tin Plate Company, from which the can-manufacturing firms secured their tin-plate. It was generally known, also, that the promoters had secured patents on the can-making machinery and had long-time contracts with the manufacturers of this machinery to sell exclusively to the merger. Finally, it was alleged that the merger had secured long-time contracts with many of the larger purchasers of cans. Third, enormous prices were offered for the plants, largely in watered stock of the merger. The American Can Company was capitalized for $88 million. The court expressed the opinion that the total cash value of all of the firms in the merger was not more than $10 million. One firm with a plant that cost $60,000 received for its plant $½ million par value of stock of the American Can Company. The promoters received $8½ million par value of stock for their services in the merger, which was nearly as much as the cash value of all of the plants. The illegal motives and objectives involved in this merger are shown in the specific provisions of the contracts. The purchase contracts contained covenants that the former owners would not engage in the manufacture of cans within fifteen years or within 3,000 miles of Chicago. One firm which refused to accept this restriction acceded when the price for its plant was increased from $300,000 to $700,000. The American Can Company closed or dismantled many of the plants which were purchased; in 1903 only 36 of the 100 plants which had been purchased were in operation. The machinery in the others was either transferred to the plants which were operating or was junked. The price of cans was increased immediately after the merger because it was believed to be practicable and also because it was necessary in order to pay dividends on the watered stocks. This increase in prices, however, induced new competitors to enter the industry, in spite of the dangers. The American Can Company fought these new competitors with all the methods available, including the purchase of all of the output of the plants of the competitors in order to prevent price cutting. Since it was heavily burdened with debt, it was unable to drive these competitors out of the industry and was compelled, instead, to cut its own prices. One of these competitors developed to a position of strength, namely, the Continental Can Company, and thereafter shared with the American Can Company a large part of that industry. The petition for the dissolution of the American Can Company was dismissed by the court in 1916, on the ground that competition had developed since the illegal organization of the corporation, and since no good purpose would be achieved by dissolving this corporation. Furthermore, it was obviously impossible for the court to restore the condition of this industry as it had been in 1900.

In addition to these larger mergers, practically all of the 70 large corporations have continued to expand by the purchase of assets of competitors and by levying tribute on the business of competitors. Armour and Swift began business as small packing plants, established additional plants, secured preferential railway rates which enabled them to secure control of practically all the equipment needed by other meat packers, such as stockyards, terminal railways, refrigerator cars, cold storage plants, fertilizer plants, and trade journals, and through these they took a part of the profits of their competitors; also, they expanded into other industries which utilized their by-products, such as leather and soap, and finally used their cold-storage plants and refrigerator cars to secure increased control of the general food industry until restricted by federal court decisions. Borden and National Dairy purchased hundreds of dairy companies in many communities, and through the profits secured control of pasteurization plants, bottle exchanges, and factories for the manufacture of milk products such as butter, cheese, and ice cream. The Aluminum Company of America began as a small fabricator of aluminum goods, expanded downward to secure ownership of the principal supplies of bauxite, from which aluminum is made, and of the larger supplies of waterpower needed for making aluminum, thus securing a complete monopoly on the production of aluminum; although this corporation shared the work of fabrication with other manufacturers, it could regulate the profits of its competitors by increasing or decreasing the price of crude aluminum, which its competitors could purchase only from this corporation. Furthermore, this corporation secured a stranglehold on magnesium, which is a substitute for aluminum, through participation in an international cartel. Very much of this expansion of corporation was made possible by the profits which had accrued from previous violations of the antitrust law.

Official complaints have been made against 35 of the 70 large corporations during their careers in regard to consolidations and purchase of assets or securities of their competitors, with a total of 87 suits. Of these suits, 43 were dismissed, 18 resulted in orders to change specific practices, 21 resulted in orders to divest themselves of specific limited properties, and only 5 resulted in general dissolution orders. The five major dissolution orders were directed to the American Tobacco Company (including, also, Reynolds and Liggett & Myers) in 1911, DuPont in 1911, Aluminum Company of America in 1912, Corn Products Company in 1918, and International Harvester in 1918. Also, in the early years of the twenties, after a generation of effort, the government ordered the two principal anthracite coal companies—Glen Alden and Philadelphia & Reading Coal—to separate from the anthracite railroads. Failure to order dissolution in other cases perhaps makes little difference, for no one of the major dissolution orders has restored competition or made a significant change in policies. Modern industry cannot possibly be restored to the earlier state of many small establishments competing against each other. In the conflict between the government and the corporations, the government has lost.

Conspiracy to fix uniform prices in an industry or part of an industry is a second method of restraint of trade. This method of restraint of trade has been held unequivocally to be illegal since the establishment of the Sherman Antitrust Act. While businessmen and their advocates have much to say about the obscurities and uncertainties of the antitrust law, no doubt can exist that it is illegal to agree to sell commodities at a uniform price or, stated negatively, to agree not to cut prices. Nevertheless, businessmen violate the antitrust law in this respect more frequently than in any other respect.

Decisions have been made against 44 of the 70 large corporations in 125 suits for price fixing. Of these 44 corporations, 26, or approximately 60 percent, are recidivists in price fixing. General Electric tops the list with 11 adverse decisions on price fixing, Westinghouse is second with 8, Allied Chemical & Dye third with 7, followed by DuPont, Pittsburgh Plate Glass, and U.S. Steel with 6 each, and by Armour, Swift, Borden, and National Dairy with 5 each. The practice of price fixing, however, is much more general than these decisions indicate. Charles M. Schwab, when asked whether the steel industry had agreements as to prices before the organization of the U.S. Steel Corporation, replied, "Yes, in all lines of business, not only in steel but in everything else. They have existed in all lines of business as long as I can remember."[49] Six methods of securing uniform prices have been used by large corporations.

The first method is the gentlemen's agreement. These agreements are made by establishments without a formal organization. They were well developed soon after the Civil War, were generally confined to small markets, were concerned with prices and with restriction of production, and were generally short-lived because the gentlemen would not live up to their promises. This method has persisted to the present time in many industries. Of the 125 decisions against 44 corporations for price fixing, 32 may be classified as gentlemen's agreements. Of these decisions 8 were concerned with collusion to make identical bids on contracts for the government.

The second method was the old "trust," in which a corporation authorized a trustee to act, in concert with similar trustees representing other corporations, to secure uniform prices and to limit production. This method of restraining trade was an invention of the Standard Oil Company in 1879. Within a decade the method was adopted in about a dozen other industries. The only one of the 70 large corporations with which we are now concerned which used this method is the American Sugar Refining Company. The sugar refiners organized a trust of this type in 1887, which was dissolved by court order in 1890, whereupon the same companies merged to form the American Sugar Refining Company.

Price fixing through trade associations is a third method of securing uniform prices. Decisions have been made against 35 of the 70 large corporations in 74 suits for using this illegal policy. Trade associations have existed in the United States since the Civil War but have become especially prominent in restraint of trade since 1920. They differ from the pools and gentlemen's agreements in the formality of organization and in their facade of legitimate activities. The ideology of the trade association was stated by A. J. Eddy in "The New Competition," published in 1911. Under Eddy's influence some associations were developed in 1911, but on advice of counsel they were halted during the election year 1912, when new legislation on restraint of trade was being discussed. They did not gain new momentum until the decade of the twenties. Twenty-two open-price associations were organized and administered by Eddy, and the movement continued to expand in spite of decisions against the Hardwood Lumber Association in 1921 and the Linseed Oil Association in 1923. Pearce made an analysis of all antitrust cases initiated by the Department of Justice and the Federal Trade Commission during the years 1935–39. He found that of 125 such cases, 92, or 74 percent, involved price fixing through trade associations.[50] Of all decisions under the antitrust laws against the 70 large corporations 9 percent found them guilty of price fixing through trade associations in 1890–1929 and 60 percent in 1930–44.

The National Recovery Administration has been suggested as the explanation of the existence and illegality of these trade associations. The argument is that those laws compelled corporations to form trade associations and to fix prices, and that the New Deal administration is respon-

sible for the origin and continuation of this method of price fixing. Information regarding the dates of origin of the policies of price fixing is
available for 51 suits against the 70 large corporations in the period
1930–44. In these suits the policy which was held by the court to be illegal was initiated prior to 1930 in more than 50 percent of the cases, and
prior to the authorization of NRA in more than 73 percent. Consequently NRA cannot be a very important factor in the origin of price fixing through trade associations.

The trade association not only provides a formal organization which
may be used for price fixing, but has been important also as an agency
for developing consensus regarding competition. The participants in
these associations hear frequently of "ruinous price wars," "cut-throat
competition," "stabilizing the industry," and "live and let live." They
have developed contempt for "price-cutters" and "price-chiselers" similar to the contempt for "scabs" by the union members. Price cutting is
one of the heinous sins of businessmen. For that reason price cutters
such as Ford, Firestone, and Macy were very unpopular among their colleagues. Because of the developed consensus regarding the wastes of
competition and the desirability of "stabilizing the industry" (which
means restricting competition) policies in restraint of trade can be executed more effectively than in former generations when businessmen
believed in free competition and free enterprise.

The cartel is the fourth method of price fixing and restraint of trade.
This is similar to the trade association except that it involves international agreements as to prices, exclusive trade territories, and other
methods of avoiding competition. Decisions have been made against 16
of the 70 large corporations in 33 cases for restraint of trade through
cartels. In addition, several of the suits initiated during the recent war,
which have not yet been decided, were against cartels with German and
Japanese corporations, with provisions for restriction of production of
commodities essential for war purposes. These cartel agreements are illustrated in the suit against the Aluminum Company of America regarding magnesium, which resulted in conviction and a fine against this
corporation in 1942. The Aluminum Company entered into an agreement in 1928 with the German chemical and dye trust, with the objective of protecting its aluminum against the competition of magnesium,
which can be produced more cheaply than aluminum and is more ser-
viceable for many purposes. According to the cartel agreement, the production of magnesium in the United States was to be restricted to 4,000
tons a year, while Germany was free to produce magnesium in unlim-

ited quantities and in addition was authorized to purchase half of the magnesium produced in the United States. When the Aluminum Company could not secure the cooperation of Dow Chemical Company in this cartel agreement, it coerced the latter by an infringement suit to become a participant, and the infringement suit was withdrawn as soon as Dow Chemical agreed to cooperate. Because of this cartel agreement, the United States had a very meager supply of magnesium at the outbreak of the war, while Germany was well supplied. The DuPont Company during the decade of the eighties entered into such cartel agreements regarding powder, and has had illegal cartel agreements during many decades since that time, as have also the Aluminum Company, General Electric, Westinghouse, and other large corporations.

Price leadership is a fifth method of securing uniformity in prices. In many industries one corporation customarily announces its prices and the other corporations adopt the same prices. This uniformity is sometimes the result of formal agreements, sometimes the result of informal understandings. The method which is sometimes used in reaching this uniformity is described in an exchange of letters between the secretary of the Minneapolis Millers' Club and the Southwestern Millers' League in 1924. The former wrote that the directors of his organization had been fixing prices but they contemplated difficulty if the Department of Justice should make an investigation and he asked for information as to the method of price fixing used by the Southwestern Millers' League. The secretary of the latter organization replied that it would be difficult to convince the Department of Justice of innocence if the directors fixed the prices and added,

> I would suggest, and it is working very well in other states, that you take a representative mill, say Pillsbury Flour Mills in Minneapolis, and use their quotations as a basis. Let them advise you of the changes and you send this information to the members of your Club. Use blank stationery and I would not put any name to the quotations, just let it appear as a regular market letter. This can be understood among your members and there need be nothing attached to it that would in any way involve anybody. . . . One of the very important features is as little information in writing as possible.[51]

This method of price leadership is the most difficult to prove in court, and no decisions have been made against the 70 corporations which can be tabulated as primarily of this type. According to evidence of the Temporary National Economic Committee, price leadership is used in the steel, cement, copper, lead, petroleum, newsprint, agricultural machinery, and other industries. The president of one of the largest of the "little steel" corporations testified that he would not dare cut the price of steel as much as ten cents a ton. Mr. Randall, president of the Riverside Metal Company, which produced about 1½ percent of the brass commodities of the United States, stated that prices in that industry were set by the American Brass Company, a subsidiary of the Anaconda Copper Company, which produced about 25 percent of the brass commodities, that these prices were adopted by the smaller corporations in the industry, and that this was a well-crystallized practice: when the American Brass Company increased its prices, the other corporations announced similar increases, and when the American Brass Company lowered its prices, the others made similar reductions. The sales manager of the American Brass Company testified before the committee that the president of the Riverside Metal Company was a "satisfactory competitor," and when asked the meaning of that phrase, replied, "He carries on his business on a very high ethical plane" (Laughter).[52]

Price fixing through patent agreements is the sixth method of securing uniform prices. This method cuts across the methods which have been described, since it may be used in gentlemen's agreements, trade associations, or cartels. For that reason, decisions on this point overlap decisions on other points. Taking this overlap into consideration, restraint of trade through patent manipulation has occurred in the practices of 39 of the 70 large corporations, as indicated in 114 decisions against those corporations. This policy of patent manipulation has been used especially by the electrical equipment companies and the chemical companies. This policy will be considered in greater detail below.

The six methods of securing price uniformity which have been described are connected with other practices in restraint of trade. Even though businessmen have developed an increased consensus in opposition to the competitive principle, they search for loopholes in their agreements, just as they search for loopholes in the statutes, and attempt to secure an advantage over other establishments in the industry. This leads to an expansion of the details covered by the agreements, regardless of whether the method is the gentlemen's agreement, the trade association, the cartel, or the patent license. Such details as the following have entered into the agreements which are designed to make price uniform: cash discounts and credit terms, date of price changes, payments to be made for return of containers, prices for damaged goods or out-of-date goods, prohibition against new type containers, prohibition against private-brand packages, standardization of models, costs of transportation.[53]

The regulation of transportation charges has been a topic of principal concern in connection with uniform prices. This concern has resulted in many industries in delivered prices, with one or more basing points, so that charges for transportation bear little relation to the actual cost of transportation in individual transactions. The costs of transportation are customarily stated as freight rates, and in several industries the trade association publishes a freight book for its members, with freight rates from the basing point to all points within the zone. In these cases the producer is not permitted to change the charge for transportation, even if errors have been made in the association's freight book, until the association publishes a new edition. Since the objective is uniformity in prices, the costs of transportation are computed in terms of freight charges even though the goods may be shipped by boat or truck. Also, in some industries the associations have adopted elaborate regulations which, among other things, prohibit the pooling of orders by small dealers for the purpose of securing car-load rates, and the reshipment of goods.

These efforts to secure uniform prices at which their goods are sold are extended in some cases to uniformity in purchase prices. In the tobacco industry the principal companies have been convicted of agreements not to compete against each other in bidding for tobacco. Substantially the same practice was used by the meat packers.

Wages are one of the costs and corporations have endeavored to keep this cost uniform. No suit has been brought against any corporation, so far as available evidence indicates, for efforts to secure uniformity in this cost.

Advertising has been regulated in some industries, as a further means of securing uniformity and of restricting competition. When competition regarding prices was eliminated, corporations in many industries turned to advertising as a method of competing. In a few industries, the trade association has taken over at least a part of the advertising and attempts to promote the sale of the products of the industry for all firms, so that the firms need not compete against each other in this respect. This is the logical outcome of the policy of restricting competition and stabilizing the industry.

Uniform prices can be maintained in most industries only if production is restricted, especially in periods of increasing demand. Manufacturers were restricting production by agreements long before the farmers were killing little pigs for the purpose of restricting production. The pools and gentlemen's agreements which followed the Civil War, as well as the current trade associations, cartels, and patent-licenses, customarily contain provisions to restrict production as a means of regulating prices. This restriction of production includes provisions in cartel agreements that foreign manufacturers will not sell their products in this country. Also, the entrance of new establishments into the industry, which would result in an increase in production, is resisted by the establishments already in the industry. In fact, many industrial leaders have demanded that the antitrust law be amended to permit producers to make agreements to restrict production when demands decrease in order to "stabilize the industry." This, obviously, would mean the abolition of competition and of the laws of supply and demand as the regulators of prices.

The elimination of competition by the methods which have been described above calls logically for the annihilation of the competitors who will not cooperate in those policies. The mergers at the turn of the century made direct attacks on competitors with relatively brutal methods, while in recent decades the attacks have involved more finesse. Two principal methods of annihilating competitors have been used, both of which result in decreased profits and financial ruin: reducing the sales of competitors, and increasing the costs of competitors.

The following are some of the methods used in the effort to reduce the sales of competitors. First, a corporation or combination of corporations which operates over a wide territory may ruin a competitor whose business is localized by cutting prices in his territory, while retaining former prices elsewhere. In some cases a secret subsidiary is used for price cutting. Several cases were reported in the earlier decades in which the employees of a competitor or the railway agents were bribed in order to secure the customers' list of the competitor, so that price cuts could be announced directly to those customers. When these price cuts are managed by a trade association, the losses are distributed among the members of the association. Second, pressure is placed upon dealers not to handle the commodities of competitors. This has been accomplished by direct bribery of dealers, by contracts which provide that no competing goods be handled, by cumulative discounts and profit-sharing devices, by buying contracts, and by full-line forcing. The last methods make it impossible for a dealer to secure certain commodities unless he takes other commodities which consumers may regard as inferior to the products of competitors. Third, competitors may be prevented from securing a sales agent. The International Harvester Company during the first decade of the century made one firm an agent for one of its models, another firm agent for another, and so on until all of the dealers in the community were tied up with the International Harvester Company in exclusive contracts. Fourth, sales persons have been bribed or secret agents have been placed in stores to promote the sale of goods in preference to those of competitors. The Federal Trade Commission published evidence that the Aluminum Goods Manufacturing Company, partially owned by the Aluminum Company of America, had secretly placed one of its agents as a clerk in the store of Marshall Field in Chicago, with instructions to recommend its own aluminum goods as superior to those of competitors. Fifth, several decisions have been made against corporations which conspired with jobbers, dealers, and trade unions to use no goods which competed with those of the manufacturers in the agreement; jobbers and contractors refuse to handle the goods of competitors and the members of the trade union refuse to work on goods of competitors. Such collusions have been the basis of convictions of the Pittsburgh Plate Glass Company, the Crane Company, the Borden Company, and the National Dairy Products Company.

The second method of annihilating competitors is by increasing their costs. First, corporations which operate in a far-flung territory force up the purchase prices in the local territory in which a competitor is operating. The meat packers did this, according to the decision of the court, by bidding up prices of livestock in the area where the competitor was operating, thus making prices so high that the competitor was ruined, while their additional costs in this local area were distributed over a wider area without disastrous results. Second, exclusive long-time contracts are made with the manufacturers of raw materials, machinery, and other necessities, so that the entrance of competitors into the industry is impeded and the chance of success limited. Similar long-time contracts are made with foreign producers that they will not sell to the local competitors. Third, pressure is put on banks and other financial institutions to refuse credit to competitors or to charge extraordinarily high rates of interest. Fourth, these organizations have subsidized sabotage in the plants of competitors. Employees have been bribed and secret agents installed in the plants of competitors, with instructions to make defective commodities, delay shipments, foment labor troubles, and in other ways reduce the efficiency of competitors. Fifth, a corporation which has a monopolistic control of raw materials and also fabricates those materials in competition with other establishments may ruin the competitors at will by increasing the price of the raw materials while holding the price of the fabricated materials constant. The Aluminum Company of America and the Corn Products Company have been accused in the court decisions against them of narrowing the spread between raw materials, over which they have no control, and the finished product, on which they were in competition, and thus ruining competitors.

Many trade associations have developed private systems of justice, with police, courts, and penal provisions, for the purpose of executing the policies of uniform prices, of restricting production, and of annihilating the competitors who refuse to enter into the collusion. This system of justice applies both to the participants in the conspiracy, in which case it has a semblance of democracy, and also to dealers and others outside of the combination, in which case it resembles dictatorship and racketeering. Businessmen, with the constant interest in profits, desire preferential advantages and seek for loopholes in their agreements just as they seek for loopholes in the law. The agreements can be enforced only if the combination develops policies of regimentation, bureaucracy, and snooping, as these policies are designated when used by governments. The DuPonts took the initiative in organizing the Gunpowder Trade Association, popularly known as the Powder Trust, in 1872. This association made various agreements until its termination in 1904 regarding price fixing and restriction of production. The increased price of powder which resulted induced new firms to enter the industry and the members of the association began to cut prices. The association employed spies to search for price cutting by its members. In the years 1881–83 the association heard and tried 203 cases in which price cutting by members of the association was suspected, and imposed fines upon those firms which were found guilty. The Sugar Institute, composed of sugar refiners, authorized the following regulations for the control of agents who were not represented in the institute: No agent may perform multiple functions in dealing in sugar; a firm which engages in the brokerage business may not act as a warehousing or trucking agency; and a warehousing agent may not engage in the brokerage business or trucking business. The Sugar Institute fixed the rate of compensation for these agents, and no member of the institute may deviate from this rate of compensation. Agents of some trade associations inspect the books of their members and also the books of dealers in order to determine whether prices are being cut. When deviations from the agreements are discovered, remonstrance is used more frequently than any other method, but the distinction between remonstrance and threats is not easily made. When the Association of Ice Cream Manufacturers, in which Borden and National Dairy were the dominant members, was attempting to eliminate the competition from counter freezers, they remonstrated with the drugstores which had installed such freezers or were contemplating such installations, threatened to establish new drugstores in the vicinity as competitors, and often purchased the counter freezers which had been installed for prices in excess of the cost to the stores. Similarly, the Corn Products Company threatened to enter the candy-manufacture business unless the candy manufacturers accepted the regulations regarding the price of corn syrup and other commodities manufactured by the Corn Products Company. The American Tobacco Company assigned a quota to a jobber far in excess of the amount he could sell, with the understanding that this quota would not be enforced unless the jobber violated the regulations imposed upon him by the corporation; if he violated these regulations and the quota was enforced, he was ruined. This was, in effect, a heavy fine for violating regulations which were imposed upon him without representation. Some associations have "white lists" of dealers with whom their members may do business, and "black lists" of dealers with whom they may not do business.

The Temporary National Economic Committee in a study of the practices of trade associations reported as to the prevalence of this system of private justice. In 92 trade associations which were found to be violating the antitrust laws in the period of 1935–39, some types of penal sanctions were found in 59, or approximately two-thirds; 28 had facilities for investigating or spying, 7 had provisions for trials, 11 for fines, 18 for boycotts; 17 used threats or coercion, 2 used violence, 1 acted in collusion with trade unions, and 1 had an agreement with newspapers not to advertise cut-rate prices.[54]

The third general method of restraint of trade is price discrimination. Decisions have been made against 23 of the 70 large corporations in 130 suits in which charges of price discriminations were made. The three motion picture corporations stand at the top of the list with 19 adverse decisions each; the American Tobacco Company comes next with 14, the Great A & P follows with 8. In these 130 suits, private parties were the complainants in 30, and even in the other suits in which action was initiated by the Federal Trade Commission or the Department of Justice, private parties had doubtless made complaint to those agencies.

Three principal types of discriminations are reported in these decisions. First, a manufacturer sells his products to an affiliated establishment under more advantageous conditions than to independent establishments; second, a manufacturer sells his products to a large corporation, whose business is of great importance, under more advantageous conditions than to smaller corporations, thus tending to give an advantage to the large corporation and ruin the small corporations; third, a corporation sells its products in one area at a lower rate than in another area with the objective of injuring competitors in the first area.

The first method of discrimination is illustrated by the decisions against the motion picture corporations. These corporations have purchased many of the local theaters in which their pictures are shown, and give to these affiliated theaters more advantageous terms than to independent theaters. In many communities new pictures are shown for a limited time exclusively in the theaters affiliated with the producers, and the price of admission is customarily higher in these theaters than in the independent theaters, giving them higher profits than the other theaters can make. Almost all of the decisions against the motion picture corporations involve complaint for this discrimination and in spite of 19 decisions against each of the three corporations, they persist in this illegal policy. In the Supreme Court decision against the motion picture corporations made in 1946, on the complaint filed in 1938, the court ordered certain discriminatory practices to cease but did not order the producers to divest themselves of their local theaters; in view of the history of this industry, nothing short of a separation of the producers and the theaters will prevent these discriminations.

Another illustration of discriminatory prices is provided by the American Can Company. This corporation was loosely affiliated with U.S. Steel in its origin and received discriminatory prices in the form of a discount of 7½ percent, which amounted to $9 million in the years 1901–12. When Continental Can developed as a strong competitor of American Can and learned of the discount received by American Can, it demanded a discount from U.S. Steel equal to that received by American

Can. For fear of antitrust proceedings, U.S. Steel was forced to grant this demand. When American Can learned that it had lost its preferential price, it demanded a larger discount. U.S. Steel promised to give an additional discount if it secured a larger share of the business of American Can. But American Can went to the other steel corporations and secured additional discounts from them, and then sued U.S. Steel under the antitrust law for its discriminatory prices; the suit was settled out of court by payment of $2½ million to American Can. Suspicion has been expressed that this suit and settlement were merely a subterfuge for the additional discrimination in favor of American Can.

The discrimination in favor of the large purchaser is illustrated in the suit against Goodyear Tire and Rubber Company and Sears Roebuck, which was finally dismissed on a technicality, although the facts of discrimination were not questioned. Goodyear entered into a contract to provide automobile tires for Sears Roebuck under a special brand name at cost plus 6 percent; these tires, except in the brand name, were identical with the tires sold under Goodyear's name. From 1926 to 1933 Sears Roebuck bought approximately 200 million casings and 17½ million tubes from Goodyear at a price of $42 million lower than the same tires would have been sold to an independent tire dealer. These tires were shipped to many different places and the costs were not significantly different from the costs of production for independent dealers. Goodyear sold 18 percent of its entire output of tires to Sears Roebuck under these contracts and received in payment only 11 percent of its income from the sale of tires. Because of this preferential price, Sears Roebuck cut the retail price of tires by approximately 25 percent and still had a profit of approximately 40 percent. The independent tire dealers appealed to Goodyear for assistance in meeting the competition of Sears Roebuck since the contracts between Goodyear and Sears Roebuck were not known to outsiders. Goodyear produced a new tire to meet the competition but it was inferior in quality and did not succeed in meeting the competition. The consequence was that approximately half of the independent tire dealers in the United States in 1926 had abandoned this business by 1933.

This price discrimination not only gave Sears Roebuck a monopolistic position in the tire sales, but also gave it great control over Goodyear. Sears Roebuck exercised its right to inspect the Goodyear books as to costs, and during the life of these contracts disallowed from half a million to one million dollars a year claimed by Goodyear as costs. When the first contract terminated in 1928, Sears Roebuck claimed that other tire manufacturers were prepared to make better offers than Goodyear had and insisted that Goodyear build a new plant in the South in order to reduce the freight charges for the southern trade of Sears Roebuck. Although the president of Goodyear asserted that this additional capacity was not needed, he was forced, in order to secure a renewal of the contract, to build a plant at Gadsden, Alabama, at a cost of $9 million. While the renewal of that contract was under consideration, Sears Roebuck forced additional concessions in the form of a gift by Goodyear of 18,000 shares of common stock of the Goodyear corporation plus $800,000 cash with which to purchase 32,000 additional shares, making a total of 50,000 shares with an approximate market value of $1¼ million.

This contract between Goodyear and Sears Roebuck was kept secret. It was drawn up without the knowledge of anyone in the Goodyear organization except the president and an attorney, although it was revealed to the directors for ratification. Even after ratification, many of the officers of Goodyear did not know the contents of the contract, and the stockholders were not informed of the contract, of the bonus, or of other payments of Sears Roebuck. When agents of the Federal Trade Commission, independent tire dealers, and other manufacturers of tires inquired about these contracts, both Goodyear and Sears Roebuck denied that such contracts existed. When the arrangements became known after about five years, the other tire manufacturers made similar arrangements—U.S. Rubber with Montgomery Ward, Goodrich and U.S. Rubber with Standard Oil. The rumor spread that Firestone attempted to make similar arrangements with mail-order houses and petroleum companies but failed because of his reputation as a price cutter.[55]

Conclusion

The statement was made at the beginning of this chapter that restraint of trade is a crime against other businessmen and against consumers. It is much more than this. The large corporations, through restraint of trade and other illegal behavior, have been the principal subversives in the sense that their behavior, regardless of their intentions, has undermined and fundamentally changed the economic and political institutions of the United States.

The economic system, as described by the classical economists, was a system of free competition and of laissez faire; the phrase "free enterprise" is currently substituted for "laissez faire." Free competition was the regulator of the economic system. The laws of supply and demand, operating under free competition, determined prices, profits, the flow of capital, the distribution of labor, and other economic phenomena. When profits in an industry were high, other businessmen rushed into that industry in the hope of securing similar profits. This resulted in an increase in the supply of commodities, which produced a reduction in price, and this in turn reduced profits. Thus the excessive profits in that industry were eliminated and the prices were lowered so that a larger supply of its commodities was distributed to the public. Through this regulation by free competition, according to the classical economists, Divine Providence produced the greatest welfare for the entire society. Free competition, to be sure, was a harsh regulator; it was a cut-throat business. The welfare of the total society was produced only by ruining the less competent establishments.

Because free competition regulated the economic system, governmental regulation was unnecessary. The economic system of the classical economists developed primarily because business revolted against the governmental regulations of the feudal period, which were not adapted to the changing conditions of the eighteenth century. Government kept out of business, after this system was established, except as it enforced contracts, protected the public against larceny and fraud, and enforced the principle of free competition by the common law prohibition of restraint of trade.

During the last century this economic system has changed. The fundamental changes have been the result of efforts of businessmen, acting individually or in small groups, to secure preferential advantages for themselves. The primary loyalty of businessmen has been to profits, and they have sacrificed the principles of free competition and free enterprise in circumstances where they believed they could secure a pecuniary advantage by doing so. Moreover, they have been in a position of power and have been able to secure these advantages. Although businessmen had no intention to change the economic and political systems, their behavior has produced this result.

The restrictions on the principle of free competition have been described in the earlier part of this chapter. To a great extent, formal and informal organizations of businessmen determine prices, profits, the flow of capital, and other economic phenomena. While businessmen state that they are merely attempting to avoid the excesses of competi-

tion, it is precisely these excesses—the cut-throat attribute of competition—which regulated the system, according to the earlier economists. For free competition as the regulator has been substituted a private collectivism, in which the public is not represented, and in which
the public receives little consideration. This system of private collectivism is very similar to socialism except that it does not include representation and consideration of the public.

Businessmen have also been active in restricting the principle of free
enterprise. Although businessmen have been vociferous as to the vir-
tues of free enterprise and have insisted, in general, that government
keep its hands out of and off of business, businessmen above all others
have put pressure on government to interfere in business. They have
not done this en masse, but as individuals or small groups which have
been endeavoring to secure a preferential advantage. These efforts of
businessmen to expand governmental regulation of business are very
numerous and they range from the early and continued pressures to secure tariff laws to protect American industries against foreign competition; through a multitude of statutes similar to the taxation of oleomargarine in order to protect the dairy industry against competition; to the
recent enactment of fair trade laws by the federal government and by
most of the state governments, which prohibit retail dealers from cutting prices on trademarked articles. The Federal Fair Trade Law was
enacted in 1937; the bill was presented by Senator Tydings as a rider to
the District of Columbia appropriations bill, where it could not be discussed on its merits; the bill was prepared, according to reports, by the
senator's law partner, who was attorney for the National Association of
Retail Druggists, and was supported by many national associations of
manufacturers and of retail dealers, who were opposed to the competitive principle, and was opposed by the Department of Justice and the
Federal Trade Commission, which had the duty of preserving the principle of competition in the United States.[56]

Businessmen have asked government to intervene in business not
only to protect them against competition, but also in order to grant them
many special privileges. Twenty-three amendments have been made to
the antitrust law since 1890; of these amendments, 11 have expanded
and implemented the law, while 12 have provided exemption from the
law for special groups and thus permitted businessmen in those areas to
engage in restraint of trade. The industries which have recently fought
for exemption from the competitive principle are the railways and insur-

ance companies. Also, businessmen are working for more general restrictions on the antitrust law. The Chamber of Commerce of the United States, in a pamphlet issued in 1938, presented a resolution that "The antitrust law shall be modified so as to make clear that the laws permit agreements increasing the possibilities of keeping production related to consumption."[57] This, obviously, surrenders completely the principle of free competition.

The interests of businessmen have shifted to some extent from efficiency in production to the attainment of special privileges from government. This has produced two principal effects. First, it has tended to "pauperize" businessmen, just as poor people who depend on special privileges of welfare organizations are said to be "pauperized." Second, it has tended to corrupt government. According to the studies of municipal, state, and federal governments made by Lincoln Steffens in the early part of this century, political corruption and graft grow primarily from the efforts of businessmen to secure special privileges. Two classes of businessmen are responsible for most of the corruption of government: first, railways, public utilities, and other branches of "big business"; second, gambling, prostitution, illicit liquor, and other business establishments connected with the vices. Because of the pressure of these businessmen for special privileges, the system of democracy has been changed into control by political bosses and political machines, which is neither representative government nor efficient government, so far as the problems of the general society are concerned.[58]

6

REBATES

Rebates are a special form of discriminatory prices which were discussed as part of the chapter on restraint of trade. Although rebates may be granted by one manufacturing firm to another manufacturing firm,[1] the cases listed under this title in the present study are limited to those which involve transportation companies and are in violation of the Interstate Commerce Act.

Like other discriminatory prices, rebates are inherent in a competitive system. Each party to a transaction makes the best bargain it can. A firm which is in a strategic position may be able to make a better bargain with a railway than another firm can. Interlocking ownership of railways and industrial firms and interlocking directorates facilitate these rebates. The firms which secure these rebates have lower costs and those which do not have rebates are unable to compete successfully. William Z. Ripley stated that railway rebates have probably contributed more than any other factor to the development of monopolies in the United States.[2] Thus the economic system contains within itself "the seeds of its own decay."

Great public indignation developed in the decade of the eighties regarding the rebates received by the Standard Oil Company, the meat packers, and other industrial corporations. The feeling that such rebates were immoral, if not in violation of the common law principles of fair competition, resulted in the enactment of the Interstate Commerce Act of 1887. This law was expanded and implemented by the Elkins Law of 1903 and the Hepburn Law of 1907. These laws defined the giving and receiving of rebates as crimes and made them punishable by fines and imprisonment.

The original law of 1887 was not implemented with funds or personnel and the enactment of the law produced little effect on rebating practices. In the period 1887–1903 only 79 indictments were returned against all railways and industrial concerns in the United States. The government won 17 of these cases and fines of $16,376 were imposed. Many of the railways and large corporations were disgusted with the rebating practices which had developed and would probably have welcomed the rigid enforcement of the law. Judge Gary, president of the U.S. Steel Corporation, wrote letters in 1903 to the presidents of 27 railway systems, requesting them to grant no rebates to subsidiaries of that corporation. During the administration of Theodore Roosevelt and subsequent to the enactment of the Elkins Law, the Department of Justice started a vigorous campaign of prosecutions against rebaters. In 1903 it secured 77 indictments and 16 convictions, with fines totaling $416,125. This campaign continued during the administration of Taft and the first part of the administration of Wilson. Practically no effort was made to enforce this law during the later part of the Wilson administration or during the administrations of Harding, Coolidge, and Hoover. The enforcement of this law was resumed in 1932 and continued well into the period of the Second World War.

The prosecutions of the 70 largest corporations for participating in rebating practices have followed the general course described above. A total of 56 decisions have been made on this charge against 26 of the 70 large corporations.[3] These are presented in Table 3.[4] The American Sugar Refining Company ranks first among the 70 large corporations with 10 decisions, Armour second with 6, Swift and U.S. Steel tie for third with 5 each. Ten of these 26 corporations have only 1 decision each, but in many of these cases 1 decision represents a large number of violations of the law. Bethlehem Steel was convicted and fined twice in 1910, one decision representing 63 counts and the other 97.

None of these decisions was made in 1887–1903, 37 in 1904–18, none in 1919–30, and 29 in 1931–44. This shows approximately the same annual average for the earlier and later periods and at least contradicts the somewhat prevalent belief that rebating ceased with the First World War. Eight of the 26 corporations with decisions of rebating had such decisions both in the earlier and later periods, indicating that rebating has continued in those corporations over a forty-year period or longer. These corporations are Armour, Bethlehem, International Harvester, Pittsburgh Plate Glass, Swift, U.S. Steel, Wheeling, and Youngstown. Five of the corporations had decisions in the earlier period but not in the later period, namely, American Sugar, American Tobacco, Corn Products, Republic Steel, and Wilson. The other 12 corporations had decisions in the period beginning 1931 but not in the earlier period; 3 of these corporations had not been in existence in the earlier period.

The original form of rebating was repayment by the railway to the shipper of part of the amount charged for shipment of freight. That simple and straightforward method of rebating soon disappeared because of the difficulty of concealing it and because of the psychological hardship of giving up money which had been received. It was replaced by more subtle forms of rebating, such as false billing in the form of false classification of shipments, underweighing, charging the lower carload rate for less than carload quantities, or by excessive payments for damages or for terminal services performed by the shipper. Many decisions were made in 1935–36 for excessive payments for terminal services performed by these corporations. Many other methods of securing partial payments of freight charges were used by some corporations. These may be illustrated by the decision against the American Tobacco Company. The Dukes, who controlled the American Tobacco Company with headquarters in Durham, North Carolina, also owned a one-mile-long railroad in Durham, named "The Durham and South Carolina Railway." The Interstate Commerce Commission decided that this railway received an excessive share of the rates from other railways on shipments carried jointly and that this was virtually a rebate to the American Tobacco Company. For instance, the rate on coal over this railway and two other railways for a distance of 338 miles was $2.29 a ton. Of this amount the Durham and South Carolina R.R. received 62 cents, although on a mileage basis it should receive only ½ cent. The commission issued a desist order against this excessive share to the Durham and South Carolina R.R.[5]

In the 66 decisions against 26 corporations, fines were imposed upon the industrial corporations in 28 cases, upon railways for granting rebates to industrial corporations in the list of 70 in 7 cases, damages were assessed in 1 case, desist orders issued in 25 cases, and orders not specified in 5 cases. The total fines imposed in the 28 cases in which the fines were specified were $492,575, with an average of $17,593 and with a range of $25 to $108,000. The average fine imposed in 1904–18 was $28,252, while in 1931–44 it was only $3,378. Fines were imposed in 62 percent of the decisions in 1904–18, and in only 41 percent of the decisions in 1931–44. These variations in orders, together with the variations in the total number of decisions, are related to the federal administrations and are not an accurate index of the practice of rebating.

In one case a suit for treble damages under the antitrust law was initiated against the Aluminum Company of America on the charge of accepting rebates in Louisiana. The amount demanded was $1,500,000, which was three times the amount of the rebates alleged to have been received by this corporation in Louisiana in specified years. The suit was settled by payment of $150,000 by the Aluminum Company, with the stipulation that the suit be dismissed.[6]

The forthright rebates as well as the concealed rebates are illustrated in the history of the meat packers. Certain railways began to pay rebates, known as "eveners," of $15 per car to the Chicago meat packers for cattle shipped from Chicago to New York. The railways were inclined to do this because they owned the Chicago stockyards, which they had constructed in 1865, and they wished to promote that business in Chicago. The effect of these rebates was to give a great advantage to the Chicago meat packers in competition with meat packers in other cities, and to make Chicago the meat-packing center.[7] This was the beginning of the monopolistic trend in this industry. As the Chicago packers grew strong with this illegal advantage, they demanded a share of the profits of the Chicago stockyards. As a means of coercion they purchased a large tract in northwestern Indiana, adjacent to Chicago, and announced a plan to construct their own stockyards on this tract. The railways, in order to prevent this, granted additional rebates to the meat packers, in the form of a share of the profits of the stockyards. When the small meat packers learned of this, they demanded equivalent rates on threats of suits against the railways. When they were compelled to pay these rebates, the ownership of the stockyards ceased to be profitable to the railways and they sold these yards to the packers. The large meat packers were then in a position to make profits on the business of their competitors and thus increase still more their monopolistic position. Also, since suitable railway equipment was lacking, Armour and Swift constructed their own refrigerator cars for meat and other perishable commodities and again were in a position to make profits on the business of their competitors. The railways made payments to the owners of these cars, when used for other shippers, which the Interstate Commerce Commission held to be excessive and to amount to rebates. Charles Edward Russell estimated that Armour and Swift received $25 million in 1905 from this one form of rebating.[8] At a meeting the Federal Trade Commission revealed that Armour and Swift, through ownership of the Denver stockyards, were receiving differential payments from the railways which amounted to rebates. In 1918 a federal grand jury indicted Armour, Swift, the Jersey City Stockyards Company, and the Pennsylvania Railway Company for rebating. The charge was that Armour and Swift agreed to route their shipments over the Pennsylvania so far as practicable in return for a lease on the Jersey City stockyards, which was owned by the Pennsylvania. This property was appraised at $16,500,000 and would ordinarily rent for $200,000 a year, but it was rented to Armour and Swift for $25,000, which was appraised as a rebate of $175,000 a year. This lease was terminated as a result of the action.[9] Again, the Federal Trade Commission made complaint against the Mechanical Manufacturing Company, which made small articles of railway equipment. This company was owned principally by the Swift family and was managed by the head of the traffic department of Swift & Company. This manufacturing business had been inconsequential until the Swifts took it over, but its profits soared when it was managed by the person who decided which railways should receive the shipments of meat from Swift & Company: the railways purchased immense quantities of these articles. The profits dropped as quickly when the Federal Trade Commission ordered the Swifts to divest themselves of this property on the ground that it amounted to a rebate.[10] Armour & Company developed a similar firm to make railway equipment, which made large profits until the Federal Trade Commission ordered the Armours to divest themselves of the Waugh Equipment Company.[11]

The American Sugar Refining Company had the most extensive record of decisions for rebating of any of these corporations. The decisions against it were all made in 1906–13. Ripley states that during eighteen months in 1905–07 fines of $586,000 were imposed on business and railway firms in the United States for rebating, and of this amount nearly $300,000 was imposed on the American Sugar Refining Company.[12]

Of the 70 large corporations 44 have no decisions against them on rebating. Most of these are either mercantile companies or are manufacturing companies in light industries such as chemicals and electrical equipment. The decisions on rebating have been limited largely to corporations in the heavy industries, in which the freight costs are a relatively large part of the total costs of production.

7

PATENTS, TRADEMARKS, AND COPYRIGHTS

Violations of laws regarding patents, trademarks, and copyrights fall into two principal classes, namely, infringement and restraint of trade.

Infringement

The record of the 70 large corporations for infringements of patents, trademarks, and copyrights consists of 130 explicit decisions, 33 stipulations, and 59 consent decrees against 53 of the corporations. Of these 222 decisions, only 21 were appraised as explicit decisions that the behavior was criminal on the basis of the penal sanction. The belief was expressed, however, that criminality was probably involved in approximately half of the cases.[1] In order to give some evidence for this belief, details will be given in regard to a relatively large number of infringement cases.

The infringement of patents will be considered first. Explicit decisions of infringement of patents have been made against 42 of the large corporations, including 4 decisions regarding royalties and 2 decisions in patent cases that unfair competition had been used. The total number of these explicit decisions is 114, with a range of 1 to 13 per corporation and an average of 2.7. In addition, infringement suits have resulted in stipulations and consent decrees in 91 cases.[2] If these 91 cases be added to the explicit decisions, 51 of the large corporations, or 73 percent, have such records in 205 infringement suits, with a range of 1 to 22 and an average of 4.3. For the purpose of describing these decisions, the 62 manufacturing and mining corporations will be considered first and the 8 mercantile corporations later.

Of the 62 manufacturing and mining corporations, 44, or 70 percent, had 133 decisions, stipulations, and consent decrees on patent infringement, as shown in Table 7. General Motors stands first with 22, General Electric second with 8, Ford third with 7. If these records constitute

TABLE 7. Decisions of Patent Infringements against 44 of the 62 Manufacturing and Mining Corporations by Classes of Decisions

Corporation	Explicit decisions	Stipula-tions	Consent decrees	Total
Aluminum Co. of America	1	—	—	1
American Can	1	—	—	1
Amer. Car & Foundry	4	—	2	6
American Smelting	1	—	—	1
American Tobacco	1	—	—	1
American Woolen	1	—	—	1
Anaconda	2	—	2	4
Armour	1	1	—	2
Bethlehem	1	—	1	2
Borden	—	1	—	1
Chrysler	—	1	—	1
Corn Products	1	—	—	1
Crane	1	—	—	1
Deere	2	—	—	2
DuPont	4	—	—	4
Eastman	1	—	2	3
Firestone	2	2	—	4
Ford	4	1	2	7
General Electric	3	2	3	8
General Motors	10	5	7	22
Goodrich	1	—	1	2
Goodyear	3	—	1	4
Intern. Harvester	2	1	—	3
Intern. Paper	2	—	—	2
Kennecott	—	1	—	1
Loew's	—	1	—	1
National Dairy	—	1	—	1
National Lead	2	—	1	3
Paramount	2	1	1	4
Phelps Dodge	1	—	—	1
Phil. & Reading Coal	1	—	—	1
Pittsburgh Plate	3	—	—	3
Procter & Gamble	1	—	—	1
RCA	1	1	—	2
Singer	5	—	—	5
Swift	—	1	—	1
Union Carbide	4	—	1	5
United Fruit	—	—	1	1
United Shoe Mach.	2	—	1	3
U.S. Rubber	1	—	1	2
U.S. Steel	5	—	—	5
Warner	1	1	1	3
Westinghouse	3	—	2	5
Wheeling	—	—	1	1
Total	81	21	31	132

adequate evidence, General Motors or its subsidiaries have infringed on its transmission, carburetor, spark plug, manifold, wheel rim, radiator shutter, oil filter, circuit control switch, amplifying apparatus, door handle, side curtain supports, lens and carrier, fifth wheel for trailers, gear-grinding machine, and the process for giving metal the appearance of wood-grain.

Three of the 62 manufacturing and mining corporations started their business on processes which the courts declared to be infringements of patents. These 3, which may be appraised as illegitimate in origin, are the Singer Sewing Machine Company, the Aluminum Company of America, and the Goodyear Tire and Rubber Company. The Singer Sewing Machine Company began business in 1851 on a patent granted to Isaac Morton Singer. The court held in 1853 and again in 1854 that this Singer machine was an infringement of the Howe patent which had been granted in 1846.[3] Singer's only defense was that the Howe patent was not valid, although the court had decided prior to 1851 that the patent was valid. In the trial of this case the testimony indicated that Singer, who had been an actor and theater-manager with no mechanical experience, submitted his application for a patent ten days after he saw one of the Howe machines.

The Aluminum Company of America began operations in 1888 with the name "Pittsburgh Reduction Company." It was under the management of Hall and had financial backing of Mellon and other Pittsburgh capitalists. The principal firm in the industry at this time was the Cowles Electric Smelting and Aluminum Company. Bradley had applied in 1883 for a patent on the process used by the Cowles Company but the patent was not granted until 1891 and 1892. According to testimony in the trial, Hall had been employed by the Cowles Company in 1887–88, had learned the details of their process, and applied for a patent on this process. This patent was granted in 1889. Each of these companies sued the other for infringement and each won its case.[4] This impasse was resolved by an agreement that the Aluminum Company of America would pay the Cowles Company $4 million for the patent of the latter on condition that the award of damages be remitted and that the Cowles Company withdraw from the aluminum industry. This agreement was probably a violation of the Sherman Antitrust Act but it removed the legal difficulties so far as infringement was concerned and at the same time it removed the only competitor in the aluminum industry and resulted in establishing the most complete monopoly in the United States.

The Goodyear Tire and Rubber Company was organized in 1898 by Seiberling and began to manufacture rubber tires for buggies. The patent on the process which he used was held by the Consolidated Rubber Company, had been declared valid by the courts, and was secured by other manufacturers on licenses. Seiberling proceeded to use the process without a license. An infringement suit against him was settled by an agreement that he would pay royalties on a license and that the Consolidated Rubber Company would take $50,000 worth of tires a month from him. Seiberling claimed that the Consolidated Rubber Company refused to take the tires as agreed, and that this failure was a deliberate attempt to ruin his business. His license to use the patent was canceled when he started a suit to compel the Consolidated Rubber Company to take the tires.[5] He continued to use the same process, without a license. In a new suit, an injunction was issued against him, but he posted bonds and proceeded with the manufacture of tires until the court decided in a suit against another company that the patent was void.[6] The disregard of patent limitations was displayed by Seiberling in other processes. Seiberling secured a license to use a patented process in the manufacture of bicycle tires on condition that he maintain the prices specified in the license. His license was soon canceled on the charge that he was cutting prices. He made a slight modification in the process and continued without a license. An infringement suit against him was withdrawn, probably as a result of a settlement out of court.[7] Later, this company was accused of infringing the patent on balloon tires. The court expressed the opinion in this case that "infringement was . . . conscious and deliberate" and awarded damages of $1,096,000 for the New York District alone and with a part of the period of infringement excluded by the statute of limitations. This award was reduced on appeal.[8] Additional decisions were made against Goodyear in later years.

Seiberling's attitudes toward patents were duplicated by the executives of two other principal rubber companies—Firestone and Goodrich—but not by U.S. Rubber. U.S. Rubber and its affiliated companies, which were known as "The Rubber Trust" at the turn of the century, were leaders in the patent pools which in violation of the antitrust law dominated the tire industry.

In its origin and development the Ford Motor Company resembled the Goodyear Tire and Rubber Company. A patent on gas engines was used to exclude prospective manufacturers of automobiles, and this patent had been held valid. Ford applied for a license to use the patent and was refused. He proceeded to manufacture automobiles without a license, using processes which were held to be an infringement of the Selden patent; this patent later was declared void.[9] Ford's contempt for patent laws persisted in his later career. Parker Rustproof Company charged that the Ford Motor Company had infringed their patent. Ford had used this process from 1916 to 1920, keeping it secret and permitting only three men in the factory to know its details. When the Parker Company discovered in 1920 that its patent was being infringed by Ford, it immediately notified Ford. Ford continued to use the process and even increased its use. In the court decisions that Ford had infringed this patent, the court stated that Ford had been notified by his own counsel that the patent was being infringed.[10]

The manufacturers of agricultural machinery had a wild history of patent infringement and patent manipulation prior to 1902, when most of them were merged in the International Harvester Company. In the earlier history the McCormick Company, although seldom selected as superior to its competitors in field trials, attained superiority as a patent manipulator. The only explicit decision against International Harvester, subsequent to its organization, was in a suit by Bucher and Gibbs on a patent on a disk harrow, which had been granted in 1906. According to testimony in the trial, International Harvester purchased one of these disk harrows in 1909 and manufactured harrows almost like it. This resulted in serious injury to the business of Bucher and Gibbs, and a decision that International Harvester had infringed the patent.[11]

A decision was made that the United Shoe Machinery Company had infringed the Mathey patent on a trimming machine which had acquired a wide sale. According to the testimony, Boulton examined this machine, made one similar to it with a few slight modifications, secured a patent on this, and assigned the patent to the United Shoe Machinery Company. This machine was sold at a lower pice than the Mathey machine and almost ruined the business of the latter.[12]

The American Car and Foundry Company has a relatively extensive list of decisions in infringement cases, of which the following is one. The Bemis Box Car Company sued J. G. Brill, subsidiary of American Car and Foundry. The court decided that Brill had infringed the Bemis patent, the master awarded damages of $122,642, and the court expressed the opinion, "The defendant's conduct, while not technically wanton, appears to have been in the highest degree reckless both of consequences to itself and of injury to the property rights of others."[13]

A decision of infringement was made against Armour & Company in a suit by the Douglas Pectin Company. The Douglas patent had been declared valid in prior suits and "Certo" manufactured under this patent had acquired a wide sale. Armour, without securing a license, developed a process which, according to the court decision, differed from the Douglas process in inconsequential respects.[14]

Procter & Gamble, after a century-long career without adverse decisions under patent laws, has been engaged in much patent litigation during the last generation. It was sued late in the decade of the twenties by Colgate-Palm Olive Peets for infringement, made a settlement, and took a license to use the patent. Subsequently, it joined with Colgate in an infringement suit against Lever Brothers, as a result of which Lever Brothers was ordered to pay damages of $5 million. Lever Brothers shortly thereafter complained that Procter & Gamble had bribed its employees to secure trade secrets; on this complaint Procter & Gamble was indicted for using the mails to defraud.[15] Also, Lever Brothers sued Procter & Gamble for infringing its patents on the "continuous process" of soap making, and in turn Procter & Gamble sued Lever Brothers for infringing its patent on floating soap. Lever Brothers won both of these suits. While appeals were pending, a settlement was made by which Procter & Gamble paid Lever Brothers $10 million on condition that the complaints be dismissed.[16]

The mercantile companies have a much higher rate of infringement of patents than the manufacturing and mining corporations which have been considered up to this point. The decisions against the eight mercantile corporations are presented in Table 8. Of these eight mercantile corporations seven, or 87.5 percent, have records of patent infringement, with Great A & P alone having no decision against it. The seven

TABLE 8. Decisions of Patent Infringements against 8 Mercantile Corporations by Types of Records

Corporation	Explicit decisions	Stipula- tions	Consent decrees	Total
Gimbel	2	—	9	11
Great A & P	—	—	—	—
Kresge	4	—	2	6
Macy	2	2	8	12
Marshall Field	1	1	—	2
Montgomery Ward	10	2	1	13
Sears Roebuck	13	4	2	19
Woolworth	1	2	6	9
Total	33	11	28	72

mercantile corporations have a total of 72 explicit decisions, stipulations, and consent decrees. The average number of decisions against the seven mercantile corporations was 10.3, while the average number against the manufacturing and mining corporations was only 3.0. Sears Roebuck stands first among the seven mercantile corporations, with 19 decisions, Montgomery Ward second with 13, Macy third with 12, and Gimbel fourth with 11. In the suits against Sears Roebuck the following commodities are involved: rubber-bladed electric fan, angle gauge, combination joint for heating plant, electric toaster, electric shaver, amplifier, battery, ironing machine, electric cooker, vacuum cleaner, antishimmy device, cream separator, lawn mower, bathtub, roofing material, film process, casting process, and control system.

The holder of a patent who believes his patent is infringed customarily sues both the manufacturer and the dealer. Because these large mercantile corporations handle the products of many manufacturers, the suits against the mercantile corporations are more frequent than the suits against any manufacturer. While the mercantile corporation is generally regarded as accessory rather than principal in the infringement, the mercantile corporation sometimes has the principal responsibility either because the small manufacturing corporation is secretly owned by the large mercantile corporation or the manufacturing corporation produces commodities on specifications drawn by the mercantile corporation.

Infringements of trademarks are less numerous than infringements of patents, as judged by court decisions. The records of the 70 large corporations on trademark infringement are shown in Table 9. This indicates that 7 of the 70 large corporations have ten adverse decisions on trademark infringements. Nine of the ten decisions were explicit and one was a stipulation. In two trademark infringement cases against

TABLE 9. Decisions of Trademark
Infringements against 7 of the 70 Large
Corporations

Corporation	Decisions
Kresge	3
Loew's	1
Montgomery Ward	2
National Biscuit	1
Sears Roebuck	1
Wilson	1
Woolworth	1
Total	10

Kresge and one against Woolworth, the decision was that the violation of law was unfair competition. Of the 7 corporations with these decisions, 4 are mercantile corporations and 3 manufacturing corporations.

In most of the cases tabulated above, the infringement appears to have been deliberate. In such cases an effort is made to palm off a commodity for the superior commodity of a competitor, and is an attempt to defraud. A few cases of this type will be described. Kresge was sued by the Mishawaka Rubber and Woolen Manufacturing Company, a subsidiary of U.S. Rubber, for selling rubber heels with a trademark alleged to infringe the Mishawaka trademark. Kresge was warned on three occasions but did not change the molds of the trademark until six months after the last warning. The court held that Kresge had infringed this trademark and awarded damages, with the interpretation that the federal courts award damages in trademark cases only when the trademark is intended to deceive.[17] Again, Kresge was sued by the Winget Kickernich Company, a manufacturer of bloomers for women and children, on the charge of using the name "Kickaway" for the purpose of palming off articles. The court decided that this was an infringement and awarded damages. On appeal, the decision that Kresge had infringed the trademark was reversed and for it was substituted the decision that Kresge had engaged in unfair competition by using the name "Kickaway."[18] A third suit against Kresge was on the charge that Kresge's "No-Deca" infringed the trademark of the "No-D-Ka Dentifrice Company." The court held that "No-D-Ka" was not a trade name and dismissed the suit under the trademark law but authorized a change in the complaint to "unfair competition."[19] Both "No-D-Ka" and "No-Deca" are misleading labels, designed to deceive customers as to the values of toothpastes and both might have been proceeded against as misrepresentation in advertising.

Woolworth was sued by the O'Cedar Corporation for infringing the name "Cedar" in its "Radiant Cedar Oil" and in other furniture polishes which contained the word "cedar" in the titles. The first suit was settled in 1925 by an agreement that Woolworth would not use the word "cedar" in its furniture polishes. The court expressed the opinion that this violation of the agreement was obviously due to the utility of the word "cedar" in selling its products. In the suit which followed, the attorney for Woolworth argued that the term "cedar" involved no misrepresentation since the polish contained an infinitesimal quantity of cedar oil. A charge of fraud, if justified, would apply equally to Woolworth and the

O'Cedar Corporation. The suit was dismissed in the district court, and reversed in the circuit court, where an injunction and damages were ordered.[20]

Wilson and Company, meat packers, was sued by Best Foods Company for infringing the trademark "Nucoa" by the name "Pecoa" on oleomargarine and by the use of packages and cartons similar to those used for "Nucoa." Best Foods had used the name "Nucoa" since 1905 and this product had acquired an extensive sale. Wilson, after failing to secure substantial sales of its oleomargarine under other names, in 1917 adopted a name and package similar to the successful brand of its competitor. It sales immediately increased, while those of its competitor decreased. This was held to be an infringement and damages were awarded.[21]

Decisions that copyrights have been infringed have been made against 5 of the 70 large corporations with a total of eight decisions. These are shown in Table 10. The decisions against Loew's are on charges of plagiarism of novels for use in motion pictures,[22] those against American Tobacco and Ford Motor Company on charges of using copyrighted materials for advertising purposes, while the other two suits were concerned with transmission of copyrighted materials over the radio. The details which are available do not suggest that infringement was deliberate in any case except those concerned with motion pictures.

The relatively small number of decisions under the copyright law is due in part to the fact that these large corporations have little to do with copyrighted commodities and in part to the fact that the standards of behavior regarding copyrights are much more liberal and tolerant than those regarding patents.

Patent Manipulation

The second class of violations of law in connection with patents, trademarks, and copyrights is the manipulation of patents and to a slight extent of trademarks for restraint of trade and unfair competition.[23] As described above, official decisions have been made that 27 of the 70 large corporations have engaged in restraint of trade by patent manipulation; reports of investigating commissions indicate that at least 7 additional corporations in the list of 70 have used the same policy. The discussion of patent manipulation in the present section is not designed to add more counts to the record of the 70 large corporations. It is designed

TABLE 10. Decisions of Copyright
Infringements against 5 of the 70 Large
Corporations

Corporation	Decisions
American Tobacco	1
Ford Motor	1
General Electric	1
Loew's	4
Macy	1
Total	8

rather to describe the general policy of patent manipulation in a manner which will assist in interpreting the criminal behavior of corporations.

Patent manipulation is a perversion of the patent system. The constitutional objective of the patent system was the promotion of science and
the useful arts. This objective was to be achieved by granting to an inventor an exclusive property right in his invention for a limited number
of years. If the invention contributed to technological efficiency, the inventor received profits, these profits stimulated others to make inventions, and thus science was promoted.

The patent system unquestionably has had some effect in stimulating
technological efficiency and science. The failure to realize this objective
more completely is due to two conditions which were not present or not
appreciated at the time this system originated. First, the inventor has
found increasing difficulty in establishing his own factory or in selling
his invention to others. This difficulty is due to the trend toward mergers
and large capitalistic enterprise, which has decreased competition and
impeded new establishments. Second, because objective criteria of invention cannot be stated, as has been learned in the experience of the
Patent Office, widespread and expensive litigation regarding patents has
resulted. The statement has been made that not one patent in ten even
pays the costs of registration. Consequently the profits which were expected to stimulate inventions have been generally lacking.

Under these circumstances, the patent system would probably have
been discarded long ago if it had not had other values than the promotion of technological efficiency. These other values lie in the area of social control and, in this respect, patents are cognate with advertising,
salesmanship, and lobbying. Although industry is necessarily concerned
both with technological efficiency and social control, its concern with
social control is relatively much greater today than it was a century ago.
The use of patents for social control has taken the form of harassment

and coercion of competitors for the purpose of maintaining prices and restricting production. For this reason patent manipulation is a perversion of the patent system and is, on a higher level, analogous to racketeering.

Trademarks have not been manipulated to the same extent as patents. The stage is set, however, for the development of manipulation in this area, for since the enactment of fair trade laws which prohibit price cutting on trademarked articles, the trademark has become a potential weapon against price cutting. Macy insisted on offering commodities at lower prices than his competitors did, won the bad graces of his competitors and of manufacturers, and was subjected to legal action. Up to date, trademark manipulation has not developed far and for that reason the following description of manipulation is directed at patents.

The policy of patent manipulation involves action in accordance with the following maxims: first, secure the maximum number and expansion of patents; second, interfere in every way with grants of patents to others; third, coerce competitors by threats and suits; fourth, make agreements for patent pools with competitors who cannot be coerced. These practices, with special reference to the 70 large corporations, are described below.

First, many corporations attempt to secure a patent on every conceivable modification in industrial processes, to make these as inclusive as possible, and, by delays in applications and by renewals, to extend these patents over the maximum time. These extensions of patents are designated "umbrella patents," "shotgun patents," "dog-in-the-manger patents," and "blocking patents." This policy of securing the maximum number of patents is feasible because of the very low level of invention to which, in the absence of objective criteria of invention, the Patent Office has been forced. This is illustrated by the fact that nearly a thousand patents on the toothbrush have been registered. Most of these "inventions" are modifications in the size and shape of the handle, or the number, size, and arrangement of the bristles. It is doubtful whether dental health would have been seriously retarded if not one patent on the toothbrush had been granted during the last seventy-five years. In general, a relatively small proportion of all patents registered have greater technological importance than these patents on the toothbrush. General Electric has secured about 300 patents on the mazda lamp but has used not more than a score of these in production. This indicates that technological efficiency is not the primary purpose of patents.

To an increasing extent the large corporations apply for and secure patents. In 1920, 63 percent of the 70 large corporations secured one or more patents, with an average of 21.6 patents per corporation. In 1942 the percentage had increased to 87 and the average to 54.5. This trend toward patent registration is especially characteristic of a small number of corporations, for 5 corporations secured 50 percent of all patents granted to the 70 large corporations in 1920 and 60 percent in 1942. These corporations are, in order of the number of patents registered, General Electric, General Motors, RCA, Westinghouse, and DuPont.[24]

Not all corporations attempt to secure patents on every invention. While the corporations which register many patents make large expenditures for inventions, the converse is not universally true. Some corporations which make large expenditures for research and make many inventions, register few patents. Thus inventions and patents are independently variable. This fact, also, tends to demonstrate that the promotion of technological efficiency is not the primary value of the patent system.

A second aspect of patent manipulation is interference with grants of patents to others, insofar as products or processes are of common interest. Corporations which secure many patents appear frequently before the Commissioner of Patents in interference proceedings in the effort to block the registration of patents by others. Also, many corporations have contracts with their employees which provide that any invention by these employees shall be the property of the corporation. Customarily no compensation other than the regular wage or salary is given for such inventions by employees and on that account some of these contracts have been declared by the courts to be invalid.

The third practice in patent manipulation is the initiation of infringement suits, generally preceded by threats of such suits. Corporations which register many patents initiate many patent suits. Among the corporations which have been prolific in infringement suits, especially during the decade of the twenties, are General Electric, RCA, and Westinghouse. Also, corporations which initiate many infringement suits against others are themselves frequently defendants. General Electric stands first in the number of patents registered and second in the number of decisions of infringements; General Motors stands second in patent registrations and first in infringements. The use of patents for social control seems to destroy respect for them as property rights; they do not have a halo of sanctity when they are used as weapons in industrial strife. Finally, both patent registrations and decisions of infringements against the 70 large corporations have increased in frequency with each succeeding decade of the last half-century.[25]

Although these large corporations initiate many infringement suits they win few, especially when the suits are carried to the higher courts. The *Federal Reporter* lists 102 patent suits initiated by General Electric (a relatively small part of all its patent suits), of which 51 percent were won by General Electric, 46 percent were lost, and 3 percent not decided. The Temporary National Economic Committee made an analysis of court decisions in a sample of infringement suits. It reported that patents were held to be valid and infringed in 39 percent of the suits decided in the district courts of the United States in 1933, in 18 percent of the infringement suits decided on appeal by the circuit courts in 1933, and in only 3.6 percent of the suits decided by the Supreme Court of the United States in 1930–39.[26] The executives and patent attorneys of these large corporations know that few of their infringement suits will be won if the defendant has funds and determination to carry the suits to the higher courts. Small corporations cannot afford to do this and dealers, who handle the products of competitors of the patent holder, are especially susceptible to suits and threats.

Infringement suits, therefore, are useful primarily as a means of harassment and coercion. If a competitor takes a license to use the patent, he must yield a profit to the owner of the patent, and at the same time may be coerced to maintain prices and limit production according to specification in the license. The patent holder has opportunity for other kinds of coercion in connection with the patent. Some licenses not only require payment of royalties on patented processes but also on processes on which licenses have expired or on processes on which no patent has ever been secured. Some corporations not only force licensees to pay royalties on articles manufactured under the patent, but also on the products of competitors which are used by the licensees. Also, some of these licenses require the licensees to make written acknowledgment of the validity of the patents, so that the licensees are deprived of the principal defense of "invalidity of the patent" if an infringement suit should develop at a later date. In such respects, the patent system in operation resembles racketeering.

The fourth practice in patent manipulation is to exchange patents and form patent pools with competitors who are so strong that they cannot be coerced. With the trend toward mergers during the last fifty years, many industries are under the domination of a small number of large corporations. Fights among these large corporations would be expensive and perhaps disastrous to all concerned. The usual substitute is an exchange of patents, patent pools, and agreements regarding patents. Furthermore foreign competition is reduced or eliminated by similar patent agreements with foreign corporations, generally in the form of cartels. A device which has been used in a few cases is to transfer the patents to a "Foundation," which with a facade of public service acts as the prosecuting agency for the corporations which own the patents. Most of the decisions against the 70 large corporations under the antitrust law, insofar as they have involved patents, have been cases which included patent pools, and few of them have been made against corporations for individual policies of patent manipulation.

Patent manipulation, with the four practices which have been described, has been used especially by corporations which are not protected against the entrance of new competitors into the industry by large capitalization or limited natural resources. Illustrations have been given previously of patent manipulation in regard to electrical equipment and automobile accessories. Such articles can be made in a shop or small factory with a small capitalization, and this competition may force prices downward. Patent manipulation is a device for preventing the entrance of such competitors into the industry, and, if competitors do appear, preventing them from cutting prices and producing more than can be sold at the existing prices. In the same manner, many small corporations attempt to protect themselves against competition by litigation regarding trivial inventions. The Miniature Golf Corporation secured a patent on its vacant-lot form of recreation. Competitors immediately developed and the Miniature Golf Corporation filed scores of suits against them during the decade of the twenties. The Good Humor Corporation engaged in patent litigation for more than a decade with the Popsicle Company and other manufacturers of ice-cream bars. The Maiden Form Brassiere Company and the Snug-Fit Foundations, Inc. were before the courts for many years regarding their patented designs.

In industries in which monopolies or near-monopolies are based on large capitalization or ownership of limited natural resources, new competitors find it almost impossible to secure a foothold. In such industries, corporations register few patents, initiate few infringement suits, and have few decisions against them for infringements. This is illustrated in Table 11. This shows for 15 large corporations in three industries the number of patents registered in 1942 and the number of decisions of in-

TABLE 11. Number of Patents Registered in 1942 by Selected
Corporations and Number of Infringement Decisions against the
Same Corporations, Classified by Industries

Industry and corporation	Patents registered in 1942	Infringement decisions
Steel industry		
Amer. Rolling Mills	12	0
Bethlehem	7	2
Inland	5	0
Jones & Laughlin	4	0
National Steel	0	0
Republic	10	0
U.S. Steel	50	5
Wheeling	4	1
Youngstown	10	0
Meat packing		
Armour	15	2
Swift	2	1
Wilson	2	0
Tobacco manufacture		
American Tobacco	2	1
Liggett & Myer	0	0
Reynolds	0	0
Total	123	12

fringement of patents during their life careers. The average number of
patents registered was 8.2, in comparison with 67.3 for the other manufacturing and mining corporations in the list of 70 large corporations,
and the average number of infringement suits decided against them was
0.9, in comparison with 3.2 for the other corporations. If U.S. Steel,
which has ramified into many specialized areas, were eliminated, the average in each column would be reduced by approximately one-third.
These corporations make little use of patent manipulation because they
are protected against competition in other ways. The failure to adopt this
higher form of racketeering is, in no sense, evidence of ethical superiority to the corporations which follow these practices.

The preceding analysis gives support to the general conclusion that
large corporations, in spite of their protestations regarding the value of
free enterprise and the competitive system, dislike free enterprise and
competition. They have used the patent system, which grants to the inventor a monopoly for a period of years, as a device for destroying the
system of free enterprise and competition.

As illustrations of the preceding general interpretation of patent manipulation, descriptions are given below of two corporations which used

this policy at an early date and of two industries in which this policy has continued to the present time.

The Singer Sewing Machine Company was the first of the large corporations to engage extensively in this policy of patent manipulation. Singer started his business, as previously explained,[27] on a patent which the court held to be an infringement of the Howe patent, and thereafter he was compelled to take a license to use the Howe patent. From the start of his business, Singer concentrated on patent manipulation. He not only secured his basic patent but immediately applied for many other patents. Also, he appeared before the Commissioner of Patents frequently in interference proceedings, sued other manufacturers, and was sued in return. Within a few years, he and other manufacturers of sewing machines began to feel rebellious against continued payments of royalties on the Howe patent. At the suggestion of a patent attorney that they would all make more money if they quit fighting each other, the three principal manufacturers—Singer, Wheeler & Wilson, and Groves & Bamler—developed a patent pool in 1856, to which Howe contributed his patent. This pool secured extensions on old patents, registered new patents on trivial details, and threatened all competitors with infringement suits. When these competitors showed a disposition to fight, the patent pool made settlements rather than permit the patents to be tested in court. In 1862 Hunt's heirs sued Singer on a contract made in 1858, according to which Singer agreed to pay Hunt $50,000 for refraining from contesting the validity of an extension on the Howe patent. The court decided against Singer in this suit and ordered him to pay a balance of $17,000 to the Hunt heirs.[28] In 1862 Singer purchased the Howe patent and the other Howe assets. By this and other methods he secured complete control of the patent pool and thus of the sewing machine industry. After the patents expired, he continued to sue competitors for infringing the expired patents.

The Eastman Kodak Company at an early date used the policy of patent manipulation. George Eastman began his career in photography, while making his living as a bank clerk, by securing two patents in 1878. He made a trip to England forthwith in order to register these patents in England. This interest in patents continued throughout his career. When he began to manufacture photographic supplies and cameras, he secured as many patents as possible, both by invention and purchase. He employed the most capable patent attorneys he could find. For a time his attorney was George B. Selden, owner of the famous patent on gas engines, which is often used as the best illustration of the atrocious policy of delays in order to prolong the life of a patent. Eastman initiated many patent suits against others, beginning in 1885 with a suit against Anthony and Company, an established firm dealing in photographic supplies. The assertion has been made that he won infringement suits on only one of his many patents, namely, the roll film-holder. The Department of Justice initiated two antitrust suits against Eastman in connection with his patent manipulations, each of which resulted in a decision against him. One of these suits began in 1915, on the charge that since 1890 Eastman had used a consistent policy of restraining trade by illegal use of patents and by other methods. This suit charged that Eastman had initiated an infringement suit against Blair and Turned of the Boston Camera Company in a vexatious and malicious manner, with the objective of ruining them as competitors, when they developed a pocket camera which cut seriously into his sales of kodaks. This suit, together with the development of a new model by Eastman, ruined Blair and Turned. They were forced to sell their assets to Eastman, with the agreement that they would not initiate suits against Eastman for prior infringements of their patents. Furthermore, according to the charge of the Department of Justice, Eastman granted other firms licenses to use his patents only if they paid royalties both on this patented process and also on products purchased from competitors of Eastman.[29] Although the court held that Eastman had violated the antitrust law, it expressed the opinion that the charge of malice had not been adequately proved.[30] The second antitrust suit against Eastman occurred at an earlier date than the one just described and was limited to a narrower field. This was the suit against the Motion Picture Patents Company, which had been organized by the Edison Company for the purpose of securing a monopoly of motion pictures. The Department of Justice charged that Eastman had agreed to sell film only to this Motion Picture Patents Company and that this company had agreed to buy films only from Eastman. This effectively eliminated all competitors and was declared illegal by the court.[31]

The manufacture of electrical equipment will be used as the first illustration of an industry in which patent manipulation is still prevalent. The General Electric Company was organized as a merger of corporations which had previously been competitors, and the control of patents was one of the primary objectives of this merger. Elihu Thompson, founder of one of the corporations which was merged in General Electric, instructed his assistants to "invent around" the patents of others,[32] and this phrase represents the policy of many corporations of the present day. Thompson secured as many patents as possible, no matter how trivial, and had a total of 691 patents to his credit during his career.[33] The other corporations in this industry adopted the same policy. Of all patents granted in 1942, totaling about 40,000, 650 were granted to General Electric, 500 to Westinghouse, and 400 to RCA, which are the three principal firms in this industry.

After the merger of competing companies to form General Electric, only one strong competitor remained, namely, Westinghouse. Sharp conflict between these two corporations continued for a few years, with much vicious propaganda regarding the defects of the competitor's products and with some raids on the stock of the other corporation in the stock market. Since the basic patents on incandescent lamps were to expire in 1896, and since this would result in a flood of new competitors, General Electric and Westinghouse made an agreement to exchange patents, and they assumed the leadership in a trade association which fixed prices and regulated production through licenses to use patents. At that time, as well as later, many infringement suits were brought against smaller and weaker firms and against dealers. These suits were organized so that they would cause the maximum difficulty to the defendants. An illustration of this is the suit by General Electric in 1901 against the Winsted Gas Company for infringing the patent on an electromagnetic machine. The court, in dismissing the suit, pointed out that the Winsted Gas Company was a small utility company which owned and used one machine of this type, that a suit could have been brought against the manufacturer of the machine, although the chance of success was small. The court pointed out also that the patent had never been used in production since it was registered in 1882 and that the patented process was such an insignificant contribution to the prior art that only an extremely broad interpretation would justify the court in holding the machine in question to be an infringement.[34]

This trade association, with its policy of patent manipulation, continued for fifteen years without interference from the government, until in 1911 an antitrust suit resulted in an order to dissolve the association. Although the association was dissolved, plans had been made for other methods of restricting competition, and additional methods were developed in later years.

In 1919, when some of the basic patents on radios were about to expire, General Electric organized the Radio Corporation of America with some of the stock held by Westinghouse and, for a time, by American Telephone and Telegraph. RCA received most of the patents which had been held by General Electric, and exchanged patents with Westinghouse. It acquired additional patents whenever possible. For nearly a decade RCA acted as the joint selling agency for General Electric and Westinghouse. These arrangements were declared by the court to be in violation of the antitrust law, and RCA was ordered to separate from the other corporations. Although this altered the formal structure, it had little immediate effect on the relationships. Both before and after this separation, each of these three corporations instituted many infringement suits against competitors. Doubtless their patents were infringed in many cases, but some corporations testified that they were compelled by suits and threats of suits to take licenses on patents which they had not used and could not possibly use. In many cases, each of the three corporations initiated a separate suit against a manufacturer or dealer in regard to the same patent; sometimes these suits were in different jurisdictions and introduced at different times, with the purpose of causing greater expense and vexation than joint suits would cause. In spite of a small percentage of victories in these suits, when carried to the higher courts, these three corporations coerced competitors into a system in which prices and production were dictated by them.

Efforts were made to establish monopolies in the motion picture industry. One of these was an agreement between Western Electric (a subsidiary of American Telephone and Telegraph) and Warner Brothers, by which Warner Brothers had an exclusive right to use patents on "talkies." General Electric, Westinghouse, and RCA were unwilling to permit another corporation to acquire an undefined area in an industry in which electricity was used, and they threatened suits. Conferences were held and agreements were made as to the boundaries of the operations of the several companies. These three companies have continuous agreements with each other and also with the American Telephone and Telegraph Company and Western Union.[35] Their negotiations regarding industrial boundary lines resemble international diplomacy. It is collectivistic planning and is a far departure from the classical ideal of a competitive self-regulating system, from the system authorized by statutes, and from the system that these corporations advocate in their advertisements and propaganda.

General Electric perhaps more than any other corporation in the list of the 70 largest corporations has used patent manipulation to develop the policy of private collectivism as a substitute for the system of free enterprise. E. S. Morrison, attorney for General Electric, is quoted as saying "that his company is largely founded upon patents and that the extent to which patents discourage competition usually controlled their attitude in regard to opening new lines of business."[36] Although recent advertisements of General Electric call attention to the strenuous efforts of that corporation to make better commodities at cheaper prices, this policy is used in a restricted part of its activities. The following office memorandum was found in the files of General Electric by a Congressional Committee.

> Two or three years ago we proposed a reduction of the life of the flashlight lamps from the old basis on which one lamp was supposed to outlast three batteries to a point where the life of the lamp and the life of the battery would be approximately equal. . . . If this were done, we estimate that it would result in increasing our flashlight business approximately 60 per cent.[37]

The significant point in this memorandum is that it proposes a poorer lamp rather than a better battery. Also, in 1939 General Electric had an exhibit at the World's Fair which showed that fluorescent lighting required less wattage than mazda lamps and was therefore cheaper to operate. The Buffalo Niagara Eastern Power Corporation wrote to General Electric that this exhibit was a violation of the agreement which had been made that "advance in lighting art should not be at the expense of wattage but should give the customer more for the same money." General Electric thereupon changed the inscription so that the customer was not informed that he could get fluorescent light cheaper than mazda light.[38] Frank B. Jowett, president of the Bell Telephone Laboratories, testified before the Monopoly Investigating Committee of the Senate in 1939 that his company had developed a long-life vacuum tube about fifteen years earlier and had used it continuously since that time in the telephone business, saving thereby about $10 million in the year 1938 alone. He stated that RCA and General Electric had cross-licensing agreements with the Bell system by which they could have manufactured and sold this long-life tube instead of their regular radio tubes. If this had been done it would have reduced the number of radio tubes manufactured to about one-fiftieth of the number currently manufactured, but it was not done.[39] Finally, General Electric has entered into international cartels which have had the effect of hampering the nation in its war efforts. These agreements are illustrated by the cartel in tungsten carbide, which was held by the court to be illegal.[40]

The chemical industry is the final illustration of the policy of patent manipulation. This is important in part because of the attempt to use foundations as an agency in the patent manipulations. The three principal corporations in the chemical industry are DuPonts, Union Carbide & Carbon, and Allied Chemical and Dye. All three of these corporations or their predecessors had made huge profits during the First World War. Their problem was to continue these profits when the German corporations resumed their activities after the war. They initiated a series of policies to protect themselves from German competition, stating these policies in terms of patriotism and specifically in terms of an increase in the strength of the American chemical industry and a weakening of the German chemical industry so that Germany might never again be in a position to wage war on America. These arguments carried great weight in the period immediately following the First World War, when patriotic fervor was at its height. The policies used by the corporations were as follows. First, they put much pressure on Congress for an embargo against importation of chemicals and thereafter for a very high tariff. Second, they requested that the chemical industry be exempt from the antitrust laws. Third, they developed an integration of the industry through trade associations, such as the American Dye Institute, the Synthetic Organic Chemical Manufacturers, and the Chemical Alliance. At the same time, several mergers were formed, so that domestic competition within the industry was reduced and regulated. Fourth, DuPonts hired German experts and induced them to migrate to America for work in the DuPont plants in order to secure access to the "know how" of the German chemical industry. Several persons were convicted in Germany of accepting bribes from agents of the DuPonts for revealing trade secrets. Fifth, while these policies were urged strenuously in the name of American safety, representatives of DuPonts were holding conferences with representatives of the German chemical industry in the effort to form cartels which would give the American firms protection against German competition. The initial conferences broke down when the German representatives discovered that the DuPonts were at the same time engaged in efforts to destroy the German chemical industry.

Finally and most significant for the present analysis, these chemical corporations exerted great pressure to take control of the seized German patents from the Federal Trade Commission, where they had been administered without bias, and transfer them to the Chemical Foundation. Authorization for this was secured by the tricky method of attaching a rider to an appropriations bill. This was passed a few days before the Armistice. The foundation was incorporated February 19, 1919, by secretaries in the office building of the DuPonts in Wilmington with a DuPont attorney as attorney for the incorporators. The chemical patents were selected by attorneys for DuPonts and Allied Chemical & Dye to a total number of 6,500. The sale of these patents occurred after the termination of the war and was in violation of the principles of international law. The Chemical Foundation, which secured the patents for $250,000 contributed by chemical corporations, was authorized to license manufacturers to use the patents. A suit against this foundation on the charge that it had been organized by fraudulent methods was dismissed; restraint of trade, which was presumably the principal objective of the foundation, was barely mentioned in the suit.[41] This foundation became the prosecuting agency for the chemical corporations, thus giving a facade of respectability to the policy of patent manipulation. During the early part of the decade of the twenties it initiated many infringement suits on patents held by it. It withdrew from much of the litigation after severe public criticism in connection with the suit for fraud and after many of the German patents were returned by Congressional action to their German owners. The foundation, however, was named as coconspirator in a suit against twelve corporations which were convicted on plea of nolo contendere and fined $240,000 for a policy of restraint of trade from 1934 to 1944.[42] This foundation has the nominal task of promoting chemistry in the United States and because of that has the general support of the American chemists. Perhaps few of them realize the subversive purpose in its organization. The support of the chemists is illustrated by the award of the Priestley medal in 1929 by the American Chemical Society to Francis P. Garvan, president of the foundation and one of the promoters of the original plan, for his outstanding services to chemistry.[43]

The Wisconsin Alumni Research Foundation (which has no organic connection with the University of Wisconsin) is another agent of the chemical and food corporations, although it purports to be a philanthropic and civic welfare foundation. From its origin in 1925 until 1946 it was an agency through which prices were fixed in violation of the antitrust law, and the policy of patent manipulations was executed. This foundation in 1946 took a consent decree in an antitrust suit, and was prohibited from collecting royalties on its patents thereafter, from initiating suits regarding the patents or making agreements by which prices were fixed or production regulated. The usefulness of the foundation to the manufacturing corporations was thereupon terminated.[44]

In conclusion, the explanation should be repeated that the constituent acts in patent manipulation are not in themselves criminal; it is not a violation of law to register a patent, to appear in an interference proceeding, to sue for infringement of a patent, or to exchange a patent with another manufacturer. They become crimes, however, when they are combined into a policy in restraint of trade. In this respect manipulation of patents is a good illustration of white collar crime in general, for it presents a surface of respectability and legality, while its inner meaning is racketeering. The climax of this procedure is the use of public service foundations as a front for criminal behavior, although neither of the two attempts in that direction has worked effectively.

8

MISREPRESENTATION IN ADVERTISING

The criminal law of fraud developed before advertising developed. It proved to be almost completely useless in protecting society against misrepresentation in advertising. Two reasons for this failure may be advanced. First, although the effects of misrepresentation in advertising were diffused widely over a society, the society made no special provision for initiating prosecutions. The individual who was injured by this misrepresentation might take the initiative but he seldom did so because the amount involved in a purchase was too small to justify this action. Second, the law of fraud became limited by many precedents regarding proof of intent, so that conviction under this law became exceedingly difficult. This difficulty was greatly increased in the impersonal transactions of modern business, with many salesmen, advertising agents, and other agents intervening between the purchaser and the persons who determined business policies. Under such circumstances, proof of criminal intent became practically impossible.

When society became convinced that it was suffering serious injury from misrepresentation in advertising, two modifications were authorized in the procedures for dealing with these frauds. First, a special staff was provided, analogous to a special police force, with the duty of receiving and investigating complaints and in other ways searching for violations of the law, and taking the initiative in prosecutions. Second, some of the procedures regarding proof of intent were modified, and the laws regarding misrepresentation in advertising approach the "strict liability" type.

These modifications were made first in the Pure Food and Drug Law, enacted in 1905, which defined violations of the law as crimes and provided penalties, generally in the form of fines. Similar laws were enacted in many states and municipalities. These laws deal both with misrepresentation in labels and also with adulteration of commodities. Only the former provisions of these laws are of interest in connection with misrepresentation in advertising. Second, the Federal Trade Commission Law of 1914 prohibits misrepresentation in advertising as well as certain other acts. The Federal Trade Commission is authorized to use three procedures in enforcing this law. The commission may accept a stipulation from the accused that he will cease from violations of the law. The commission accepts a stipulation only if the accused raises no controversy regarding the fact of violation of the law. Also, the commission may order the accused to desist from violations of the law. Finally, the commission may appeal to a court for enforcement of its order, with fine or imprisonment for violation of the order of the court.[1]

The decisions by the Federal Trade Commission against the 70 large corporations for misrepresentation in advertising are presented in Table 12. This table shows that 85 decisions have been made against 26 of the 70 corporations. In 42 of these cases stipulations were accepted, in 34 desist orders were issued without being referred to courts, and in 9 desist orders of the commission were referred to and sustained by the courts. Desist orders of the commission which have been referred to the courts and not sustained are not included in this tabulation.

Sears Roebuck stands first in the number of adverse decisions with 18,[2] and Montgomery Ward second with 12. Gimbel ranks third with 11, Procter & Gamble fourth with 8, and Macy fifth with 5. The 26 corporations with adverse decisions have an average number of 3.3, and a range of 1 to 18. Of the total decisions, 88 percent were made in the years 1933–44 and only 12 percent in the years 1914–32. This does not justify a conclusion that false advertising has been more prevalent in the later years.

One of the significant conclusions from this tabulation of decisions by the Federal Trade Commission is that no adverse decisions were made against 44 of the 70 corporations. Of these 44 corporations, 27 may be classified as "nonadvertising" corporations. They sell all or practically all of their products to expert buyers and do little or no public advertising for purpose of sales. While they spent large sums in advertising after the beginning of World War II, this was for purposes of general goodwill and propaganda regarding governmental policies and most of the expenditures for this purpose could be deducted from income taxes. Because these 27 corporations do not engage in advertising for sales purposes, they do not come within the jurisdiction of the Federal Trade Commission.[3] Of the 44 corporations with no adverse decisions, 17 are listed as

TABLE 12. Decisions under the Federal Trade Commission Act against 26 of the 70 Large Corporations for Misrepresentation in Advertising, Classified by Types of Decisions

Corporation	FTC stipu- lations	FTC desist orders	Court deci- sions	Total
Allied Chem. & Dye	1	—	—	1
American Woolen	1	—	—	1
Armour	1	—	—	1
Borden	1	1	—	2
Chrysler	1	2	—	3
Corn Products	1	1	—	2
Firestone	—	1	—	1
Ford	1	—	1	2
General Electric	2	—	—	2
General Motors	—	1	1	2
Gimbel	5	3	3	11
Goodrich	—	1	—	1
Goodyear	—	1	—	1
Intern. Shoe	2	—	—	2
Kresge	1	—	—	1
Macy	5	—	—	5
Marshall Field	1	1	—	2
Montgomery Ward	4	8	—	12
National Dairy	1	—	—	1
Procter & Gamble	6	1	1	8
RCA	1	—	—	1
Sears Roebuck	4	11	3	18
Standard Brands	1	—	—	1
U.S. Rubber	—	1	—	1
U.S. Steel	2	—	—	2
Westinghouse	—	1	—	1
Total	42	34	9	85

advertising corporations. This includes 3 motion picture companies, 2 manufacturers of agricultural machinery, 2 meat packers, 2 tobacco manufacturers, and 8 other corporations. If the 27 "nonadvertising" corporations be excluded from the base, we find that decisions have been made on misrepresentation in advertising against 60.5 percent of the corporations which engage in advertising for sales purposes.

The decisions on misrepresentation under the federal Pure Food and Drug Law and analogous laws of states and municipalities are presented in Table 13. This gives a total of 11 decisions against 4 of the 70 corporations. These decisions are concerned principally with weights which are less than shown on the labels; some of the cases tabulated above involve short weights in articles which had no labels. Of the 70 large corporations 20 are manufacturers of or dealers in foods and drugs. Decisions

TABLE 13. Decisions against 4 of the 70
Large Corporations for Misrepresentation
under Pure Food Laws

Corporation	Number of decisions
Armour	5
Corn Products	2
Great A & P	3
Swift	1
Total	11

have been discovered against only 4 of these. The explanation of the small proportion of corporations with adverse decisions in this category and of the small number of decisions is that reports regarding violations of the Pure Food Law with names of offenders were made only in the years 1924–27.[4] The cases tabulated above were taken almost entirely from the *New York Times Index* and consequently were ordinarily limited to New York City and vicinity. For instance, Armours was fined in New York State in 1938 for selling butter with the label "Made in USA," when the butter in fact was imported from Siberia. The United States Attorney stated at the time of the trial that Armours had violated the law regarding butter ten times and been convicted three times. This case is counted, however, as one adverse decision.[5]

The total number of decisions under the Federal Trade Commission Law and the Pure Food laws, so far as misrepresentation in advertising is concerned, is 97 and these have been made against 28 corporations. This includes one case in which Gimbel Brothers was enjoined against representing silks to be Cheney silks when they were not so in fact.[6]

The number of articles advertised falsely by the 70 large corporations and other large corporations, according to decisions of the Federal Trade Commission, is enormous. Among the articles found in the ordinary middle-class home, the following have been advertised falsely, according to decisions of the Federal Trade Commission.

In the kitchen: Kelvinator, Quaker Oats, Wheaties, Cream of Wheat, Swan's Down Cake Flour, Fleischmann's Yeast, Knox Gelatine, Kraft-Phenix Cheese, Carnation Milk, Horlick's Malted Milk, Diamond Crystal Salt, Morton's Salt, Welch's Grape Juice, Nehi.

In the laundry: Ivory Soap, P & G Naphtha Soap, Rinso, Chipso, Palmolive Soap.

In the bathroom: Scott's Tissue toilet paper, Dr. Lyon's tooth powder

(or almost any other toothpaste or tooth powder), Shick Dry
Shaver, Wildroot Hair Tonic, Ingram's Shaving Cream, Marlin
razor blades, Drene, Herpicide.

In the medicine chest: Phillips' Milk of Magnesia, Piso, Zonite, Ab-
sorbine Jr., Pond's Extract, Retonga, Smith Brothers Cough Drops,
Bayers' Aspirin.

On the dressing table: Cutex, Peroxide, Ingram's Milkweed Cream,
Coty's cosmetics, Vivadou, Djer Kiss Talc, Mavis Talcum Powder,
Elizabeth Arden cosmetics, Murine Eye Wash.

In the man's wardrobe: Hart Schaffner & Marx suits and Cluett Pea-
body shirts.

In other parts of the house: Fanny Farmer candy, Life Savers, Wur-
litzer piano, Philco radio (or Zenith, Magnavox, or others), Hoover
Sweeper, Remington Typewriter (or almost any other standard
typewriter), and the Encyclopaedia Britannica.

In the garage: Buick automobile (or almost any other automobile),
equipped with Goodyear or almost any other standard tire, with
Perfect Circle Piston Rings and lubricated with Quaker State Oil.

The articles listed above, on which decisions of misrepresentation in
advertising have been made, have been selected because they are generally known. Although this list gives an impression that misrepresentation in advertising is very prevalent, it does not give even an approximate measurement.

Assertions regarding the extent of misrepresentation in advertising
vary widely. Allen R. McIntyre stated in 1936, "The truth-in-advertising
campaign in the United States has been so successful that it is no longer
necessary to place emphasis on it. You simply cannot be untruthful and
stay in advertising."[7] On the other hand, Kenneth Collins, of the advertising departments of Macy's and Gimbel's stores, said, "We draw all
sorts of codes of fair conduct, but the indisputable fact remains that lies
continue to be very prevalent."[8] Paul E. Murphy, advertising manager
of the Loeser Department Store, said, "Advertising is being reduced to
the level of a burlesque script and its practitioners to the status of
Minsky comedians."[9] One of the members of the Federal Trade Commission is reported to have concluded that of the total expenditures for
advertising, which range from one to one and a half billion dollars a year,
approximately a half-billion are for making fraudulent claims.[10] These
assertions, also, do not give conclusive evidence as to the prevalence of
misrepresentation in advertising.

The closest approach to general statistical evidence on this point is provided by the Federal Trade Commission. This commission makes annual reports of its examination of several hundred thousand current advertisements in periodicals and by radio. It reported that 10 percent of these were apparently misleading in 1935, 7 percent in 1941. The commission does not describe the method by which it selects these advertisements for examination. Consequently one is not justified in concluding that from 7 to 10 percent of all advertisements are misleading or that the percentage decreased in six years from 10 percent to 7 percent. These reports do indicate that misrepresentation is concentrated in certain industries, for of all the questioned advertisements, 33 percent were on drugs, 12.7 human food, 3.6 animal food, and 13.5 cosmetics, a total of 65.3 percent in the area of food and drugs. In addition, 10.2 percent were advertisements of specialty and novelty goods.[11]

These surveys by the Federal Trade Commission, as well as the decisions enumerated previously, do not constitute accurate measurements of the prevalence of misrepresentation in advertising. The commission tends to concentrate on a particular industry in the effort to clean that industry's advertising. In one year many complaints and decisions are made against shoe firms, in another against candy firms, and in another against electric firms. For several years, the commission was attempting to reduce the fraud in advertisements of vitamins. In 1941 it issued desist orders against 25 firms for misrepresentation in advertising vitamins. These advertisements claimed with practically no qualifications that the vitamins advertised would restore vigor, aid digestion, eliminate sterility, prevent miscarriage, increase sex vigor, decrease blood pressure, reduce neuritis, reduce insomnia, stop falling hair, cure hay fever and asthma, cure alcoholism, prevent tooth decay, eliminate pimples, make chickens lay more eggs, and keep the dog in good health.

The Federal Trade Commission in recent years has made adverse decisions on advertising in slightly fewer than 1,000 cases a year. If the decisions of misrepresentation in advertising under federal, state, and municipal laws regarding food and drugs were available and could be added, the total number of decisions would be much larger than 1,000 a year. But even if all such decisions were enumerated, they would certainly be far short of the total number of violations of the legal principle of honesty in advertising.

One of the principal reasons for the inadequacy of these decisions is the organized efforts of manufacturers and dealers to prevent the implementation of the laws which are designed to prevent dishonesty in advertising. These manufacturers and dealers are organized. In the drug business, the Drug Institute is the over-all association, with five principal constituent groups, namely: the Proprietary Association, which is composed of the large manufacturing firms; the United Medicine Manufacturers Association, which is composed of the smaller firms; the American Pharmaceutical Association; the National Association of Wholesale Druggists; and the National Association of Retail Druggists. Some of these have subgroups, such as the National Committee of Manufacturers of Antiseptics, and all of them are organized in smaller regions. The food interests are similarly organized, with such groups as the National Manufacturers of Flavoring Extracts, the National Manufacturers of Soda Water Flavors, the International Association of Ice Cream Manufacturers, the International Apple Association. Also, the advertising agencies have a national association, and the newspaper publishers have a national association.

These associations not only oppose the enactment of laws which limit dishonesty, but work consistently to prevent the vigorous enforcement of the inadequate laws which are enacted. Dr. Wiley was the principal influence in arousing the public so that the first Pure Food and Drug Law was enacted in 1906, and he was responsible for the enforcement of that law. Many efforts were made to impede his program. First the whiskey industry offered him employment as a consulting chemist and this offer was interpreted as a method of getting him out of his responsible position. Then, the Secretary of Agriculture, under whose direction Dr. Wiley worked, impeded the enforcement of the law. For instance, Dr. Wiley had initiated a suit under this law against the Coca-Cola Company. The Secretary ordered this suit dropped and he reversed his order only when a newspaper editor threatened full publicity regarding the order. The Secretary then ordered that the suit be transferred from the courts of the District of Columbia to the court in Chattanooga, where the plant of the Coca-Cola Company was located and where public sentiment was strongly in favor of the company. There the company won the suit, but this decision was reversed on appeal to the Supreme Court.[12]

In later years, pressures against enforcement of these laws regarding advertising have continued. These are described as follows:

Business men seeking protection from bureaucratic interference go to their representatives with a tale of woe, or appeal to political officials higher up. In the past, on more than one occasion, the Secretary of Agriculture has overruled his subordinates in the Food and Drug Administration when their interpretation of the law brought strong protests from the food or drug interests. . . . Officials are loath to discuss political intervention, but they admit that they must reckon with it. On more than one occasion Congressmen or Senators have asked sharply why their constituents are being proceeded against by the Bureau. If the reasons given are unsatisfactory, the Administration wins an opponent in Congress; and if bureaucrats are to escape criticism, unfavorable publicity, or a cut in their appropriations, they must be discreet in their relations with the legislative body.[13]

Because of these pressures, both the Federal Trade Commission and the Food and Drug Administration have adopted conciliatory policies. They use penal methods only as a last resort and attempt by addresses to national associations and by individual conferences to secure compliance with the law without formal action. The result is that we have misrepresentation in advertising without adverse decisions, such as are illustrated in the following paragraphs.

Misrepresentation has been used in advertisements of milk, without official decisions against the dairy companies. In 1936 the Consumers Union tested samples of milk from the Borden dairy and from the National Dairy Products and found that the butterfat content and bacterial content were almost identical in Grade B milk and Grade A milk, both being well within the legal limits. But Grade A milk was advertised as superior and sold for three cents a quart more. Also, certified milk was found to be almost identical with Grade A milk, although it was advertised as superior and cost the consumer seven cents a quart more. At a later date these two corporations, with others in their association, conducted a general advertising campaign to sell more milk. They used methods in advertising which led to the query: Is milk a medicine or a food? They advertised vitamin B, C, and D milks, metabolized vitamin milk, iodine milk, iron milk, copper milk, milk as a reducing food, milk as a cure for fatigue, milk as a cure for hang-over, and milk as a food for the complexion: "Each glass of milk you drink is a calcium treatment—look what milk does for the baby's skin."[14]

Three of the four principal tobacco companies were charged in 1943 with misrepresentation in their advertisements of cigarettes, but the

cases were dismissed. The American Tobacco Company advertised that
"Luckies pay 35 per cent more" and "Get the cream of the crop." The
advertisements apparently claim that Luckies are superior to other cigarettes and this claim is definitely misleading, according to the complaint,
which asserts that all tobacco companies pay 35 percent more for cigarette tobacco than for other tobacco and all get the cream of the crop.
Reynolds Tobacco Company claimed that "Camels give a lift," or "aid
digestion," or "don't get your wind." According to the complaint of the
Federal Trade Commission these claims are false and the only "lift"
from Camels goes to the athlete or prima donna who receives $1,000 for
the testimonial. When *Reader's Digest* reported an investigation which
concluded that the various cigarettes differed in nicotine content by
amounts which were negligible, Lorillard's advertisements placed great
emphasis on the smaller nicotine content in Old Golds than in other cigarettes and did not reveal the fact that the difference between Old Golds
and either of two other brands would amount to one-twenty-fourth of an
ounce in 365 cigarettes. The only large cigarette company not included
in these complaints by the Federal Trade Commission was Liggett &
Myers, whose advertisements of Chesterfield cigarettes have been confined principally to "They Satisfy."[15]

The preceding discussion of the prevalence of misrepresentation in
advertising may be summarized as follows: Official decisions for misrepresentation in advertising have been made against 28 of the 70 large
corporations in 97 cases. Although this appears to give the large corporations a fairly clean record, the appearance is misleading. Approximately 27 of the 70 large corporations do not advertise for sales purposes. Of the remaining corporations 28, or 60 percent, have official
decisions against them. Moreover, since official reports of the decisions
under the Pure Food and Drug Law with names of offenders are published only for four of the forty years of the history of this law (and these
records were not used in the tabulations in this chapter), the enumeration of decisions under the law is a very small fraction of the total number of decisions. Finally, because of the pressure of organized interests,
prosecutions are limited to the extreme cases. This justifies a conclusion
that the number of official decisions tabulated above is far short of the
total number of official decisions made against the 70 corporations, and
the total number of decisions made is far short of the number of violations of these laws.

The methods of misrepresentation in advertising may be classified in three groups. First, some advertisements are designed to sell products which are physically dangerous, with the dangers unmentioned, minimized, or denied. Most advertisements of this class relate to drugs or cosmetics. None of the large manufacturers of drugs or cosmetics is included in the list of the 70 large corporations and consequently the abundant evidence of fraud in advertisements of these commodities is not applicable here. Only 2 of the 70 large corporations have had decisions against them on the ground of misrepresentation regarding physically dangerous articles. Montgomery Ward and Sears Roebuck have advertised electric fence controls, and in addition Montgomery Ward has advertised a coal-tar hair dye, which have included misrepresentations of this type.[16]

Secondly, many advertisements are designed to sell products by exaggeration of values. This is equivalent to giving short weights. The extreme of this procedure is illustrated by a case in Chicago in 1935, in which two men sold to a blind man for $5 a pint bottle of hydrant water with an aspirin dissolved in it, with the assurance that it would cure his blindness; these salesmen were imprisoned for taking money under false pretenses. The advertisements of large corporations often follow the same principle except that they are less extreme and are not followed by imprisonment. Garments are advertised and sold as silk or wool when they are entirely or almost entirely cotton. "Alligator shoes" which are not made from alligator hides, "walnut furniture" which is not made from walnut lumber, "turtle-oil" facial cream which is not made from turtle-oil, "Oriental rugs" which are not made in the Orient, "Hudson seal" furs which are not the skins of Hudson seals are instances of such misrepresentation. Caskets are advertised as rustproof which are not rustproof, garments as mothproof which are not mothproof, garden hose as three-ply when it is not three-ply, and radios as all-wave reception when they do not receive all waves. Electric pads are advertised with switches for high, medium, and low, when in fact they do not give three different degrees of temperature. These corporations have sold storage eggs as fresh eggs, old and reconditioned stoves as new stoves, and worn and reconditioned hats as new hats. Facial creams are sold as "skin foods" and as "corrective of wrinkles." The Corn Products Company advertised its Linit "Makes the skin soft and smooth, relaxes the nerves, lubricates the skin, lifts the facial muscles," but the Federal Trade Commission decided that the only effect of Linit was the smoothness produced by the starch in it adhering to the skin.[17] Some of these cor-

porations have advertised that their tea and coffee were selected from
the best plantations but the Federal Trade Commission learned that
these corporations secured their tea and coffee from regular importers
and that it, on the average, was not different from the tea and coffee sold
by other firms. None of these advertisements is so close to the truth as to
be included in the slight exaggerations which grow out of pride in one's
own accomplishments.

The third class of misrepresentations in advertisements, seldom
found without one or both of the other classes of misrepresentations,
does injury to the competitors. Gimbel Brothers advertised certain silks
as Cheney silks, which were in fact not Cheney silks, and were sued by
Cheney for the injury done to his firm.[18] Montgomery Ward advertised
gas furnaces as containing features which no other gas furnace contained, when in fact, the furnaces of competitors contained the same
features.[19] Consumers Research Service, which claimed to be unbiased
and impartial, was strongly biased in favor of Chrysler cars as a result of
payment of commissions.[20] Of the 85 decisions by the Federal Trade
Commission, 12 contain this injury to competitors in very obvious form.

In modern industry all, or practically all, misrepresentation in advertising is competitive misrepresentation. The process has been revealed
clearly in certain prominent cases, which will be described briefly as illustrations. General Motors initiated the 6 percent installment purchase
plan in 1935,[21] and it was copied within a few months by the other automobile manufacturers who felt compelled to misrepresent their interest
rate in order that General Motors might not have an advantage over
them. These advertisements induced customers to believe that the interest rate on the deferred payments for an automobile was 6 percent, but
the Federal Trade Commission after making its own calculations concluded that the actual interest rate was nearly 12 percent. This exaggeration of nearly 100 percent was, in principle, taking money under false
pretenses. Again, all of the important automobile companies were ordered in 1936 to cease and desist from two forms of false advertisements. First, they quoted a price which did not include the necessary
and customary parts and accessories, and when these were added the
price was increased approximately 10 percent. In addition, "handling
charges" independent of the transportation costs were added, thus further padding the advertised prices. Second, they advertised a picture of a
car which was not the car for which the price was given, without explanation that the picture and price did not belong together. The evidence

does not indicate which one of the companies initiated these false advertisements, but all of the companies followed the same pattern.[22]

Three of the four principal tire manufacturers, beginning with Firestone, developed advertising campaigns in 1938, with special prices on the Fourth of July and Labor Day. The reductions advertised for these special sales ranged from 20 percent to 50 percent. When the Federal Trade Commission investigated these prices, it found that the reduction advertised as 20 percent was actually only 8 percent, and the reduction advertised as 50 percent was actually only 18 percent. In addition, Firestone was declared guilty of misrepresentation on two other points: the claim that because of a scientifically developed tread Firestone tires stopped 25 percent quicker, and the claim of safety based on the use of Firestone tires in the races at the Indianapolis Speedway. The commission found that Firestone tires did not stop 25 percent quicker than other tires, and that the use of Firestone tires especially constructed for races was no assurance of safety of tires constructed for regular passenger cars.[23]

Procter & Gamble has a long list of decisions on false advertising and is far ahead of any other manufacturing corporation in the number of adverse decisions. It has been appearing before the Federal Trade Commission with regularity since the early part of the decade of the twenties. It has been engaged in a strenuous fight with other soap manufacturers, and charges of patent infringement, bribery of employees, false advertising, and unfair competition in general have been made. At the same time it was accused of entering into a criminal conspiracy with other soap companies to fix prices, it took a consent decree on this charge. This is a good illustration of the trend in modern industry—reduction of price competition while competition in salesmanship continues.[24]

Accessories to misrepresentation in advertising have been included in the decisions of the Federal Trade Commission during the last decade. The commission has named the agencies which conduct advertising for other corporations as accessories. Many of these advertising agencies which have been named are small and unimportant, but practically all of the well-known agencies which have participated in the "truth in advertising" campaigns have been included. Young and Rubicam have conducted at least two of the advertising programs which have been declared false by the Federal Trade Commission, namely, Swan's Down Cake Flour and Sal Hepatica, and also this was the principal agency for

the advertising of drug products of the corporations which were origi-
nally merged in Drugs, Inc. J. Walter Thompson has been the agency
through which false advertisements of Fleischmann's Yeast and other
products of Standard Brands have been disseminated.

The Federal Trade Commission has included, also, within its decisions
the newspapers, journals, and radio systems which are the media for
false advertisements. The President's Commission on Social Trends reported on the basis of a survey of newspapers that only eight were found
which did not carry advertisements that were patently false; of these
eight newspapers one was the *Christian Science Monitor* and the other
the *United States Daily.* In the earlier years the religious journals were
notorious as accessory to misrepresentation in advertising, and many of
them have not improved their standards. Even the *Journal of the American Medical Association* has been a participant in false advertising,
according to findings of the Federal Trade Commission, although it has
the stated policy of accepting no advertisements unless the statements
in it have been checked and been found true. This journal has for many
years published advertisements of Philip Morris cigarettes, which in
earlier years claimed that these cigarettes cured irritated throats and in
later years that they were less irritating to the throat than other cigarettes, and which cited opinions and experiments of physicians as proof.
Many, if not all, of the physicians who performed the experiments and
gave the testimonials, including some physicians of prominence in the
profession, were paid by the Philip Morris Company. The competing tobacco companies employed equally prominent physicians, who performed experiments which demonstrated that Philip Morris cigarettes
were not less irritating to the throat. Philip Morris made a grant of
$10,000 a year to the Department of Otalaryngology of St. Louis Univer-
sity, which insisted upon complete freedom in the investigation. This
work, at the end of two years, resulted in a report that no accurate
method of judging throat irritations or the effects of the substances
under discussion had been devised, and consequently that no justification could be found for claims that one cigarette was less irritating than
another. Philip Morris gave no publicity to this report, and the advertisements of their cigarettes continued to appear in the *Journal of the
American Medical Association* with the old claims of scientific proof.[25]

9

UNFAIR LABOR PRACTICES

Many corporations have committed crimes against their employees. Evidence for this statement is provided principally by the decisions under the National Labor Relations Law. This law contains both a prohibition and a mandate. It prohibits employers from interfering with employees who desire to organize unions for collective bargaining, and it imposes upon employers the positive obligation of participating in good faith with employees in such collective bargaining. A violation of this law is defined as "unfair labor practice." Although a violation of this law is not explicitly designated as a "crime," it may properly be regarded as a crime since the law is enforced in the last instance by a penal sanction.[1]

This law was not a sudden invention of "The New Deal," but was the culmination of a century-long trend in labor legislation and in court decisions regarding labor. The courts, after variations in decisions, held finally in 1842 that employees have a legal right to organize for collective bargaining.[2] Despite this decision, many employers fought vigorously against the formation of unions among their employees and society was frequently disrupted by conflicts between labor and management. Congress appointed many committees to investigate these conflicts and to recommend actions that might protect society against such disruptions. The La Follette Committee on Civil Rights listed 34 such Congressional committees, which over a fifty-year period reported violations of the civil rights of employees. Many of these committees recommended that collective bargaining be adopted as a general policy in American industry.[3] These recommendations were adopted first in situations where labor conflicts were particularly disastrous to society. Laws which were designed to promote or require collective bargaining in the railway industry were enacted in 1888. These laws were expanded in several subsequent years until in 1932 by the Norris–LaGuardia Act collective bargaining was made obligatory upon the railways. Also, because strikes were interfering with war efforts during the First World War, collective bargaining was made obligatory by the War Labor Act. This requirement ceased with the termination of the war. Finally, in 1933 collective bargaining was made generally obligatory. This law, which was modeled on the railway labor law and the War Labor Law, was designed to promote industry and was a part of the National Industrial Recovery legislation. The labor sections of this law had little effect because they were not adequately implemented. About the time the NRA legislation was declared unconstitutional, the principle of the labor section of those laws was enacted as "The National Labor Relations Law" in 1935. This law was much more adequately implemented than the preceding law had been.[4]

Many employers fought vigorously against the enactment and enforcement of these laws. The National Association of Manufacturers and the National Metal Trades Association were very active in this fight. Industrial leaders on several occasions expressed open defiance of the law, regarding the enactment rather than the violation of the law as a "crime." Sayre, commissioner of the National Metal Trades Association, is quoted as advising the members of that association to disregard the law. William S. Knudsen, vice-president of General Motors, is quoted as saying in 1934 that General Motors would neither recognize any union in the American Federation of Labor nor commit itself to hold elections in which employees could express their preference as to unions.[5] Labor leaders interpreted the sit-down strikes which developed in the plants of General Motors as a device to compel this corporation to obey the law.[6]

Three arguments were used by employers in their expression of opposition to this law. First, the law was said to be unconstitutional. Attorneys for the National Metal Trades Association published an analysis of the law, with the conclusion that the law violated the Constitution of the United States. The Supreme Court, however, decided in 1936 that the law was constitutional. Second, the law was said to be biased in favor of unions, since the law prohibited employers from coercing employees but did not prohibit unions from coercing employees to join the unions. Finally the employers claimed that even if the law were equitable in principle, it was not equitable in operation, since it was administered by "communists and other radicals."

Many employers petitioned for and secured injunctions against enforcement of the orders of the National Labor Relations Board, with the result that the laws of 1933 and 1935 had little effect until the latter law was declared constitutional by the Supreme Court in 1936.[7] Also employers' associations exerted continuous pressure on Congress to repeal or modify this law. Congress appointed committees to investigate the operation of the law. The biased and partisan nature of such investigations is illustrated by the report of the committee of which Howard W. Smith was chairman; this report, which attacked both the principle and the administration of the law, was submitted by three members of the committee without being referred to the minority of two, who apparently approved both the principle and the administration of the law.[8]

An argument which has been used to defend the administration of this law is that the courts have upheld the decisions of the National Labor Relations Board with very few exceptions. Bowman, in a statistical analysis, concluded that the decisions of this board were sustained in a larger proportion of the cases referred to the courts than had been true of the Interstate Commerce Commission, the Federal Trade Commission, or any other quasi-judicial commission in the federal government. The courts sustained the decisions (although not all of the specific orders) in 89.3 percent of the labor cases referred to them in 1938–39, and in 96 percent in 1940–41.[9] In view of the widespread opposition of employers to this law, with frequent statements in open defiance of the law, many violations of the law may be expected. This expectation is realized in the records.

Of the 70 large corporations whose records are being described, 43, or 62 percent, were officially declared to be engaged in unfair labor practices in the period 1934–44. These decisions are listed in Table 14. Against these 43 large corporations 149 decisions were made, of which 7 were made under the Act of 1934, 142 under the Act of 1935. Of these 149 decisions, 68 were referred to and sustained by courts as to the unfair labor practices; a few decisions by the board which were not sustained by the courts when referred to them are excluded from this table. Nineteen of the total number of cases involved stipulations by the employers, of which 15 were made before the board without court action and 4 before the courts.

Ford Motor Company stands first among the 43 corporations in the decisions regarding unfair labor practices, with 15 adverse decisions. Armour, General Motors, and Phelps Dodge tie for second rank with 9 decisions each, while Swift and Wilson tie for the next rank with 8 decisions each. The average number of decisions for the 43 corporations is 3.4, with a range of 1 to 15. Of these 43 corporations, 31, or 72 percent,

TABLE 14. Decisions by National Labor Relations Board against 43 of the 70
Large Corporations for Unfair Labor Practices, by Relations to Court Decisions

Corporation	Sustained by court	Not referred to court	Total
Allied Chem. & Dye	3	2	5
Aluminum Co. of America	3	—	3
Amer. Car & Foundry	2	—	2
Amer. Radiator & Stand. San.	1	1	2
Amer. Rolling Mills	2	1	3
American Smelting	2	2	4
Armour	3	6	9
Bethlehem Steel	2	3	5
Chrysler	—	1	1
Crane	—	1	1
Deere	1	1	2
DuPont	1	2	3
Firestone	—	2	2
Ford	5	10	15
General Motors	3	6	9
Glen Alden Coal	1	—	1
Goodrich	—	3	3
Goodyear	2	1	3
Great A & P	—	1	1
Inland Steel	2	1	3
Intern. Harvester	—	2	2
Jones & Laughlin	3	1	4
Kennecott	2	—	2
Kresge	—	1	1
Marshall Field	1	2	3
Montgomery Ward	4	1	5
National Lead	3	2	5
National Steel	2	—	2
Phelps Dodge	1	8	9
Pittsburgh Plate Glass	1	1	2
Procter & Gamble	—	1	1
RCA	—	1	1
Republic Steel	2	5	7
Sears Roebuck	—	1	1
Singer	1	1	2
Swift	5	3	8
U.S. Rubber	0	1	1
U.S. Steel	—	1	1
Westinghouse	1	1	2
Wheeling	1	—	1
Wilson	6	2	8
Woolworth	1	—	1
Youngstown	1	2	3
Total	68	81	149

are recidivists. This is a larger percentage of recidivism than is found among prisoners in state and federal prisons except among habitual and professional criminals.

The unfair labor practices, according to these decisions, are concentrated in a few industries, namely meat packing, automobile, steel, nonferrous metals, rubber, and the chemical industries. Of the 70 large corporations three are meat packers and each of these had adverse decisions under this law with a total of 25. Three automobile manufacturers are included, with a total of 25 decisions against them. Four rubber companies in the list have adverse decisions. Nine steel companies have a total of 31 adverse decisions, with at least 1 for each company. Seven nonferrous metal mining and fabricating companies are included, of which 6 have 25 adverse decisions. On the other hand no adverse decisions have been made against any one of the 3 tobacco companies, 3 motion picture companies, 2 paper companies, and 2 dairy companies.

The absence of decisions against corporations in an industry should not be interpreted as evidence that no unfair labor practices exist in those industries. More generally, the enumeration of adverse decisions which has been presented should not be regarded as an accurate measure of the unfair labor practices of the 70 large corporations. Several reasons for this caution may be mentioned. First, since most complaints of unfair labor practices are made by representatives of unions, a corporation which has prevented the unionization of its employees even by exceedingly unfair methods may have few or no complaints before the National Labor Relations Board. Second, most complaints are settled in their preliminary stages and do not reach the National Labor Relations Board. Of 12,281 complaints against all employers in the United States, only 2.7 percent went to the final stage of decision by the National Labor Relations Board.[10] Probably a large proportion of these settlements would have resulted in decisions of unfair labor practices if the procedures had continued. A research study by the Twentieth Century Fund reported that 70 percent of the complaints in the steel industry in 1933–36 were settled in favor of the employees.[11] To some extent, the cases which reach the National Board are cases against corporations which are most hostile toward the law and most uncompromising in their dealings with their employees. Third, these laws were relatively futile until 1937. Late in 1936 the Supreme Court declared the law constitutional and in 1937 Congress expanded the scope of the law and made more adequate provision for the administration of the law. The result was a significant increase in the number of complaints and the number of decisions. Of the 149 decisions against 43 large corporations, only 16 were made in the four years 1934–37, while 133 were made in the seven years 1938–44. Fourth, some unions have little confidence in governmental regulation and prefer to depend upon their own bargaining strength rather than make complaints under the National Labor Relations Law. Fifth, some decisions regarding unfair labor practices have been made by other agencies than the National Labor Relations Board and these decisions are not included in the preceding tabulation. Finally, some corporations are involved in interstate commerce much less than others and therefore come within the scope of the law less than others.

The methods of violation of the National Labor Relations Law have a wide range. The complaints, as decided by the National Labor Relations Board, are listed for the 149 decisions against 43 large corporations in Table 15. This gives a total of 653 counts against these 43 corporations. These complaints involve much duplication and, particularly, "interference," "restraint," and "coercion" seem to be almost identical. The complaints may, however, be divided into two principal classes, namely, refusal to bargain collectively and interference with the efforts of employees to develop an organization for collective bargaining.

"Refusal to bargain collectively" is the method of unfair labor practices in 46 cases decided against 25 of these corporations. In no one of these cases was the refusal to bargain collectively the only method of unfair labor practices. Several corporations have taken no positive steps to prevent the organization of a union among their employees; their rep-

TABLE 15. Complaints of Unfair Labor Practices against 43 of the 70
Large Corporations by Types of Complaints

Type of complaint	Number of corporations	Number of complaints
Refusal to bargain collectively	25	46
Interference	39	139
Restraint	39	126
Coercion	39	134
Company union	34	78
Discrimination	33	84
Intimidation	4	9
Espionage	13	24
Violence	5	10
Other interference	2	3
Total		653

resentatives have met and talked affably with representatives of the employees whenever requested; but they have rejected all suggestions of collective bargains and have made no countersuggestions. This has been held by the courts to be an unfair labor practice in the sense that it is a failure to participate in good faith in collective bargaining. Not far removed from this method is the practice of some corporations of listening to the proposals of the representatives of their employees and later, without making an agreement, announcing as a policy the proposals of the labor representatives. This, also, has been held to be an unfair labor practice. According to the Supreme Court in the H. J. Heinz case, collective bargaining terminates in agreements and, at least in this case, the National Labor Relations Board was justified in the order that the agreement be written.[12]

The second class of unfair labor practices is interference with the efforts of employees to develop their own organization for collective bargaining. Each of the 43 corporations against which decisions have been made by the National Labor Relations Board has engaged in this class of unfair labor practices, with a total of 605 counts. Several of the specific methods of interference are elaborated below.

The National Labor Relations Board has decided that 35 of the 70 large corporations have engaged in unfair labor practices in the form of a "company union," with a total of 78 decisions. Swift stands first in this list, with 8 adverse decisions. Republic Steel ranks second with 7 decisions and Bethlehem Steel, Ford, and Phelps Dodge tie for third rank with 5 decisions each. Many of the corporations which have used this unfair labor practice developed company unions during the First World War. Almost all of these company unions ceased their existence with the termination of that war, although a few persisted. The other company unions were developed either during the NRA period or shortly thereafter. The court decided in 1930 that company unions of railway employees did not satisfy the obligation of collective bargaining.[13] This was a prominent case and was doubtless known to the attorneys of the corporations which developed company unions in other industries in 1933–35. The illegality in a company union is the domination of the union by the corporation. Many corporations which did not want collective bargaining in any form, attempted to evade the law which made collective bargaining obligatory by developing unions under their own control. The United States Bureau of Labor Statistics issued a report in 1937 regarding 126 company unions in American industries. Of these unions, 96 were organized entirely on the initiative of the employer and in the other cases the initiative of the employees was merely nominal. Of these company unions 64.8 percent derived their financial support entirely from the corporation and only 26.8 percent of them held regular meetings at least once a month.[14] For these reasons company unions are called "phony unions" and they are a device for avoiding rather than participating in collective bargaining.

Discrimination is a second specific method of interference with collective bargaining. This consists in dismissal or demotion of employees who join a union and refusal to rehire employees who have participated in strikes. It is aimed particularly at leaders among the employees. In the 149 decisions against 43 large corporations, 84 include a finding that 33 corporations engaged in unfair labor practices in the form of discrimination. These decisions range from 1 to 11 per corporation, with Ford Motor Company standing first with 11 adverse decisions. Phelps Dodge is second with 8 decisions, and Armour, National Lead, Republic Steel, and Wilson tie for third rank with 5 each. The total number of employees discriminated against, as reported in 64 of the 84 decisions, was 3,277. In 36 of these 64 decisions the number of employees discriminated against was fewer than 10 each, and these were usually leaders in the unions. When larger numbers were involved, the point at issue was generally the rehiring of strikers. In these discrimination cases the employers are almost unanimous in the defense that they had dismissed or demoted employees because of inefficiency and not because of union activities. The managers of the Chevrolet and Fisher Body plants in Baltimore made a defense of this nature, but the testimony indicated that employees had first been advised by the plant managers to get out of the union, then threatened with dismissal if they did not get out, with the assurance that the corporation was going to break the union, and finally were dismissed with the explanation that they were inefficient.[15] A few decisions of discriminations have been made in cases in which an employee was dismissed after making complaints to or testifying before the National Labor Relations Board. The law states explicitly that dismissals for this reason are unfair labor practices.

A third type of interference with collective bargaining is espionage or the employment of labor spies. The National Labor Relations Board has found 13 of the 70 corporations guilty of unfair labor practices in the form of espionage, in a total of 24 cases. The investigation of the La Follette Committee indicates that at least 13 additional corporations among the 70 have used espionage, although no decisions have been made against them on this point by the National Labor Relations Board. The La Follette Committee made an extensive investigation of espionage in the automobile, rubber, and steel industries. The committee was hampered in its efforts to discover the facts because all of the corporations in these industries, as well as their trade associations and labor-detective agencies, destroyed their records as soon as the investigation was authorized and before subpoenas were issued. The only document found in the labor files of General Motors was a copy of an address on labor by the president of the corporation. During the period of the investigation the labor spies were ordered to report orally and never in writing, and they were paid in cash and not by check. Although the regulations of the Securities and Exchange Commission required corporations to report all expenditures of $20,000 or more, the Chrysler Corporation did not report an expenditure of $72,611 in 1935 in payment of a bill of Corporations Auxiliary (a labor-detective agency). It avoided the report to the Securities and Exchange Commission by paying this bill by four checks, each of which was less than $20,000, to Corporations Auxiliary, two firms affiliated with Corporations Auxiliary, and attorneys for Corporations Auxiliary.[16] These illustrations of the efforts of corporations to conceal the employment of labor spies from the Congressional committee imply willful violation of the law.

General Motors, according to the report of the La Follette Committee, was the largest patron of the spy services of the Pinkerton Detective Agency. In addition, it employed spies from sixteen other agencies during 1933–36 at a total cost of $994,855. It had more than 200 labor spies in its six plants at one time. Three spies shadowed practically all labor leaders who came to Detroit, shadowed conciliators from the Department of Labor, and lecturers who came to the city. For a time, these spies rented an office adjoining the union office in Detroit, established a dictaphone in the union office, tapped the telephone wire in the union office and also the telephone wire in the residence of the president of the union. These spies attempted to secure membership and even executive positions in the union and often succeeded in these efforts. One of General Motors' spies was an executive in the local union in Flint and attended the national convention of the union at the expense of this corporation. If, as often happens, the identity of the spy becomes known, the damage is often greater than it would have been if his identity had not been discovered, for many members withdraw from the union when they learn that they have spies in their midst. When spies were discovered in the Flint local, the membership quickly dropped from 6,000 to 200. At the time of the La Follette hearings, the Lansing local of the Fisher Body plant had only five members, all of these being Pinkerton agents. Spies are required to operate on principles of expediency, and consequently often hold legal and moral codes in low esteem. It is, therefore, not surprising that General Motors, suspecting that information was "leaking" through labor spies, set the spies from one agency to spy on those from another agency. A reporter for the *St. Louis Post-Dispatch* summarized the evidence regarding the espionage system of Jones & Laughlin in Aliquippa:

> "An elaborate system of espionage permeated not only the plants but extended into the churches, school, lodges, and even the homes."[17]

Senator La Follette made the following summary of the evidence on this point secured by his committee:

> "The evidence is overwhelming . . . that the use of this labor espionage is . . . one of the most effective methods of destroying genuine labor collective bargaining activities on the part of the workers."[18]

A fourth type of unfair labor practices is violence and threats of violence. The National Labor Relations Board has found 5 of the 70 corporations guilty of unfair labor practices in the form of violence in 10 cases, and 4 corporations guilty of intimidation in 9 cases, a total of 19 such decisions against 7 corporations. These are confined principally to the steel and automobile industries. The actual use of violence is more extensive than these decisions indicate. The La Follette Committee gave a list of the corporations which purchased gas-guns and other gas equipment to the value of more than $300 each in 1933–37, and 26 of the 70 corporations were thus prepared for organized warfare. Republic Steel stood at the top of the list of such corporations, with an expenditure of $79,712. During this period it purchased 142 gas-guns, while the Chicago Police Department purchased only 13, and it purchased 6,714 shells and grenades for gas-guns, while the Chicago Police Department purchased only 757.[19] Many other purchases were made, of which the committee did not secure evidence, and this is true especially of machine guns. Although the National Firearms Act of 1934 requires the registration of all machine guns in the possession of private parties, the

La Follette Committee reported that Youngstown Sheet and Tube Company possessed eight machine guns which had not been registered under that act.

The corporations customarily claim that they secure this equipment to protect themselves against violence by unions. This argument is not entirely without justification, but the decisions of the National Labor Relations Board place the responsibility for violence squarely upon the corporations in the cases listed above. It is significant, also, that violence ceased entirely while the La Follette Committee was making its investigation. Corporations sometimes attempt to conceal their responsibility for violence by organizing "loyal employees" or "citizen's committees." This is generally recognized in certain industries as a clever technique for fighting unions, but the responsibility for resulting violence cannot always be avoided. When the union was attempting to organize the employees in the Delco-Remy plant of General Motors in Anderson, Indiana, the "loyal employees" attacked an organization meeting of the union, smashed the furniture, and destroyed the records. They evicted from the shops 91 employees who were suspected of being in sympathy with the union. On one occasion a rumor spread that CIO organizers were to arrive in the city by train. Many "loyal employees" left the plant—more than 300 by one gate—and went to the railway station, armed with blackjacks. When the organizers did not arrive, the "loyal employees" returned to their jobs, receiving full wages for the time they were absent. The leader of one group of "loyal employees" was found to be an operator for a detective agency.[20]

From many reports by the National Labor Relations Board and the La Follette Committee on the use of violence by corporations, one detailed account will be selected. This is taken from the National Labor Relations Board's decisions regarding violence in the River Rouge plant of the Ford Motor Company in 1937. Two things should be stated as a background for this particular case of violence. Henry Ford is quoted as saying in 1937, "We'll never recognize the United Automobile Workers' Union or any other Union."[21] In accordance with this sentiment, Ford organized a Service Department under the supervision of Harry Bennett, an ex-pugilist, with as many as 600 staff members at one time, equipped with guns and blackjacks. Frank Murphy, who at the time was governor of the State of Michigan and had been mayor of Detroit, is quoted as saying, "Henry Ford employs some of the worst gangsters in our city."[22]

In 1937 the United Automobile Workers Union was attempting to organize the employees in the River Rouge plant of the Ford Motor Company. A public announcement was made that the organizers would distribute literature at this plant at a specified time. Reporters and others gathered in advance. When a reporter asked the guards what they were going to do when the organizers arrived, one guard replied, "We are going to throw them to hell out of here." When the organizers arrived, they went with their literature up on an overhead pass to one of the entrances. They were informed that they were trespassing upon private property. According to many witnesses, they turned quietly and started away, and as they were leaving were assaulted by the service staff of the plant. They were beaten, knocked down, and kicked. Witnesses described this as "a terrific beating," and as "unbelievably brutal." This occurred not only on the overhead pass, but continued after the organizers had reached the adjoining public highway. One man's back was broken and another's skull was fractured. The cameras of reporters, who were taking pictures of the affray, were seized by the guards and the films destroyed. A reporter taking a picture from the highway was observed by a guard, who shouted, "Smash that camera." The reporter jumped into the automobile of another reporter and they were chased by the service staff at eighty miles an hour through the streets of Detroit until they secured refuge in a police station. According to prearranged plans, women organizers arrived later to distribute literature. They got off the streetcar on the highway at the entrance to the plant and were immediately attacked by the service staff and pushed back into the streetcar. One woman was knocked down and kicked. While these assaults were being committed, city policemen were present and did not interfere; also, the director of the Service Department was present.[23]

The record of violence in other Ford plants is even more extreme than the one presented above.[24] And the records of violence by the Ford Motor Company can be duplicated by other corporations.[25] The significant thing is that employers have used violence frequently for the purpose of preventing a union-organization movement, even though Congress had enacted a law which prohibited an employer from interfering with the efforts of employees to organize for collective bargaining.

A fifth method of interfering with collective bargaining is the bribery of union leaders for the purpose of avoiding bona fide collective bargaining. Although no decisions have been made against any of the 70 large corporations explicitly on this complaint, presumably because the unions make most of the complaints, two or three of the decisions describe this practice as occurring and evidence is available in other sources that the practice is used. The motion picture industry provided an illustration which is not entirely free from interpretative factors. The employees in this industry began to organize as locals of the International Alliance of Theatrical and Stage Employees during the period of the NRA. The Motion Picture Producers' Association fought this movement and were successful in destroying it. Consequently the Hollywood local held no union meeting from 1933 to 1937 and on that account it lost its autonomy and control passed to the national officers. The national officers at this time were William Bioff and George E. Brown. The stagehands were notified in 1936 that an agreement had been made and that employment was to be on a closed shop basis. This announcement was a complete surprise to the stagehands, for they had not been consulted and were given no opportunity to agree or disagree with the conditions of the contract. Union members who raised questions were dismissed by the producers. Two interpretations have been made of this transaction. The first is that the presidents of the motion picture companies, under fear of death, paid Bioff and Brown an amount alleged to be more than a million dollars and agreed to a contract for a closed shop; Bioff and Brown were convicted of extortion, in accordance with this interpretation. The second interpretation is that the presidents, in the effort to prevent real collective bargaining, bribed Bioff and Brown and secured a contract which had no semblance of collective bargaining.[26]

The preceding analysis of violations of the National Labor Relations Law, together with other data, justify the classification of corporations into three groups from the point of view of labor policies. First, a few corporations have entered into predatory collusion with trade unions for the maintenance of prices and restriction of production in violation of the antitrust law. Official decisions have been made against 3 of the 70 corporations on this charge.[27] Second, some corporations offered little resistance to the organization of unions and to collective bargaining or, after some resistance, accepted collective bargaining in good faith long before the law made it obligatory upon employers. From 7 to 10 of the 70 corporations may be classified in this group. Third, some corporations have fought bitterly against trade unionism and collective bargaining. Some of these have been subtle in their methods, using tactics which would not antagonize the public, while others have been violent. Even those which have been violent have generally had sufficient sympathy of newspaper owners and editors to avoid much public criticism. These 70 corporations, however, do not fall into two distinct classes, one cordial and the other hostile toward collective bargaining. Rather they constitute a continuum, with the most cordial at one extreme and the most hostile at the other. The distribution, however, is distinctly skewed toward the hostile extreme.

Violations of the National Labor Relations Law have been principally an expression of a long-continued hostility toward trade unionism and collective bargaining. Many corporations had fought the unions in their own industries and had broken those unions. Some industrial leaders had vowed that they would never recognize the unions or permit their employees to organize. When the National Labor Relations Law prohibited them from interfering with their employees in the effort to develop unions, they had a sincere belief that this was a bad law and many of them continued to use the same tactics they had used before the law was enacted. Their violations of the law were an expression of an ideology which originated prior to the law and persisted after the enactment of the law. This ideology contains the propositions: the business belongs to the employer and he may manage it as he sees fit; the employer is not willing to permit ignorant workmen to dictate to him how to manage his business; if his employees do not like the conditions of work they can look elsewhere for work; when trouble develops regarding labor, it is due to outside agitators. This ideology is essentially the individualistic theory of the preceding century, which had been rather completely abandoned so far as relations to competitors are concerned and retained only in relation to employees.

In spite of this opposition, the membership of the national unions increased enormously after the enactment of the law. From a membership of about 3 million in 1933, the national unions increased to 11 million in 1938. This increase certainly reflects a belief of employees that the danger resulting from union membership decreased after they secured the protection of the federal government in their legal right to bargain collectively. Presumably it means, also, that employers have not interfered as much with the union movement as they had prior to the enactment of the law. However, it does not mean that many corporations have accepted collective bargaining in a cordial spirit. They have continued efforts to modify the law and succeeded with the enactment of the Taft–Hartley amendment in 1947. Also, they have continued to snipe at organized labor and are waiting for a favorable opportunity for a knockout fight.

Corporations, as indicated previously, are not uniformly and equally antagonistic toward collective bargaining. Two factors seem to be related to the variations in antagonism. The first of these is the organization of employers. Employers developed associations to fight collective bargaining in the last part of the nineteenth century. The Stove Founders Association was formed in 1886, the National Association of Manufacturers in 1895, the National Founders in 1898, and the National Metal Trades Association in 1899. Also, many city, state, and regional associations have been developed.[28]

The National Association of Manufacturers is the general nationwide and industry-wide association of employers. After twenty years of militant activity against unions, this association weakened somewhat during the decade of the twenties. It was revived in 1932 by Girdler, who represented the extreme antagonism of the steel industry, and thereafter it was dominated by the larger corporations. Contributions to this association increased from $240,000 in 1933 to $1,439,548 in 1937. A rough statistical relationship exists between the size of the contribution to the National Association of Manufacturers and the number of adverse decisions by the National Labor Relations Board. Among the 70 largest corporations, 46 contributed more than $2,000 each in 1933–37, and of these corporations, 33, or 72 percent, had adverse decisions by the National Labor Relations Board in 1934–44. If the 46 corporations be arranged by the size of their contributions to the National Association of Manufacturers, the upper fourth (12 corporations) included 10 which had a total of 40 adverse decisions by the National Labor Relations Board, while the lower fourth (12 corporations) included 7 which had a total of 11 adverse decisions.

While the policies of these associations are in part a reflection of the policies of the individual members, the associations have held their members to militant activity and have secured converts. Any corporate member of the National Metal Trades Association which entered into collective bargaining with its employees was forced to resign from the association.[29] When the labor provisions of the NRA were adopted in 1933, Gerard Swope of General Electric advised corporations to accept this law and to dissolve the National Association of Manufacturers, the National Metal Trades Association, and the other labor-fighting organizations. He was called a "radical" by the officers of some of these associations.

In addition to the formal association, some informal associations have been organized. The personnel directors of several of the large corporations held informal conferences once a month over a period of twenty years. Among the corporations represented in these monthly conferences were Bethlehem Steel, DuPont, General Electric, General Motors, International Harvester, U.S. Rubber, and U.S. Steel. The labor problems and labor policies were discussed in these conferences, and some consensus was reached as to unified policies.

A second reason for variations in corporate policies regarding collective bargaining is the variations in the situations in which the corporations operate. One of the situational variables has been analyzed by labor economists under the title "the organizability of labor." Christenson found in a study of collective bargaining in Chicago that employers tend to be cordial toward collective bargaining if the demand for their products is relatively inelastic and if the labor costs are a relatively small part of the total costs of production.[30] In such situations, increases in wages can be passed on to consumers without loss of profits to employers. This is an illustration of the variables in the situations in which corporations operate, all of which might enter into the determination of policy. It has not been possible to make specific comparisons of the 70 corporations with reference to such variables.

Although it has not been possible to provide a specific and definite explanation of the violations of the National Labor Relations Law by large corporations, the following suggestions have been presented: First, corporations which violate the law are continuing the policies which they had prior to the enactment of the law. Second, violations of this law are so prevalent that any violator has the support of the cultural standards in his part of our society. Third, the organization of employers for union fighting has tended to hold corporations to a unified policy. Fourth, the antagonism of corporations toward collective bargaining, which varies from one corporation to another, is an adjustment to the specific facts of that situation, in which the possibility of passing on to consumers any increase in wages is a significant part.

A special problem is, Why do some corporations use violence in fighting collective bargaining? Two facts are available in answer to this question. First, violence has been most prevalent in "company towns," in the South, and in certain West Coast areas. In the "company town" the local government is largely under the control of the corporation and consequently the corporation is relatively immune in the use of violence. Even in the more completely industrialized cities, such as Detroit and Akron, the corporation has great power in government and is seldom punished for using violence. The extraordinary use of violence in the South and in certain West Coast areas is probably related to the race prejudice in those areas, for the dominant race prejudice is easily transferred from a minority race to any other powerless group. Second, violence is most prevalent in plants in which the employees are most removed from the middle-class standards. In industries in which the employees approach "the white collar class," the use of violence is infrequent.

The preceding analysis has been confined to violations of the National Labor Relations Law. These 70 corporations violate, also, other labor laws. Without an organized search of reports nine decisions have been collected incidentally and are included in the tabulation in chapter 2. Doubtless an organized search of the reports of state labor departments and of the reports of various federal boards would reveal many times this number of decisions. A brief report will be made regarding some of these other laws which are violated, with illustrations from decisions against the 70 corporations.

The Fair Labor Standards Act of 1938 fixed minimum wages and minimum hours of work, regulated overtime pay, child labor, and certain other conditions of employment. Courts have made decisions under this law against Armour and Swift in two cases each, and against Borden, Great A & P, National Dairy, Pittsburgh Plate Glass, and Wilson in one each, a total of nine decisions against seven corporations. Prior to the enactment of this law a suit was initiated against Montgomery Ward for overtime work by a woman. The court allowed the claim and ordered payment, but on appeal a higher court reversed the decision on the ground that the law limited the women employees to nine hours a day and her overtime work was illegal. Although this decision released Montgomery Ward from the obligation of paying the overtime wages in this case, it is a decision that Montgomery Ward violated the law regarding hours of labor of women.[31]

The violations of this law are much more prevalent than the few cases enumerated would indicate. A Department of Commerce release in 1947 revealed that 51 percent of the 40,000 business firms inspected in the preceding year were violating the major provisions of this law. A routine inspection of lumber establishments resulted in the finding that approximately three-fourths of them were violating this law. During the first three years of this law, restitution of approximately $16 million was made to 525,000 employees under the provisions of this law, principally for overtime pay.

Some corporations have violated state labor laws. The Anaconda Copper Company was charged with violation of mining laws and neglect of the orders of inspectors, with the result that many accidents, some of which were fatal, were occurring. A suit which was initiated resulted in a decision, affirmed by the Supreme Court, that this corporation had violated the state mining laws.[32] New York state officials reported recently that 11 war workers were killed and 511 seriously disabled by skin diseases occasioned by violations of health laws in the plants of Anaconda and of Habirshaw Cable and Wire Company (subsidiary to Phelps Dodge). During the decade of the thirties a disaster, described by Senator Holt of West Virginia as "the most horrible industrial disaster in the history of the world," occurred at Gauley Bridge, West Virginia. The New Kanawha Power Company, subsidiary of Union Carbide & Carbon, planned a tunnel at Gauley Bridge and let the contract for construction to the firm of Rinehart and Dennis of Charlottesville, Virginia. Although the contract contained careful specifications to safeguard the health of employees on this project, the New Kanawha Company offered a premium price for speed in construction. The objective of this speed was to complete the project before it could be inspected by the Federal Power Commission. The tunnel was to be drilled in part through silica and this results in silicosis of workers unless state and federal laws are carefully observed, especially as to wet drilling. In the rush which was required by the New Kanawha Company, these laws were not observed. The result was that out of 1,500 workers on this project, an appalling number, estimated variously between the limits of 200 and 500, died from silicosis while many others were permanently injured.[33]

10

FINANCIAL MANIPULATIONS

The term "financial manipulation" is used here to refer to practices of corporations or of their executives which involve fraud or violation of trust. These practices include embezzlement, extortionate salaries and bonuses, and other misapplications of corporate funds in the interest of executives or of the holders of certain securities; they include public misrepresentation in the form of stock market manipulations, fraud in sale of securities, enormous inflation of capital, inadequate and misleading financial reports, and other manipulations.

Charges have been made by minority stockholders, by official investigating committees, and by authorities in economic history that at least 59 of the 70 largest corporations have engaged in these financial manipulations; the total number of these charges is 150, or an average of 2.5 for the 59 corporations. This enumeration is far from complete and probably some of the 11 corporations against which no charges have been discovered have participated in the same practices.

On these 150 accusations against 59 corporations, only 17 official decisions of courts or commissions against 15 of the 70 corporations have been discovered. In addition, definite settlements have been reported in 10 suits against 8 corporations or their executives. This gives a total of 27 decisions against or settlements by 22 of the 70 corporations. This number of cases is included among the "other" violations of law in the tabulation in Table 3.[1]

The present chapter is an analysis of the 150 charges against the 70 corporations rather than of the official decisions. The law has been very inadequately implemented as to such financial manipulations. Manipulations which have been repressed by the Securities and Exchange Commission during the last decade were, in fact, in violation of law two generations ago, when the government was not organized to discover financial manipulations or secure proof of them. Furthermore, the judicial decisions have tended to change, without change in the statutes. Stock market manipulation by pools were held to be fraudulent in England fifty years ago,[2] and judicial decisions in the United States showed a trend in that direction prior to the explicit prohibition of such frauds in the Securities and Exchange Law.[3]

Violation of Trust

Executives and directors of a corporation are trustees, in the eyes of the law, and have the duty of managing the affairs of the corporation in the interest of the corporation as a unit. At the same time, these executives have personal interests and other interests. While every person in a position of responsibility confronts this situation,[4] many corporate executives make strenuous efforts to secure positions with such multiple and conflicting interests.

A total of 64 accusations of violation of trust have been made against executives of 41 of the 70 large corporations. These include violations of trust in the interest of the particular executive, of a small group of executives, of a particular group of security holders, of investment banks, and of other corporations with which these executives are connected. These several types of violation of trust will be illustrated by selected cases.

A prominent case in which an executive used corporate funds for his personal affairs is that of Seiberling, the organizer and practical dictator of the Goodyear Rubber Company until 1920. When control of this corporation was secured by an investment bank, the discovery was made that Seiberling was short $3,744,729 in his accounts with the corporation. His explanation was that he regarded the corporation as "his corporation," and used personal funds for corporate purposes on many occasions, just as he used corporate funds for personal purposes on other occasions. No official decision was made in the suits against him, but according to reports Seiberling made a settlement by agreeing to repay $3 million to the corporation.[5]

Closely related to the embezzlement by an individual officer of a corporation are many cases in which officers used their positions for the purpose of making a profit at the expense of the corporation. Havemeyer, president of American Sugar Refining Company, is reported to have purchased huge quantities of sugar on his personal account shortly before the enactment of the tariff law for which he had been working, held the sugar until the price rose, and then sold it at a considerable profit to the corporation. Many similar incidents were reported in the steel industry at the turn of the century.[6]

In 1915 Coleman DuPont offered to sell to the DuPont Corporation the shares of stock of that corporation he owned. The executives and directors of the corporation formed a syndicate and purchased these shares for their personal accounts, after the same persons refused to purchase them as members of the board of the corporation. Three members of the DuPont family who had not been admitted to the syndicate brought suit on the charge that this was a fraudulent use of the corporation's credit for personal benefit and a violation of trust as directors of the corporation. Judge Thompson of the federal court decided in 1917 that the action was fraudulent and he severely castigated the participants, stating that Pierre DuPont, who was conducting the negotiations, was "a double-dealer and faithless officer" and that his behavior was "trickery and concealment." The judge stated, also, that the pamphlet which was distributed among the stockholders in 1916 as an explanation of the transaction misrepresented the facts. The court ordered the director to submit this proposition to the stockholders for a vote. Although the court had explicitly charged the executives with bad faith and betrayal of trust, the circular prepared by the executives and distributed among the stockholders preparatory to the vote stated regarding the persons in the syndicate, "Against these men the decision makes no finding of bad faith, betrayal of trust, or wrong-doing." The court ordered that this circular be withdrawn. When the stockholders voted on this question, they supported the board in the refusal to purchase the Coleman shares. According to the opposition, the outcome of the vote is explained by the fact that the members of the syndicate owned a large proportion of the shares and also were in a position where they could control the proxies. The original complainants, not satisfied with their moral victory, appealed the decision, which was reversed in 1919.[7]

Executives of corporations have organized personal companies to render services to the corporations. In doing this they act as both buyers and sellers of the services and make bargains which are advantageous to their personal companies. The United Metals Selling Company, which was organized by the promoters of the American Smelting and Refining Company for their personal benefit, has been described above, and also the conflict on this issue with the Guggenheims who wanted to substitute their own personal selling company.[8] Another illustration of this duplicity is the literage firm organized by Havemeyer, while president of the American Sugar Refining Company; the activities of this literage firm were limited largely to the sugar company and their charges were reported to be higher than the charges of other literage firms.[9]

The Chicago Stockyards Company was owned by a New Jersey corporation which, in turn, was controlled by a Maine corporation through ownership of shares and through contracts which provided that all earnings of the New Jersey corporation above a specified percentage were to be the property of the Maine corporation. The Maine corporation was organized in 1911 by J. Ogden Armour and F. H. Prince. All of the 80,000 shares of the Maine corporation except 10 were held in the name of F. R. Pegram, a bookkeeper in the office of F. H. Prince & Co. of Boston. The names of Armour and Prince did not at any time appear as directors or stockholders. The treasurer of the Maine corporation was changed at least every two years, in order that no person might get an intimate knowledge of the corporation. When this Maine corporation was organized, Prince was president and director of the New Jersey corporation and advised the stockholders that they accept the proposed contract with the Maine corporation; he did not reveal that he was one of the promoters of the Maine corporation. The executives of Armour & Company had testified in court and in other official hearings that Armour & Company had no connection with the Chicago Stockyards Company. Through the Maine corporation J. Ogden Armour, president of Armour & Company, controlled the Chicago Stockyards Company and also drained off the lion's share of the profits to himself. When these facts became known, stockholders of the New Jersey corporation instituted suits, one of which was for $50 million. These suits were dismissed in the federal court on the ground of "no jurisdiction."[10]

Another type of violation of trust is the action of a parent company to the injury of a subsidiary. The Inland Steel Company owned 80 percent of the stock of the Inland Steamship Company. The directors of the steamship company sold the assets of the steamship company to the steel company, with the same persons acting as buyers and sellers. Minority stockholders of the steamship company charged in a suit that the price paid for the steamship company was insufficient and that they had been illegally deprived of their property. The court decided that the method of acquisition was illegal and ordered additional compensation to the minority stockholders.[11]

The Radio Corporation of America was organized by General Electric and Westinghouse Electric in 1919 for purposes which were held by the courts to be illegal. As a result, RCA was ordered in 1932 to separate from the two other corporations. Subsequently minority stockholders of RCA initiated suits, one for $500 million, another for $270 million, and others for smaller amounts. These suits charged that in 1932, prior to the separation, RCA gave 6,500,000 shares of its capital stock with a market price of $40 a share to General Electric and an equal amount to Westinghouse, in return for the right to manufacture, sell, and distribute radio apparatus controlled by these two corporations. These rights were the point at issue in the antitrust suit which was under way and which terminated within a few weeks by a consent decree in which General Electric and Westinghouse abandoned their so-called rights. The minority stockholders merged their suits and General Electric, without acknowledging fault, agreed to settle for $1 million.[12]

Another form of violation of trust is favoritism of one group of security holders at the expense of other security holders. The stockholders of the American Tobacco Company in 1904 voted on a plan of reorganization, in which the information was supplied to them by the executives of the corporation. The stockholders discovered later that the reorganization was very favorable to certain securities which were held principally by the executives of the corporation.[13] The Goodrich Company in 1935 proposed to issue $45 million in bonds. Holders of other securities fought this proposal on the charge that it would put $10 million of new bonds ahead of previous mortgages.[14] In 1943 Oscar B. Cintas petitioned for an injunction to restrain American Car and Foundry from paying dividends on the common stock until dividends on preferred stock were paid. The court granted this injunction and ordered prior payment of more than $2 million of dividends on preferred stock.[15] A plan for the reorganization of Wilson & Company in 1943 was restrained by injunction on the ground that the plan eliminated accrued dividends on preferred stocks.[16] In 1941 holders of the preferred stock of U.S. Rubber petitioned for an injunction against payment of dividends on common stock until the dividends on the preferred stock for 1933–37 had been paid.[17] Another form of favoritism is the granting to unsecured bank creditors of precedence in reorganization proceedings. Charges were made that this occurred in the reorganization of Paramount Pictures during the decade of the thirties. A. J. Sabath, chairman of the Congressional Committee on Reorganizations, stated that the Paramount reorganization was marked by "collusion, fraud, and conspiracy."[18]

Another form of violation of trust is the use of knowledge or power by an executive in the interest of another corporation. Stockholders of Montgomery Ward have charged on several occasions that Sewell Avery, president of that corporation and also chairman of the board of U.S. Gypsum, had used his position to compel Montgomery Ward to make purchases from U.S. Gypsum which it could have made elsewhere more advantageously. In no case, so far as discovered, has the court sustained these charges. Another case involves the relation between Anaconda Copper and the Chicago, Milwaukee Railway. Ryan was president of Anaconda and a director of the Chicago, Milwaukee Railway; William Rockefeller, with whom Ryan was closely associated, was a director in each of these corporations. The railway was induced to electrify its Puget Sound Division at a cost reported to be $180 million, with the copper alone costing $4 million. This was profitable to Anaconda but was said to be a principal reason for the bankruptcy of the railway. The Interstate Commerce Commission started an investigation of this transaction but was stopped by an injunction secured by the directors of the two corporations.[19]

Many charges are made that violation of trust occurs in the interest of investment bankers. Since representatives of banks sit on many boards, the financial policies are often controlled in the interest of the bankers. An instance of this is the bond conversion plan of the U.S. Steel Corporation which was promoted by agents of J. P. Morgan and Company. In 1902, one year after the organization of the corporation, an announcement was made that $200 million preferred stock was to be converted to 5 percent bonds. This proposal appeared economical, but it concealed a profit of $10 million which the promoters expected to make from the conversion. Ripley and other economists discovered the "joker" and criticized the proposal so severely that several suits were initiated and the transaction was canceled, not however until the promoters had made a profit of $6 million.[20] Many instances of this nature are reported in the financing of many corporations. When the Securities and Exchange Commission required competitive bidding on security issues, both the investment banks and the corporations controlled by investment banks naturally fought strenuously against the requirement.

The Goodyear Rubber Company was for a time controlled in the interest of an investment bank. In 1920–21 this corporation was in financial difficulties and was required to give control to Dillon Read & Co.

through an issue of management stock in order to secure financial aid. Clarence Dillon was put in charge of the Goodyear Company and in that position his first responsibility was to the welfare of the Goodyear Company. He violated this trust egregiously. He made a contract with Leonard Kennedy & Co., alleged to be a corporation-management firm, to manage the business of the Goodyear Company. The contract provided that Kennedy & Co. was to supply a president and a treasurer at salaries of $50,000 and $15,000, respectively, and was to have no other duties. For this service Kennedy & Co. was to receive $250,000 a year for five years plus 5 percent of the net earnings in excess of $10 million a year. Under this contract Kennedy & Co. received nearly a million dollars in twenty-five months, with an expense of $65,000 a year for the two officers. Later investigation revealed that Kennedy & Co. consisted of one man and a secretary in a small office, that Kennedy & Co. was owned by the Nassau Company, and that 80 percent of the stock of the Nassau Company was owned by Mrs. Clarence Dillon. Consequently, Kennedy & Co. was essentially an alias for Clarence Dillon. Several suits were started against the Goodyear Company and against Dillon Read by minority stockholders on the charge that Dillon Read had misappropriated corporate funds and violated its trust. These suits, after much negotiation, were settled out of court, with the agreement that Dillon Read would surrender the management stock and return the corporation to the stockholders, that an 8 percent security issue (on which Dillon Read had made a huge profit) would be converted to a 5 percent issue, that the Goodyear Company would pay the legal fees of all parties, and that all suits would be dropped.[21] Dillon Read is reported to have made enormous and illegal profits while holding a position of trust in the organization of the Chrysler Corporation.[22]

Another type of behavior which may involve fraud and violation of trust is the appropriation of enormous salaries and bonuses by executives. Accusations have been made on this count against the executives of 25 of the 70 large corporations in suits and other sources. These huge awards are described in the accusations as illegal appropriations by officers who are in a position to manage the corporation in their own interest. On the other hand, the defense is made by the executives that the number of persons qualified for executive positions in large corporations is small, that large awards are necessary in order to secure good executives, that these huge payments are incentives to greater efficiency, and that they are therefore economical in the long run. Baker, however, in a statistical analysis found a slight tendency for corporations which paid high salaries to have smaller earnings and greater fluctuations in earnings than those which paid low salaries.[23]

Stockholders are seldom able to determine from the corporate reports the salaries paid to their executives. In some of the earlier cases, such as American Sugar Refining Company and American Smelting and Refining Company, not even the directors knew the salaries of the executives. Recently Liggett & Myers was indicted and fined for false reports to the Securities and Exchange Commission, designed to conceal a special fund for executive bonuses.[24] In some cases an executive received a salary from the parent corporation and additional salaries from each of several subsidiary corporations. John D. Ryan, chairman of Anaconda, received in 1928 a salary of $150,000 and a bonus of $273,265 from that corporation, and salaries and bonuses from two subsidiary corporations amounting to $321,557 and perhaps additional compensation from other subsidiaries.[25] The executives of such corporations protest vigorously against publicity regarding salaries and bonuses.

These huge salaries were paid in depression years and at other times when the corporations were unable to pay dividends. The accusation was made that William M. Wood, president of American Woolen Company, received a salary and bonus of approximately $1 million a year, with additional payments to cover his income taxes, although his corporation had paid no dividends on common stock for many years. Due to criticisms on this and other points, Wood was replaced by Noah as president and an announcement was made that economy measures would be introduced. These economy measures did include elimination of pensions to wage earners who had retired and who had no other income, but left the salary and bonus of the president at $373,000 in 1934, when the corporation had a net loss of $5,500,000 and at $400,000 in 1935, when the corporation still had no profits.[26]

These accusations against a few of the corporations will be elaborated. Suits were initiated against officers of General Motors, resulting in a decision that the bonus plan had been operated fraudulently and in an order that eight officers of this corporation reimburse the corporation in the amount of $4,348,044 plus interest estimated at $2,222,000 for the period 1930–36, with earlier illegal appropriations exempted by the statute of limitations. By vote of the stockholders in 1918 the bonus policy was adopted as a general plan for special compensation for employees who rendered exceptional service to the corporation. One month later the plan was amended by making directors eligible for awards from the fund. President Sloan's compensation for the years 1923–28 was salary $795,000, "living allowance" $199,327, cash dividends under the bonus plan $4,749,200, stock in the corporation under the bonus plan which in 1928 had a market value of $14,428,800, or a total compensation of approximately $20 million in six years. Suit was brought in 1936 against the officers of the corporation for fraudulent appropriation of corporate funds. The court expressed the opinion that the bonus plan had been extraordinarily wasteful of corporate funds prior to 1930, over which the court had no jurisdiction because of the statute of limitations, and that subsequent to 1930 it had been fraudulent in four respects. First, the methods of calculating the earnings, of which the bonus awards were a percentage, included paper transactions within the corporate system which should not have been included as earnings. Second, the participants in the bonus system made a gentlemen's agreement in 1929, when the plan was modified, that the awards to particular persons should not be less than under the preceding system, with the result that $1,540,830 was appropriated by the executives without the approval of the finance committee. Third, an amendment was made in 1920, without notice to the stockholders, that bonus stock forfeited by executives who severed their connection with the corporation should revert to the bonus fund and hence be divided among the remaining participants rather than revert to the treasury of the corporation. Fourth, Raskob, who had been chairman of the finance committee which organized and administered the bonus system, resigned in 1928, when he was appointed chairman of the National Committee of the Democratic Party. After the finance committee had twice refused Raskob's request that they purchase his shares in the corporation which handled the bonus funds, a new chairman of the finance committee purchased Raskob's shares at $50 a share, without authorization of the finance committee or of the board of directors. Subsequently the board adopted a general plan for purchase of shares of persons retiring from the bonus fund at $34.25 a share. Raskob gained $4,261,000 by his illegal sale to the corporation; this was declared illegal by the court but protected by the statute of limitations.[27]

President George Washington Hill of the American Tobacco Company has been the object of much criticism by stockholders and of many suits on the charge of receiving illegal compensation under the bonus plan of that corporation. One suit, in which the accusation was made that the annual salary and bonus of the president amounted to $2,500,000, was dismissed by the federal court on the ground that it was not within the jurisdiction of the federal court. In this suit, Judge Manton, who was presiding in the Second Circuit Court, suggested to Louis Levy, attorney for the American Tobacco Company, that he needed to borrow $250,000. This attorney passed on the information to the assistant to the president of the corporation, who mentioned it to Lord & Thomas, advertising agency for the American Tobacco Company, which lent Judge Manton $250,000. The suit against the president of the company for illegal compensation was then dismissed, with Judge Manton casting the deciding vote on a bench of three judges. Judge Manton was convicted of receiving a bribe, Levy was disbarred from practice in the federal courts, nothing was done to Lord & Thomas or to the American Tobacco Company, and the assistant to the president, who made the arrangements for the bribe, was promoted to the position of vice-president of the corporation, the day after Judge Manton rendered his decision. The decision of the circuit court, to be sure, was affirmed by the Supreme Court, but this was entirely on the ground that the suit was a state rather than a federal case, and a dissenting opinion characterized the president and five directors of the American Tobacco Company as "wrong-doers."[28] The complainant immediately started a new suit in the state court of New Jersey. This new suit was soon withdrawn, with the explanation that the bonus policy of the American Tobacco Company had been modified. Several years later it was revealed that the corporation had paid the complainant $263,000 to drop the suit, put approximately the same amount in escrow to pay his personal income tax, paid $320,000 to the law firm of Chadbourne, Stanchfield, and Levy, and $70,000 to the attorney of another complainant. Altogether the corporation had paid nearly $1 million to settle the case against its president, although the bylaws of the corporation did not authorize payment of expenses of suits against the executives.[29] In another suit the New York Supreme Court ordered Hill and four executive associates to reimburse the American Tobacco Company by $2,018,033 which had been taken illegally as compensation; this was settled for $1,500,000.[30]

Similar stockholders' suits on complaints of illegal appropriations of compensation by executive officers were initiated against Bethlehem Steel,[31] Union Carbide & Carbon,[32] Warner Brothers,[33] and Loew's.[34]

Public Misrepresentation

Public misrepresentation of the financial affairs of corporations has been reported against 40 of the 70 large corporations. These misrepresentations range from technical misrepresentation, which has little significance as an indication of criminality, to intentional fraud. The misrepresentations include stock watering, specific fraud in the sale of securities, market manipulations, misrepresentation in corporate reports, and other forms of misrepresentation.

Stock watering is one of these types of misrepresentation. Commissions and other investigating agencies have reported stock watering by 19 of the 70 corporations at the time of the original mergers with which the corporations began and by 8 additional corporations on other occasions. This makes a total of 27 of the 70 large corporations on which such reports have been made, and an organized search of the records would certainly show many more cases.

The principle of the law in regard to capitalization is clear: stock may be issued only in return for property or services, and deliberate overvaluation is fraudulent. The difficulty is that no clear-cut criterion of the value of property and services has been developed or used by the courts.[35] A prevalent practice in the mergers of corporations, especially in the years 1898 to 1903, was to issue preferred stock with par value approximately equal to the tangible assets of the constituent companies and an equal amount of common stock with no tangible assets; the common stock was a payment for the promotional services, which were generally in violation of the antitrust laws. The dividends which have been paid on this watered stock are evidence that crime—at least white collar crime—pays.

The United States Steel Corporation was organized in 1901 with capitalization of $1,402,000,000. The U.S. Commissioner of Corporations reported that the tangible assets of this corporation were approximately half the capital and that all of the common stock was water. The Anaconda Copper Mining Company, capitalized at $75 million, was a merger of mines which had been purchased by the promoters for $39 million. The International Paper Company, with a capital of $55 million, was a merger of plants appraised by the United States Industrial Commission at $15 million. The American Tobacco Company was organized in 1890 with capital of $25 million; the U.S. Commissioner of Corporations estimated the tangible assets of the constituent companies at $5,370,000. The process of inflation of capital has been repeated several times in the subsequent history of the American Tobacco Company and many of the other corporations.

The inflation of the capital is sometimes eliminated at a later date. When this is done, the motive is generally something other than honesty. When Walter C. Chrysler began to manage the property of the bankrupt Maxwell Company in 1920, he found an item of $25 million on the books for "good will." He retained this in the Maxwell record until 1925 and thereafter in the Chrysler record until 1932, when it was written down to $1. This writedown was due to the fact that the bonus for executives was calculated as a percentage of earnings employed in operations: the smaller the capital, the higher the percentage of earnings and the higher the bonuses.[36]

The Sugar Refineries Company, predecessor of the American Sugar Refining Company, was an old-fashioned "trust." It issued trust certificates of $50 million to the constituent companies, which had a combined capital of $7 million. When this form of organization was declared illegal, the companies merged in a corporation with a capital of $50 million. At a later time, an affiliated corporation was organized with the name "National Sugar Refining Company," as a merger of companies "outside of the Sugar Trust." The preferred stock of this corporation was equal to the values of the physical plants, and the entire issue of common stock with par value of $10 million was given to Havemeyer, president of both corporations, for his work as promoter. The court declared that this issue of common stock was illegal, since it did not represent any value, and denied the stockholders, i.e., Havemeyer, all rights in connection with the stock except the right to vote that the stock be retired.[37] This is one of very few cases among the 70 large corporations in which watered stock has been held by the courts to be illegal. The decision in this case was perhaps affected by the fact that the American Sugar Refining Company was in very bad repute at the time.

The DuPont Company until 1899 was a partnership with simple and straightforward financial methods. In that year it was incorporated with a capital of $2 million. Eugene DuPont, the president, died in 1902 and the other members of the family discussed the advisability of selling the corporation. Three young DuPont cousins proposed that they buy the business. They had practically no money, but one of them, Coleman DuPont, had been a promoter in the street railway industry and had learned the methods of corporate finance which were customary in the public utilities. These three cousins proposed that they buy the stock of the $2 million corporation for $12 million and pay for it with 4 percent bonds of the new corporation which they proposed to organize. This offer was accepted. The young DuPonts thereupon organized a new corporation with capital of $20 million and pledged the stock as security for

$12 million in bonds, which were given to the former owners in payment for the property. They had left $8 million par value of common stocks as promoters' profits at an expenditure of $8,500. In the same manner they purchased the properties of competitors in the powder industry and merged these with their former holdings. In 1905 the stated assets of these combined properties were $59 million and they had been acquired by the young DuPonts at a cash expenditure of $14,000.[38]

The early financial history of General Motors resembled wildcat speculation. Its history began with the Buick Company, which had common stock with par value of $500,000 in the early part of 1905. None of this was paid up and $303,000 had been issued to Durant for promotional services. The stock was increased later in 1905 without increase in tangible assets to $1,500,000. John J. Carton, attorney for the company, stated that the capital was increased because the company needed additional credit.[39] Durant developed a grandiose plan in 1908 for a merger of automobile companies, and J. P. Morgan and Company agreed tentatively to underwrite one-half of the proposed capital. While the plan was being discussed, the stock of Buick and Maxwell began to change hands with astonishing rapidity. Durant was suspected of buying up the stock without notifying the stockholders of the proposed reorganization. The attorneys for Morgan suggested to Durant that the stockholders be informed of the plans. When Durant refused to give this information to stockholders, Morgan withdrew from the project. Durant went ahead without Morgan's assistance and organized General Motors Corporation, with capital of $13,500,000. The only assets of General Motors were those of the Buick Company and the new corporation was, in fact, merely a change in name with an immense inflation of capital. With this capital stock and a small amount of cash, Durant bought stock of other automobile corporations, including Maxwell, Oakland, Oldsmobile, and Cadillac. These acquisitions were reported to have been consummated in some cases without authorization of the directors and to have resulted in unauthorized profits to Durant.[40] Within two years the indebtedness was so great that the corporation was taken over by the bankers with complete control. The new management wrote off $12,531,319 of the stated assets and decreased the indebtedness. At the same time, the bankers took a reward for their services. This is illustrated by one issue of notes to the amount of $15,000,000, discounted at $2,500,000; for underwriting and selling this issue the bankers took preferred stock in the corporation with par value of $5,169,000. In 1915 Durant regained con-

trol of the General Motors Corporation, with the assistance of the Du-
Ponts, who were looking for opportunities to invest their huge war profits. Pierre DuPont became chairman of the board of General Motors and
Durant president. General Motors increased its capital in 1916 from
$68,492,580 to $102,223,500 without change in its material assets.
Durant was forced out of the corporation in 1920, when it was discovered that he had incurred personal indebtedness of $25,000,000 in the
stock market.[41]

One of the purposes in stock watering, especially in the mergers, was
the reward to promoters and underwriters. The following profits in such
promotions are stated generally in par value of stock, which was generally considerably above the market value at the time of the mergers.
The profits to the promoters and bankers in the organization of the Anaconda Copper Mining Company in 1898 were about $36,000,000 and in
the organization of the American Smelting and Refining Company
about $8,100,000. The promoters of National Biscuit Company received
$30,000,000 and of American Can Company $17,000,000. The estimate
was made that the promoters and bankers who participated in the organization of the U.S. Steel Corporation and of the principal mergers preliminary to it received a total of $162,500,000 for their services.

A second type of public misrepresentation is fraud in specific security
issues. Eight of the 70 large corporations are reported to have engaged
in these practices. In 1920 the Goodyear Company issued a stock dividend of 20 percent, which had the effect and presumably had the purpose of creating an impression of prosperity. About the same time, this
company issued a prospectus as a part of a campaign for the sale of additional securities. On the basis of this prospectus and of conversations
with an agent of the corporation, Mandelbaum purchased $30,000 in
shares of the Goodyear Company in October 1920. In that month the
company became unable to meet its obligations and appealed to a banking group for relief. Mandelbaum sued the corporation on a charge of
fraud, claiming that the officers knew early in 1920 that it was on the
verge of bankruptcy and misrepresented the financial condition of the
corporation in the hope of securing additional funds; he charged, also,
that the prospectus carried real estate and machinery which had been
written up by $3,379,000 and failed to show that Seiberling, the presi-
dent, was indebted to the corporation by more than $3,000,000, for
which no security had been given, and that other officers of the corporation had large and unsecured loans from the corporation. In 1922 Mandelbaum sold his stock at a loss of $23,650. The suit was dismissed by

the court, with the opinion that the intent to deceive had not been sufficiently demonstrated.[42]

Since the Securities and Exchange Commission was established and the approval of that commission was required for security issues, many of the earlier practices have been stopped. A consent injunction was issued against the Anaconda Copper Mining Company in 1936 on complaint by the Securities and Exchange Commission, and proposed issues of securities have been rejected by the commission and withdrawn as follows: $9,900,000 by Inland Steel in 1937, $14,879,000 by American Smelting and Refining Company in 1937, $30,000,000 by Montgomery Ward in 1940, while a proposed $500,000 issued by Borden was stopped temporarily.[43]

A third type of public misrepresentation is manipulation of the stock market by pools, wash sales, and other methods of creating fictitious values. Accusations have been made against 10 of the 70 large corporations for using these procedures. The American Tobacco Company was accused of market manipulation in 1893 and again in 1895. On the latter occasion the quarterly dividend was passed and the stock dropped from 117 to 63. It is alleged that the officers of the corporation bought stock at this low point. The corporation soon announced new purchases, a cash dividend of 20 percent, and a scrip dividend of 20 percent. The stock promptly rose to 180, where the officers sold the stock which they had purchased for 63.[44]

After Rogers and his associates organized the Anaconda Copper Mining Company, they sold the stock to the public and thus lost control of the corporation. It is reported that they regained control by organizing a pool, raiding the stock until the price dropped to 33, when they purchased stock. This procedure, according to reports, was repeated several times during the early history of the corporation.[45] Pools in copper stocks were reported as late as 1928–29, with the National City Bank as one of the participants.[46]

When Judge Gary became president of U.S. Steel, he introduced a reform by prohibiting the treasurer from giving any financial information to directors or officers prior to the public announcement in the press. He stated in regard to this:

I always thought that the use of inside information by directors—very common at the time—was akin to robbery of their own stockholders, and I had no hesitation in making my disapproval of it so clear that everyone on the board could understand it.[47]

Nevertheless, market manipulation was used in the sale of the securities of the U.S. Steel Corporation. James R. Keene, famous for his ability as a market manipulator, was put in charge of the sale of these securities and by judicious buying and selling at the same time he forced the price upward.[48] As stated previously, this method of creating prices on the stock market has been held by the English courts for several generations to be fraudulent and at the present time is so held in the United States by the Securities and Exchange Commission and by some courts.

This increasing opposition to market manipulation is probably the explanation for the use of a different method of "creating a market" for the shares of Standard Brands, when this company was organized in 1929. J. P. Morgan gave to persons on a preferential list an option to purchase 722,600 shares of the total of 12,648,108 shares of common stock of the new corporation at $10 below the opening market price. All of the persons on this preferential list were politically or socially prominent, and the rights which were given them were equivalent to $10 per share. He gave this right to Calvin Coolidge for 3,000 shares, to Bernard Baruch for 4,000 shares, to Charles D. Hiller (Republican National Committeeman from New York State) for 2,000, and to others, to make a total gift of $7 million. The explanation given for these gifts was that they helped make a market for the shares and were equivalent to expenditures for advertising.

A fourth form of public misrepresentation is the annual report which conceals from the stockholders and the public the actual financial operations of a corporation. Of the 70 corporations, 23 have been criticized by accountants and economists for failure to give correct and adequate information in their annual reports.[49] The explanation of the misrepresentation in annual reports is that they are one of the devices for public control and manipulation—control of prices on the stock market, control of legislation, securing credit, determining taxes, negotiating with trade unions, determining bonus awards of executives, and many other policies. Some of these motivations are shown in the following descriptions.

Charles E. Smith, president of the Philadelphia and Reading Railway in 1861–69, testified that he resigned as director of the railway in 1876 because of fraud in the annual reports. More specifically, he testified that money which had been borrowed by the corporation was shown in the report as income and a dividend of 10 percent was paid to stockholders on this income.[50] The Congressional Committee which investigated this railway reported that the railway was under the control of a group interested in huge salaries and in stock market manipulation. Other corporations at the turn of the century had little more respect for financial facts than did this corporation. American Smelting and Refining Company, American Sugar Refining Company, Anaconda Copper Mining Company, American Tobacco Company, and other corporations at that time issued annual reports which prevented stockholders and the public from determining the true financial conditions of the corporations.

Ripley in 1927 charged that the National Biscuit Company had never made an accurate annual report, that stockholders and the public could not determine from the reports how the corporation was being managed, and that its real earnings were concealed.[51] When the Federal Trade Commission, on an order from Congress, was investigating the food industry, the National Biscuit Company refused to fill out the schedule submitted by this commission unless the commission agreed to give no publicity to its data; it did not fill out the schedule until the court issued a mandate for it to do so.[52]

The Ford Motor Company, customarily among the least inclined of the large corporations to financial manipulation, included in its financial report for 1920 a "good will" item of $21,262,833. This item had not been used in earlier years and it was apparently used at this time in order to bolster its credit. The American Woolen Company, according to a statement of its president, had net earnings in 1921 of $14 million, but the annual report showed them to be $9 million, because "if you show big earnings you will never get them: your employees will insist upon an advance in wages."[53]

The accountants have mentioned several corporations that showed fictitious earnings in the early years of the depression by burying current losses in the surplus account or by decreasing the usual annual reserve for depreciation. Union Carbide & Carbon reported a net income of $18,029,522 but buried losses of $49,548,105 in the surplus account.[54] United Fruit Company reported a net income of $6,779,363 in 1931 and of $5,707,221 in 1932. The net income would have been only $1,040,930 in 1932 if the allowance for depreciation had been the same in that year as in 1931.[55] A charge was made in a suit against Balaban and Katz, subsidiary of Paramount Pictures, that dividends of $1,000,000 were paid in 1933, although the corporation would have had a loss of $1,515,419 if the usual allowance for depreciation had been made.[56] One of the devices of some corporations is to invest in their own stock, pay themselves dividends on these stocks, and record the dividends as income. In 1933 the New York Stock Exchange prohibited this practice in the corporate reports which are required by the Exchange. The National Lead Company in 1932 reported an investment of $10,308,616 in its own securities, and dividends of approximately $500,000 on these securities were included as a part of its income.[57] Other corporations which use this practice conceal the items in general classes. Allied Chemical and Dye Company was criticized for this practice by James W. Gerard, a stockholder, and by the listing committee of the New York Stock Exchange. This listing committee stated that "the balance sheet in its present form is misleading," and ruled that the stock of Allied Chemical and Dye would be removed from the list of the Exchange if reports were not made as required. The annual reports of that corporation for several years had carried an item of $93 million as "investment in marketable securities" without revealing that this included $31 million of its own securities, on which it had been paying dividends to itself of about $1 million a year and entering them as profits. Not only did the stockholders and the New York Stock Exchange fail in the efforts to secure annual reports from this corporation which would honestly and accurately reveal its financial transactions, but the Securities and Exchange Commission also failed.[58]

Similarly, in periods of prosperity, many corporate reports conceal a part of the profits. In general, when a corporate report stated that the net earnings for a year are $25 million the stockholders and the public have no assurance that the earnings are not $50 million or $1 million, or even a loss of $10 million.

Miscellaneous Manipulations

Several other cases of manipulations have been described which do not fall appropriately into the classes of violation of trust or public misrepresentation. Some of these are minor transactions, while others involve questions of national policy.

One of these manipulations is coercion to buy or sell securities. The Chrysler Corporation was prosecuted in England in 1935 for coercing P. de la Poer and the Suffolk Investment Company, which had a sales agreement with the Chrysler Corporation, to sell shares in their firm to Chrysler at a price below the market on threat of cancellation of the sales agreement. The court decided that Chrysler had violated the law, awarded damages of $197,000 plus interest amounting to $75,000, and imposed a fine upon the Chrysler Corporation. The judge castigated Walter Chrysler as a man of low business morals.[59] Likewise, the Federal Trade Commission reported that subsidiaries of Borden and of the National Dairy Products Company, with other milk companies in Philadelphia, had coerced milk producers to buy securities of the dairy companies on threat of refusal to purchase their milk.[60]

"Check kiting," which is a customary technique of professional criminals, is used also by white collar criminals. The financial plan in the organization of the Anaconda Copper Mining Company (known at first as the Amalgamated Copper Company) was as follows: Marcus Daly was to purchase certain copper mines for the syndicate at the price of $39 million. Rogers was to write a check for $39 million for these properties, with the understanding that the check was not to be deposited for a specified number of days. In the meantime, Rogers organized the Amalgamated Copper Company with capital of $75 million and transferred to that company the deeds to the mines which he had purchased, receiving for this all of the stock of the Amalgamated Copper Company. Rogers then took the stock of the Amalgamated Copper Company to the National City Bank and, with it as security, borrowed $39 million, which he deposited in the bank so that the check given to Marcus Daly could be cashed.[61]

The U.S. Rubber Company in 1896 had bills amounting to $180,000 against C. H. Fargo Co. It lent $50,000 more to that company, with the knowledge that the company was hopelessly insolvent, on condition that the debts to U.S. Rubber be given priority and that this agreement be concealed from other creditors. When banks and other agencies made inquiries, U.S. Rubber and the Fargo Co. flatly denied that special arrangements had been made. When the Fargo Co. shortly went into bankruptcy, the U.S. Rubber Company presented its preferred claims. The matter was referred to the court, which decided that the agreement between U.S. Rubber and the Fargo Co. was fraudulent, and that U.S. Rubber had no priority. On appeal, this decision was sustained, with a scathing criticism of the agreement and an order that all other claimants be satisfied before the claims of U.S. Rubber should be considered. The U.S. Supreme Court, however, restored U.S. Rubber to a position of equality with other claimants.[62]

A more general case of manipulation is the procedure by which U.S.

Steel acquired the Tennessee Coal and Iron properties in 1907. These properties were threatening competition with U.S. Steel and the latter had desired to secure control of them. Representatives of J. P. Morgan and Company visited President Theodore Roosevelt and expressed a conviction that a certain bond house in New York City would fail and would pull down with it many other financial institutions so that the financial depression would become general, unless that bond house were given financial support. Morgan was willing to give that financial support by purchasing for U.S. Steel the shares of Tennessee Coal and Iron which were held by the bond house, provided this would not make U.S. Steel liable under the Sherman Antitrust Act. President Roosevelt, believing this statement and that this purchase of the shares from the bond house was necessary in order to prevent a ruinous panic, gave assurance of immunity from prosecution under the antitrust law. Economists subsequently threw doubt on the entire argument of the representatives of J. P. Morgan and Company, claiming that the financial depression was practically ended at the time President Roosevelt gave this assurance, that Morgan could have made a loan to the bond house and staved off a disaster as effectively as by purchasing the stock, and that President Roosevelt had been the victim of a trick.[63]

Another case of manipulation which has had wider significance concerns the Firestone Rubber Company and Liberia. During the decade of the twenties, the Firestone Company was much disturbed by the English rubber pool and, with the cooperation of President Herbert Hoover, attempted to develop rubber plantations in Liberia. Firestone proposed to the government of Liberia that he invest in rubber lands in that country. He laid down extremely severe conditions, including a loan to the government of Liberia under conditions which gave him control of the financial policies of that nation. Although the government of Liberia needed the loan, they objected strenuously to the conditions proposed. On the strong advice of the State Department of the United States, the government of Liberia agreed to accept a loan from parties in the United States, provided the loan did not come from Firestone. Secretary of State Kellogg sent a cablegram in 1925 that Firestone had assured the department that he had no thought that the loan would come from the company which he had organized to develop rubber in Liberia. With that assurance the government of Liberia accepted the proposal for a loan, together with the condition that foreign advisers be placed in control of the financial policies of the nation. The company which actually provided the loan, however, was the Finance Corporation of America, which was organized by Firestone solely for the purpose of providing the loan. The fears of the government of Liberia were fully realized in subsequent years and finally the League of Nations stepped in to assist the government of Liberia in stopping the exploitation. The committee of the League of Nations reported, among other things, that the money expended since the Firestone loan had been "squandered as a result of the deplorable advice" of the American financial advisers in Liberia.[64]

11

WAR CRIMES

This chapter is concerned with violations by the 70 large corporations of the laws which relate to war. It includes, first, the violations of the special regulations in the two world wars; second, the avoidance of war taxes; third, a summary of the decisions on restraint of trade so far as these relate to war; fourth, interference with war policies by these corporations in order to maintain their competitive positions; fifth, violations of embargoes and neutrality; and sixth, treason. Few official decisions have been made against the large corporations on these charges. These decisions are included in Table 3 among the "Other" violations. The materials in this chapter are presented not because they add significantly to the number of decisions against the corporations but because they may throw light on the attitudes and motives of the large corporations and thus aid in the interpretation of their behavior.

Violations of Special War Regulations

In preparation for World War I, Congress enacted in 1916 a national defense act which included a prohibition against "profiteering" and made profiteering a crime. This law was designed to prevent increases in prices and to limit profits. President Wilson defined "fair prices" and "fair profits" as those which prevailed in the prewar period. Altogether 12 suits were initiated against 11 of the 70 large corporations in World War I, with only two official decisions against these corporations.

Reports of commissions are more valuable than decisions of courts as to the extent of violations of war regulations. The Federal Trade Commission, on order of Congress, investigated several industries, reported widespread violations of the law against profiteering, and recommended suits under the antitrust law in several cases. Also, the Congressional Committee on War Expenditures made general surveys and reported enormous increases in profits in certain industries. The price index of steel, taking the price in the year ended July 30, 1914, as 100, rose to 370 in July 1917 and then decreased to 218 in 1918. If profits for 1910–13 be taken as 100, the annual average profit before taxes in 1914–18 was 228 for U.S. Steel, 291 for the Big Five Meat Packers, 312 for General Motors, 324 for Anaconda Copper, 420 for Republic Steel, 723 for Bethlehem Steel, and 952 for DuPont.[1] These increases in profits were computed from the published statements of the corporations and their actual profits were probably far in excess of the published statements. The Iron and Steel Institute compiled these published statements for steel corporations and announced that the annual profits increased only from 6.9 percent in 1915 to 9.0 in 1918. Accountants for the Federal Trade Commission, after examination of the records of the steel corporations, reported that the annual profits increased from 7.4 percent in 1915 to 20.0 percent in 1918.[2] The assets of the corporations increased enormously and a large part of their growth was financed by reinvestment of profits. The assets of DuPonts increased from $74 million in 1913 to $308 million in 1918, and of Anaconda from $140 million in 1914 to $254 million in 1918. Although the officers of the DuPont company divided among themselves more than $15 million in bonuses during the war years, the corporation still had profits of more than 100 percent on the investment during the four war years.[3] The Federal Trade Commission made the following generalization regarding the Big Five Meat Packers, including reference to profiteering during the war. "They have attained their dominant position primarily as a result of unfair practices and illegal methods."[4]

The methods by which these great increases in profits were secured are described as follows by the Congressional Committee on War Expenditures, with special reference to the leather commodities:

1. The purchase of leather equipment and the fixing of prices therefore during the war was largely controlled by the leather tanners and their representatives.
2. The amount of leather and leather equipment purchased was excessive and far beyond the reasonable needs of the government.
3. The prices paid for such supplies were exorbitant and unnecessary.[5]

The first and last points apply generally to the industries which were investigated by the Congressional Committee. The prices for an industry were generally fixed by dollar-a-year representatives of that industry who were serving in Washington. For instance, in fixing the prices of steel, Judge Gary was both buyer and seller, for he was chairman of the steel committee of the Council of National Defense and also chairman of U.S. Steel. He submitted prices for steel, to which the Secretary of the Navy Daniels reacted by a note to Baruch, "It looks as if there was a great rake-off on the products." After much resistance, Daniels was forced in order to secure steel to capitulate and accept the price suggested by the steel industry. The steel corporations then gave much publicity to the statement: "These steel prices are a wonderful monument to the patriotism of the steel manufacturers." Baruch was asked in 1935 by a Senate committee about the patriotism of the steel manufacturers in World War I and he replied that he did not agree with the statement quoted above and added, "I told Judge Gary that my personal inclination was to take over the steel industry."[6]

The Nye Committee in its report in 1935 made the following statement regarding the shipbuilding industry during World War I:

> The record of the present ship-building companies during the War, whenever examined, was close to being disgraceful. They made considerable profits. On Treasury audits they showed up to 90 per cent. They secured cost-plus contracts and added questionable charges to the costs. They took their profits on these ships after the war-time taxes had been repealed. They secured changes in contract dates to avoid war taxes. They bought from the Government very cheaply yards which had been built expensively at Government cost. In one case this was pre-arranged before the yard was built. One yard did not build necessary additions until it was threatened with being commandeered. Knowingly exorbitant claims were filed against the Government for cancellation. Huge bonuses were paid to officers. Profits were concealed as rentals. After the war was over keels for $181,847,000 worth of destroyers were laid, which was probably the largest post-war favor done by any Government to any munitions group.[7]

Efforts were made at the close of the war to recover excessive payments to corporations and to prosecute for fraud. These efforts were seldom successful, in part because of the personnel in administrative offices in the postwar period. The Bethlehem Steel Company was sued for fraud in contracts for war materials. This corporation refused to make ships for the government except on a contract which provided for a bonus for savings on the estimated costs, and the Emergency Fleet Corporation was forced to accept this contract in order to secure ships. Bethlehem made immense profits on this contract because it made immense savings on the estimated costs. The Department of Justice subsequently charged Bethlehem with fraud in overestimating the costs so that the bonus payments would be enormous, and sued for over $11 million in excessive costs. The court ruled that Bethlehem's action was akin to daylight robbery but did not include the element of deceit which is necessary in fraud. A minority opinion of the Supreme Court held that the court should not submit supinely to reprehensible behavior and indicated ways in which the nation might be protected.[8]

The United States sued the Aluminum Company of America for overcharges during World War I and recovered $1,540,738.[9] This suit grew out of accusations of fraud, but the decisions of the Court of Claims did not include a finding of fraud. When the Army and Navy expressed an urgent need for more powder, the DuPonts insisted that their facilities were adequate for all needs and for months they resisted the requests of the government for expansion of the powder plants. When they yielded on the general question of need, they used additional months in higgling regarding prices and profits. In the fall of 1917 the War Department, without consulting the War Industries Board, which had jurisdiction, signed a contract with the DuPonts for the building and operation of a plant to be owned by the government. The War Industries Board protested so vigorously against the huge profits allowed the DuPonts that the contract was canceled and a new contract written, which reduced the DuPonts' profits to 40 percent on construction and 30 percent of operation. During the negotiations, the Secretary of the Navy in disgust called the DuPonts "outlaws." The plant cost the government $90 million for construction and $25 million for operation for a short period at the end of the war and no powder was produced for use in the war. Later, the DuPonts purchased the plant for $3½ million and dismantled it, so that it could not be used by competitors, and also purchased at 4.3 cents a pound powder which they had sold the Army for 47.5 cents a pound and which had been damaged while stored in their plant. The difficulty in proving the accusations of fraud grew out of the fact that many of the records, which according to the contract were to be preserved, had been destroyed or misplaced.[10]

No official decisions have been discovered regarding defective materials in World War I, although many accusations were made by Congressional committees, some involving charges of fraud. The Committee on War Expenditures presented much evidence regarding the defects in airplanes constructed for war purposes and pointed out the persons responsible for the defects. Similar accusations were made regarding many other industries. Also, the Federal Trade Commission presented much evidence regarding inferior food sold by the large packing companies to the Army. The following extract from a letter from the sales manager of Morris and Company to another executive of that corporation is an illustration of the evidence:

> We examined some of this stock of butter before shipping to Alexandria (for Camp Beauregard) and found all we tested to be very fishy and we feel that the stock was well sold at the price you mention.[11]

Also, the superintendent of a branch house of Armour and Company wrote to the manager of the dressed-beef department on February 23, 1918:

> This has been a very unsatisfactory week because of the great quantity of bad-condition beef we had to sell. . . . 90 per cent of our beef unloaded this week was very stale. . . . Wilson bought beef from Arch Street that was so bad that we bathed it in vinegar and soda before we showed it to them. . . . I certainly do not know what they are going to do with this beef.[12]

The American Legion and other persons were dismayed and disgusted at the profiteering in World War I and insisted that policies be developed to take the profits out of any future war: that dollars be drafted as well as men. A War Policies Committee was appointed to make recommendations to this end, but it was diverted to some extent from its primary purposes. At any rate, when World War II arrived the recommendations of this committee were forgotten or neglected and men were drafted but dollars were not drafted.

The record of World War II is not essentially different from that of World War I. Twenty-four decisions have been made against 12 of the 70 corporations for violations of regulations of World War II. These are shown in Table 16. Of these decisions 9 were under criminal laws, 12 were injunctions against further violations, 1 was a decision of an administrative board with a penalty, 1 was a government claim for losses due to fraud, and 1 was a private claim for price violations. Fifteen of the decisions were concerned with prices, 4 with violations of priority regulations, 4 with fraud in production of war goods, and 1 with a violation of blackout regulations.

Violations of price regulations took several forms.[13] One was the straightforward quotation of prices in excess of the ceiling price. An injunction was issued against Montgomery Ward for pricing 156 items in its 1942 catalogue above the ceiling prices and against the same corporation regarding 434 items in its 1943 catalogue.[14] The violations of price regulations generally involved more subtle methods. Three meat packers—the only meat packers in the list of 70 large corporations—had adverse decisions for upgrading meat, that is, charging for a certain grade of meat a price which was allowed for a higher grade. Some of the meat packers, also, had decisions against them for tie-in sales, that is, requiring a dealer to take a large quantity of meats of less popular type in order to secure meat of the type desired. Injunctions were issued against Armour for tie-in sales on butter in Newark, Boston, and Philadelphia. The charge was made in Philadelphia that 44 violations were recorded against this corporation in the period February to October 1943.[15]

These decisions regarding price regulations, however, are presumably a very small fraction of all violations of price regulations. The OPA did not take one-tenth of the known cases to courts, but instead held

TABLE 16. Decisions against 12 of the 70
Large Corporations for Violations of
Regulations of World War II

Corporation	Number of decisions
Anaconda	4
Armour	4
Great A & P	1
Inland Steel	1
Jones & Laughlin	1
Kresge	1
Montgomery Ward	2
National Steel	1
Swift	2
U.S. Steel	3
Wilson	1
Woolworth	3
Total	24

conferences, gave advice, and issued warnings. Only those who engaged in violations in the most persistent and flagrant manner were referred to courts. Furthermore, the OPA issued no reports of court cases in which the names of defendants were listed. The statistics presented above were collected almost entirely from newspaper reports, principally the *New York Times* because it has an index.

As in World War I, the regulations for World War II were made chiefly by representatives of the large industries and in their favor. It has been reported, for instance, that the regulations regarding cheese were written under the direction of a representative of the large cheese corporations, and that they gave so much advantage to the larger corporations in the cheese industry that a large proportion of the smaller producers disappeared.[16] A representative of the International Paper Company was the executive of the paper division of the OPA, which granted two increases in the price of newsprint in 1943; these increases in prices were accompanied by big increases in the salaries and bonuses of the executives of the paper companies. The profits after taxes of corporations in the steel industry were approximately 100 percent higher in 1940–43 than in 1936–39, and they continued to increase in the later years of the war. Substantially the same increase was found in the meat industry and the chemical industry.

Four decisions were made against 3 of the 70 large corporations for violating priority regulations, so far as could be gleaned from newspaper accounts. Two of these were against subsidiaries of U.S. Steel, and one each against Jones & Laughlin and National Steel. The decision against Weirton Steel, a subsidiary of National Steel, is most indicative. This corporation was convicted in November 1945 of fraud in securing scarce materials under priority rights, and fined a total of $148,125. The corporation had applied for air-conditioning apparatus for a company hospital, on the ground that it was the only hospital in the community, that the air was dirty, and that the hospital could not be kept clean without air conditioning. The War Production Board, after an investigation of the hospital, granted priority for this purpose. The air-conditioning equipment was not installed in the hospital but in the barroom of an exclusive country club, in which the members were limited almost entirely to the executives of this corporation. Other scarce material was secured by the corporation for industrial purposes in connection with the plant and was used to make an addition to the country club, install plumbing fixtures, ornamental stair rails, and a new kitchen.

Official decisions on charges of fraud have been against only 1 of the

70 large corporations, although accusations with substantial bodies of supporting facts have been made against many others. The Anaconda Wire and Copper Company was convicted in Indiana in 1943 and in Rhode Island in 1944 for such fraud, and indictments were voted against this corporation in two other states on the same charge. A government suit for $6,000,000 for losses due to this fraud was settled for $1,626,000 as to three of the plants. The government charged that 90 percent of the wire and cable produced on its orders was defective, and that adequate inspection had been avoided by tricks and manipulations. Employees of the corporation testified that these tricks had been used since 1932 and that the manager had instructed the employees to be careful not to get caught, for "If you do get caught, it's your neck, not mine or the corporation's."[17] Also, a subsidiary of National Lead Company was indicted for fraud in the inspection of bullets for machine guns and rifles for the armed forces, but no outcome of this suit has been discovered. The Truman Committee of the Senate reported in 1943 that tests of steel manufactured by the Irvin plant of the Carnegie-Illinois Steel Company, a subsidiary of U.S. Steel, had been consistently "faked," that this was known to the executives of the corporation, that these executives interfered with the efforts of the Senate Committee to secure evidence in regard to these accusations, and that 26,000 tons of inferior steel had been delivered from this plant to the United States government as a result of these fraudulent practices. The court, while convinced that the records of the corporation had been falsified, was not convinced that the materials delivered were defective, that the United States had suffered damage, or that the corporation had gained financially from the falsifications, and therefore dismissed the suit.[18]

Tax Evasion

The policy of the government in both world wars was to reduce war profits by heavily graduated taxes. The corporations avoided payment of their share of the costs of war by many methods, some of which were illegal. One of these methods was the padding of costs in order to reduce the profits reported for tax purposes. Reserves for depreciation were increased, interest on investments was included as costs, salaries and bonuses of officers were increased enormously, raw materials were given fictitious values, inventories were manipulated, and profits were concealed by intercompany transactions.[19] In the Second World War the Navy disallowed $49 million in costs which were claimed by manufacturers on cost-plus contracts.[20] Expenditures for advertising, which could be deducted from income as a necessary cost, were immensely increased by many corporations, although these corporations had nothing to sell to the readers.

A second method of avoiding taxes was by juggling financial data. Two cases of this nature in World War I came to the courts, both involving the Aluminum Company of America. A subsidiary of this corporation made its return for 1916 and 1917 for the normal income tax on the principle of receipts and expenditures, but calculated the special munitions tax on the principle of accrual. By this shift it reduced its total tax by $166,910. The Bureau of Internal Revenue refused to allow this shift and, on appeal, the court ordered the corporation to pay the additional tax.[21] Also, this corporation, in reporting on the normal income tax, filed a separate return for each subsidiary of the system, but in calculating the excess profits tax made a consolidated return for the entire system. The question at issue was whether a sale of $1,694,355 by one subsidiary to an affiliated corporation could be included as income. The Bureau of Internal Revenue refused to approve this shift in methods of calculating taxes and ordered the corporation to pay an additional $650,632. The court, on appeal, sustained the bureau and stated:

> If the intercompany dealings had shown a book loss of $1,694,355 instead of a book profit of that amount, it is quite certain that the plaintiff would not be asking us to take the intercompany dealings into account in figuring the group net income for 1918.[22]

A third method by which these corporations avoided payment of taxes was the recovery for amortization of war expenditures; that is, the government reimbursed corporations which had constructed plants in excess of their peacetime needs by refunding portions of their taxes. A total of approximately half a billion dollars was repaid to corporations for amortization, most of this during the administration of Andrew Mellon as Secretary of the Treasury. Ten of the large corporations in the list of 70 asked for a total of $115,000,000 refunds initially, and later added $37,000,000 to these requests. The Aluminum Company of America, in which Andrew Mellon had been the chief stockholder, claimed $6,852,697 for construction in excess of peacetime needs, and later increased this claim to $18,258,000. The amount allowed was $15,268,000 and was based on the average production for the years 1921–23 as representative of peacetime needs. The production of this corporation in 1921 and 1922 was very small as compared with

1920, 1923, and later years. While appearing before the Treasury Department, they insisted that they used only 56 percent of the capacity of the plant which had been expanded for war purposes, but at the same time they were appearing before the Federal Trade Commission on a charge of restraint of trade for refusing to sell to certain parties, and argued that the capacity of their plant was insufficient to enable them to sell to these parties.[23] U.S. Steel Corporation claimed refunds for amortization of $75,520,512. The Treasury Department under Mellon made an appraisal in 1923 of $55 million. The Couzens Committee of the Senate in 1926, with the same data, concluded that not more than $19 million should be refunded. Later, when Senator Couzens was under attack and not able to act vigorously on the amortization questions, the Treasury raised the allowance to $23 million, later to $33 million and finally in 1930 to $55 million. Vice-President Garner stated that two weeks after the last refund of $33 million to U.S. Steel, the Court of Claims made a decision which, if applied to U.S. Steel, would have reduced its total allowance by $26 million.[24] A Congressional Committee had the duty of investigating any refund in excess of $5 million but all of the Republican members of this committee gave their proxies to the chairman of the committee on a standing vote to approve the decision of the Secretary of the Treasury. Senator Couzens had been insistent that the refunds to the Aluminum Company of America as well as to other corporations should be investigated and urged that Haney, who had a reputation as a vigorous prosecutor of grafters, be placed in charge of the investigation. It is reported that Mellon threatened to resign if Haney were made director of the investigation. Under a less vigorous director, the commission reported that approximately half of the refunds to corporations for amortization were illegal.[25] At any rate, much of the taxes paid by profiteers during World War I were recovered in this form, and the corporations which made huge profits from the war failed to meet the share of the costs of the war which the legislators had intended to place on them.

Similarly, taxes paid during World War II were recovered by many corporations, at least in appreciable part.

Restraint of Trade on War Materials

Decisions have been made against 21 of the 70 large corporations on charges of restraint of trade in materials directly necessary for war, and many other decisions on charges of restraint of trade on materials indirectly connected with war.[26] The more direct offenses occurred principally in the steel, powder, and chemical industries. The Secretaries of the Navy, with considerable regularity since 1890, have accused the Bethlehem Steel Company and the Carnegie Steel Company, both before and after the latter became a part of the U.S. Steel Corporation, with collusion to make identical bids on armor plate for the Navy and with participation in international cartels which were designed to prevent foreign steel corporations from bidding on armor plate for the U.S. Navy. Similar accusations have been made with regularity regarding shipbuilding for the Navy. Likewise, the same charges have been made against the DuPont company regarding powder for the Army and Navy. The DuPonts paid German and English corporations which had purchased land in New Jersey with the intention of constructing powder plants there, to withdraw. When the courts held the DuPont Corporation to be a combination in restraint of trade and ordered its dissolution in 1911, Coleman DuPont attempted to secure a conference with President Taft to discuss the terms of the dissolution. One of the DuPonts reported that President Taft refused to see Coleman because the latter "was as slippery as an eel and as crooked as a ram's horn." Alfred DuPont added regarding Coleman DuPont: "The trouble was that you just could not trust him." Furthermore, both the powder company and the steel companies were accused of selling war materials to foreign governments at lower prices than to the government of the United States. The companies have denied this categorically, but the evidence is quite convincing as to some incidents. Secret correspondence between executives of DuPont shows that this corporation made a price of 54½ cents a pound on powder to the Estonian government, while selling the same powder to the United States at 71 cents a pound. One executive of the corporation cautioned another to be careful that the price to Estonia be "regarded with the utmost secrecy," since "we cannot take the chance of this reduced price being divulged."[27]

Maintaining Competitive Positions

Many large corporations interfered with war policies in both world wars in order to maintain their competitive positions in the war and postwar periods. The Vinson Committee of the House presented much evidence on this as to World War II. Delays in converting to war industries for fear of loss of civilian customers to their competitors, opposition to the establishment of government plants for fear that they might be continued as competitors after the war, hoarding of materials and of labor that were greatly needed elsewhere, political pressures to secure war contracts that could not be carried out effectively, and other corporate policies have been described in the reports of these Congressional committees. Elaboration and illustration of these charges will be limited to one corporation, although many others would serve equally well.

In 1940, when responsible government officials were demanding that the facilities for the production of aluminum be expanded, the Aluminum Company of America gave assurance that its existing facilities were entirely adequate for all military and civilian needs, with a considerable surplus for the Allies. Stettinius, who had authority on this question, accepted these assurances and decided that no expansion was necessary. Before the end of that year reports were circulated that the airplane firms were being delayed by lack of aluminum, and a short time later a public drive was started to induce citizens to contribute their aluminum pans and kettles to the war purposes. Even after everyone agreed that expansion of aluminum facilities was necessary, the Aluminum Company, having a monopoly on aluminum, was in a position to drive a hard bargain with the government and did so, using months in the process of bargaining. The first proposal of the government was that new plants be constructed in the TVA region, which had a large supply of power and ready access to the supplies of bauxite and to the plants which would use the aluminum. The Aluminum Company refused to participate in any plan for construction on this site, since this would subject the plant to inspection and regulation by the TVA and to the possibility of repurchase by the government. After much delay, the government made a contract with the Aluminum Company, which was described by Senator Truman as the worst contract the government ever made with anyone. The corporation was given a veto power on sites, on installation and production rates, and a profit of 15 percent on construction. The only redeeming feature of the contract was that the price of aluminum was reduced from 19 cents a pound to 15 cents a pound. This reduction was the reverse of the effort of this corporation in the earlier war and is not explained by increased patriotism of the corporation. The explanation is that a contract was being made at the same time for the production of aluminum by the Reynolds Metal Company, so that the Aluminum Company at last had a competitor. Finally, the Aluminum Company strenuously opposed the development of the lime-soda process, by which low-grade bauxite could be used in the production of aluminum, because the corporation did not have a monopoly on low-grade bauxite. Despite this opposition, Secretary Ickes continued experimentation on the process through the Bureau of Mines. When bauxite from abroad was shut off by submarine warfare, the Aluminum Company requested and secured a loan of $54 million from the government to construct plants in which this lime-soda process could be used.

Violations of Embargoes and Neutrality

Documentary evidence indicates that several of the 70 large corporations have violated embargoes and neutrality, although no official decisions have been made against any of them on these charges. The DuPonts, as manufacturers of powder, have been accused more frequently than any other corporation and a survey of the accusations against this corporation will be presented. In 1915 Coleman DuPont wrote to another director of his corporation that an embargo on powder to European countries was being discussed and might be enacted, and he inquired whether it might not be wise to construct a powder plant in Canada so that shipments of powder could be continued if an embargo were enacted. After the Treaty of Versailles had limited trade in munitions in Germany, the DuPonts engaged indirectly in such trade. They made cartel agreements with the Nobel firm in England, which was connected with German corporations, even before the Treaty of Versailles was signed. These agreements were extended in 1926–27 and included exchange of confidential information regarding the processes of manufacture of powder. Representatives of the DuPonts, when accused of this, explained that the agreement referred only to nonmilitary powder, but they admitted under pressure that the processes of manufacturing military powder could not be distinguished from the processes of manufacturing nonmilitary powder. Also, this agreement was not signed but it contained a statement that it was a "gentlemen's agreement." Major K. V. Casey, an executive of the DuPont Corporation, wrote to another executive of that corporation in 1924:

> Both the Army and Navy have indicated that they are desirous of keeping secret the development work which we do for them. If we were to agree to exchange information with any foreign firm and at the same time accept help in selling powder abroad from our own Army and Navy, we would create a condition which would at some time or other bring discredit to us.[28]

Furthermore, the DuPonts acquired stock in the English and German powder firms and the three developed German subsidiaries under joint ownership. Thus before 1930 close corporate ties had been developed with the German firms, with exchange of information which the Army and Navy wished to keep secret. On February 1, 1933, Felix DuPont, vice-president of the corporation, made an agreement with Mr. Giera, an international spy, to act as special agent for the corporation in Holland and Germany in the sale of powder and explosives, at a time when such sales were in violation of the Treaty of Versailles. This contract was discussed in the executive committee of the corporation on February 3, 1933, and the contract was destroyed. The executive committee consulted Sir Henry McGowan of the Imperial Chemical Industries of Great Britain (successor to Nobel), who objected to the contract on the ground that it would interfere with more general plans for trade with Germany. On April 14, 1933, Giera was paid $25,000 for immediate cancellation of the contract in lieu of six months' notice, which was required by the contract.[29] The wishes of the chairman of the British corporation carried more weight than the wishes of the Army and Navy of the United States. Furthermore, the Remington Arms Company, which became a subsidiary of DuPonts in 1933, paid royalties from 1929 to January 1, 1934, to a German munitions firm for the use of German patents, in violation of the embargo on such transactions by the Treaty of Versailles. These incidents show that the Soviet accusation that Germany was rearmed by America in violation of the Treaty of Versailles is not entirely without foundation.

The report of the Nye Committee contains detailed documentary evidence that the DuPont company was similarly engaged in trade in munitions with Russia, with Japan, and with South American countries in violation of the policies of the State Department in many cases and of laws in some cases. A total of 12 such occasions are reported. The DuPonts have expressed great contempt for embargoes and for the State Department. In 1932 one of the executives of this corporation wrote:

> Regarding the attempt of Mr. Hoover and his "cooky pushers" in the State Department to effect embargoes on munitions sent out of this country, I do not believe that there is the least occasion for alarm at present.[30]

Other executives of the DuPont company referred to plans for embargoes as "crazy ideas," and as "unfavorable legislation." One executive, after being informed that the State Department was opposed to agreements with foreign firms regarding poison gas, wrote to the home office:

> If we were in possession of complete technical details, which would enable us to construct and operate the proposed chemical warfare plant, we would undertake the project regardless of the attitude taken by the State Department.[31]

On the other hand, the executives of this corporation expressed great respect for the executives of foreign corporations in their industry. Lammot DuPont expressed hearty agreement with the following statement written by Lord McGowan of the British Imperial Chemical Industries:

> Everything possible is being done to ensure that no prospective political or legislative action on the part of government be permitted to influence relations between DuPont and ICI.[32]

Similarly, at a time when the government of the United States was expressing indignation against the Japanese government for aggression in Manchuria, interoffice correspondence in the DuPont company stated:

> There might be some value in a continuance of friendly relations between Mitsui and DuPonts from the international point of view and that DuPont felt some embarrassment in refusing to deal with Mitsui at this time, it being necessary to reverse our previous position if we were to take the stand of not selling the process.[33]

In other words, the DuPonts felt less embarrassment in violating an American embargo than in breaking business relations with a Japanese corporation.

Treason

Although the accusations of treason have been made with little regard to the statutory definition of this crime, 3 of the 70 large corporations have been accused of treason in the sense of revealing military secrets to other nations. The DuPonts were accused of making an agreement with the German powder manufacturer in 1889, which was repeated in later years, by which, in return for $100,000, the DuPonts agreed to report to the German powder corporation the quantities and types of powder purchased by the United States government, and to exchange secret information regarding improvements in the processes of manufacturing powder, including the processes which were invented or to be invented by the United States Army and Navy. Army regulations prohibited the description of tests of munitions except by permission of the Secretary of War, and limited the persons who might witness such tests to persons approved by the Secretary of War. On some occasions the War Department had refused to testify before Congressional committees regarding the processes used in the manufacture of powder on the ground that this information might thus become known to foreign nations. In spite of this caution, the DuPonts agreed to keep the German powder manufacturers regularly apprised of all improvements.[34] Likewise the Aluminum Company of America, in its illegal cartel agreement regarding magnesium, made arrangements for officers of the Magnesium Development Company (owned jointly by the German and American participants in the cartel) to visit the American airplane factories. These visits were made during most of the decade of the thirties and almost up to the entrance of the United States into the war. Some of these officers were Germans and were carrying out the Nazi program of learning the details of the military equipment of prospective enemies. Finally, according to the report of Drew Pearson, RCA was instrumental in revealing to the enemies of the United States the secret of radar, which had been invented by members of the U.S. Signal Corps and used by them experimentally for a period of six years prior to 1938. William D. Hershberger, who had been employed as a civilian by the Signal Corps and whose duties had made him acquainted with radar, resigned and shortly thereafter was employed by RCA. Within approximately a year, in 1938, RCA filed a patent on radar, with William D. Hershberger listed as one of two inventors. This patent, if granted, would not only be an appropriation by a private corporation of an invention made by a public agency, but also would reveal to all other nations this process which the Army desired to keep secret. The Army opposed the granting of this patent and all publicity regarding the topic; it was successful in preventing publicity regarding this invention until the end of the war. But in the same year RCA filed, applications for patents were granted and publicity was given to them, and also in Germany and Japan, where patents were not granted. At the end of the war an inquiry was made by the Department of Justice regarding the prosecution of RCA, but this was stopped when the chief of the Signal Corps, who was pushing for prosecution, was given an important position in RCA.[35]

Conclusion

The general conclusion from the preceding description is that profits are more important to large corporations than patriotism. The executives of large corporations, with few exceptions, wished to win the war. But, like trade unions, the corporations wished to secure advantages from the war and promote their positions. When trade unions did this during the war period, they were accused of treason.

The evidence for the proposition that profits take priority to patriotism consists, to a slight extent, of the decisions of courts and commissions, and to a much larger extent of the documentary evidence published by Congressional commissions. This documentary description of the overt behavior of the corporations was generally in conflict with their verbal claims of patriotism. On a few occasions the verbal statements have been forthright and have agreed with their overt behavior. Lammot Du-Pont, chairman of the DuPont Corporation, is reported to have made the following statement in the meeting of the Resolutions Committee of the National Association of Manufacturers in 1942:

> Deal with the government and the rest of the squawkers the way you deal with a buyer in a seller's market. If the buyer wants to buy, he has to meet your prices. Nineteen hundred and twenty-nine to nineteen hundred and forty-two was the buyer's market—we had to sell on their terms. When the war is over, it will be a buyer's market again. But this is a seller's market. They want what we've got. Good! Make them pay the right price for it.[36]

Eugene Grace, president of Bethlehem Steel, is reported to have said: "Patriotism is a very beautiful thing, but it must not be permitted to interfere with business." And Pierre DuPont is reported to have said: "We cannot assent to allowing our patriotism to interfere with our duties as trustees."[37]

In a secret conference of the National Association of Manufacturers, where the members were discussing the question of whether they should announce as a policy "First Win the War," Lammot DuPont is reported to have made the following statement:

> The way to view this issue is this: Are there common denominators for winning the war and the peace? If there are, then we should

deal with both in 1943. What are they? We will win the war (a) by reducing taxes on corporations and high income brackets, and increasing taxes on low incomes; (b) by removing the unions from any power to tell industry how to produce, how to deal with any employees, or anything else; (c) by destroying any and all government agencies that stand in the way of free enterprise.[38]

This statement, obviously, means "First Realize Our Own Interests," and is definitely in contrast with the resolution adopted at the same time by the CIO, that the first objective of that organization was to win the war.

The significant point of this chapter is this: The large corporations in time of war, when Western civilization was endangered, did not sacrifice their own interests and participate wholeheartedly in a national policy, but instead they attempted to use this emergency as an opportunity for extraordinary enrichment of themselves at the expense of others. Since these corporations lacked the consideration for the general social welfare in an emergency that endangered all civilization, they will be even more incapable of participating in national policies in ordinary years. They are driven by self-interest and the desire to secure an advantage over others which makes them constitutionally unable to engage in the cooperative life of society.

12

MISCELLANEOUS VIOLATIONS OF LAWS

Decisions have been made against 25 of the 70 large corporations for 73 miscellaneous violations of law. Fines were imposed in 16 of these cases, adulterated commodities confiscated in 23, injunctions issued in 15, damages awarded in 16, and settlements accepted by the complainants and the court in 3 cases. The number of decisions against each of these 25 corporations is shown in Table 17. Swift stands at the top of the list with 18 decisions.

Of these 73 decisions, 32 were concerned with health and safety. Seventeen decisions were made against Swift on charges of adulteration of foods, 9 against Armour, 2 against Great A & P, and 1 each against National Biscuit, National Dairy, and United Fruit. Almost all of these were reported by the Pure Food and Drug Administration for the years 1924–27, which were the only years in which the names of offenders have been published. One of the 32 cases, which does not involve adulteration of foods, was against the Boston Blacking Company, a subsidiary of the United Shoe Machinery Company, for shipping explosives not marked as required by law.[1]

Eight decisions were made against five corporations for transacting business without the licenses required by law. Four of these are against Kresge for selling milk of magnesia without a druggist's license or glasses without an optometrist's license. Two decisions were for transaction of business in a state without a license from the state as required by law, and one was for construction on a navigable river without a license from the Federal Power Commission.

Five decisions have been made against four of the large corporations for maintaining a public nuisance. All of these were suits for damages, four from fumes and one from water pollution.

Eleven decisions have been made against five of the large corporations for libel, false arrest, and assault. Of these decisions four were

TABLE 17. Decisions against 25 of the 70
Large Corporations for Miscellaneous
Violations

Corporation	Number of decisions
American Can	1
American Smelting	3
American Sugar	6
Armour	9
Chrysler	1
Corn Products	1
Ford	1
Goodyear	3
Great A & P	6
Intern. Shoe	1
Intern. Paper	2
Kresge	5
Loew's	2
Montgomery Ward	3
National Biscuit	1
National Dairy	1
National Lead	1
Phelps Dodge	1
Procter & Gamble	2
Swift	18
Union Carbide & Carbon	1
United Shoe Mach.	1
United Fruit	1
Woolworth	1
Youngstown	1
Total	73

against Great A & P, three against Montgomery Ward, two against
Loew's, and one each against Goodyear and Swift. Of the four decisions
against A & P stores, two involved unlawful detention by the manager of
customers who were accused of thefts. In one of these cases the manager detained a Negro girl twelve years of age, accused of picking up a
piece of candy, until her parents paid $5 for her release.[2] The other two
charges against A & P stores involved an unlawful accusation of theft
against a former employee of the store, and assault and battery upon a
customer by the manager of the store.[3] Two of the decisions against
Montgomery Ward were for accusing customers of theft and one for accusing a former employee of theft.[4] One decision was made against
Swift for accusation of a former employee of theft,[5] and one against
Goodyear for an assault upon a customer by the manager of a branch in
Evansville, Indiana.[6] In contrast with the preceding cases, the two deci-

sions against Loew's were for libel of Russian princes and princesses in the picture *Rasputin and the Empress* and both decisions were made in London.[7]

Seven decisions have been made against four of the large corporations for fraud and false pretenses. Three of these were fraud in customs duties, two fraud in taxes, one fraud in regard to water meters, and one fraud in the tire industry. The most striking of these cases were the decisions against the American Sugar Refining Company for fraud in customs duties. This fraud was reported to have continued from 1891, when the corporation was organized, until the date of the suits against the corporation. A civil suit was initiated in 1907 and resulted in a fine of $134,411 plus $2 million in settlement of all civil liabilities. A criminal suit, initiated in 1909, resulted in the conviction of four employees and several federal employees in the customs service. These convictions included the general superintendent of the refinery in which the fraud occurred, who was sentenced to two years in prison and a fine of $5,000; President Taft commuted this sentence to thirty days in jail. It included also the secretary of the corporation, who was sentenced to eight months in prison, a fine of $8,000 and costs; this sentence was commuted to fine and costs. The other employees who were convicted were wage earners at the pier, and their sentences were one year in prison and these were not commuted. In addition to the federal employees who were convicted, thirty employees in the customs service were dismissed.

Two methods were used in this fraud. First, samplers at the pier were bribed by employees of the corporation to take the samples from low-grade sugar, on which the duties were low, rather than from the average sugar in a cargo. The charge was made that these samplers received approximately $200 per cargo for this fraud. Second, seventeen Fairbanks scales, belonging to the Sugar Company, were used in weighing the sugar. In each of these a hole had been made, in which a plug could be inserted with the result of decided reduction in the weight shown although the scales were accurate without the plug. The charge was made that through this device approximately 75 million tons of sugar had been imported duty-free during the preceding six years. Although estimates were made that the loss to the government since the origin of these frauds had been $30 million, the government claimed a loss of $9 million within the period permitted by the statute of limitations. The claim was made that the corporation gained enough by these frauds to pay 6 percent annually on its capital stock.

The executives of the corporation, which alone could benefit by these frauds, professed ignorance and expressed a desire that the perpetrators be prosecuted. Their explanation was that the employees had committed the frauds of their own accord out of loyalty to the stockholders. The charge was made, also, that these frauds had been reported to the Treasury Department from time to time over a period of ten years. One member of the staff who was insistent that an investigation be made was removed from his position. This creates a suspicion that higher executives in the Treasury Department were aware of the frauds. Furthermore, when the suits against the American Sugar Refining Company were decided, the investigations revealed that many other large corporations were using similar methods to escape customs duties and that these frauds were found in Boston, Philadelphia, and New Orleans, as well as Brooklyn. The American Sugar Refining Company settled the government's claim for insufficient duties in the New Orleans district for $52,185.[8]

At about this time the City of New York instituted a claim that the American Sugar Refining Company had secretly connected pipes with the city water system, one of the pipes being ten inches in diameter, and had systematically withdrawn large quantities of water through the pipes without meter attachments and without payment to the city. The charge was made that this had continued for several years. The Law Department of the City of New York claimed $525,600 for the unmetered water but a settlement was made for $295,422.[9]

A decision, which has been classified as a case of false pretense, was made against the Goodyear Tire and Rubber Company. The manager of the Atlanta branch, according to the complaint, called five other tire dealers in the city, asking their prices on tires. He gave his name as "Vandergriff," who was a well-known trucker in the city. The other tire dealers, thinking that Vandergriff was a good prospect, called him again and again, causing him much annoyance. An injunction was granted against the manager of the Goodyear branch and the court expressed the opinion that the manager's action was criminal.[10]

The other decisions against these corporations include two cases of bribery, two cases of trespass, and one case of each of the following: larceny, violation of the prohibition law, violation of state insurance law, violation of air traffic law, violation of building law, contempt of court, and refusal to compensate an employee for an invention which the corporation had appropriated. Not included in this tabulation are many actions against several automobile manufacturing companies under the prohibition law. These automobile corporations, in order to retain control over their local agencies, had a contract by which the manufacturer retained ownership of automobiles sold on the installment plan until the final payments were made. Some automobiles sold in this manner and technically owned by the manufacturing company were used illegally in the transportation of liquor. These automobiles were confiscated by prohibition agents and actions by the manufacturers to recover the automobiles were systematically denied by the courts.

In addition to the decisions listed above, 17 decisions have been made against 13 of the large corporations for violations of contracts. These are not included in the tables in this chapter and in chapter 2, and no claim is made here that these violations of contracts were criminal. They are additional evidence, however, that many corporations are not reliable. Decisions have been made against corporations for violations of contracts in hundreds of other cases, of course, and the small number presented here has been selected primarily because they raise questions about the reliability of the corporations. Of these decisions three were against Montgomery Ward, two against Gimbel and Youngstown, and one each against Ford, General Motors, Goodrich, Great A & P, International Harvester, Jones & Laughlin, Kresge, Swift, U.S. Rubber, and Westinghouse Electric.

The Ford Motor Company agreed to take the entire output of hubcaps of Charles A. Myers Company if the latter would enlarge his plant. Myers made this enlargement but Ford refused to take the entire output. Myers was awarded $11,024 as damages for the violation of contract.[11] In a suit by the Gloversville Silk Mills Company against Gimbel, the charge was made that the latter had ordered gloves for which it refused to pay. The court decided against Gimbel and ordered payment.[12] Cyrus McCormick signed a contract for a certain number of binders manufactured on the Gordon patent. Another firm made an invention and secured a patent. McCormick concluded that this new patent was superior to the Gordon patent and refused to take the binders according to the contract. The court awarded damages of $250,000.[13] Kresge made a contract with the trustee in bankruptcy of the Titus Company that they would pay cost price for salable merchandise and that the price for damaged and out-of-date merchandise would be settled by agreement. The trustee claimed that Kresge had refused to abide by this contract, and the court decided that this claim was correct.[14] A truck driver, who wished to secure a tire as quickly as possible in order to complete some hauling work which he had agreed to do, placed an order for a tire with a local branch of Montgomery Ward, with the agreement that the tire would be ordered by wire. The agent, instead, ordered the tire by letter, with the result that the truck driver did not secure the tire in time and lost the work which he had contracted to do. On suit for damages, he was awarded $600.[15] Swift & Company agreed to pay for a minimum amount of power for the season for its cottonseed oil mill. Because the crop failed that year and the mill was operating for a small fraction of the season, the minimum amount of power was not used and Swift refused to pay for that minimum. In a suit, the court decided against Swift and ordered payment.[16]

Six decisions against five corporations were on violations of contracts on leases of buildings. Two of these consisted of "jumping leases."[17] A decision was made against Great A & P for nonpayment of rent and against Saks & Company, a subsidiary of Gimbel, for refusing to pay rent on vaults under the city sidewalks.[18] Goodrich Tire and Rubber Company rented a building with the stipulation that it would paint no sign on the building. However, it did paint a sign on the building and persisted after the owner of the building had called their attention to the violation of the agreement.[19] Montgomery Ward made a contract to rent a building for twenty years, with an agreement that alterations would be made in certain respects. The owner of the building made alterations, as specified, at a cost of $40,000. Within a few years Montgomery Ward took steps to terminate the lease, but the court held the corporation to its agreement.[20]

In general, the decisions enumerated above, as well as the violations of contracts, indicate that large corporations are persistent in their effort to secure differential advantages and ruthless in the pursuit of their interests. These miscellaneous offenses, however, do not show the settled policies that are shown in restraint of trade, misrepresentation in advertising, infringement of patents, and unfair labor practices.

PART III

PUBLIC UTILITY CORPORATIONS

13

RECORDS OF FIFTEEN
POWER AND LIGHT CORPORATIONS

Public utility corporations are interesting in the present study of white collar crimes both from the point of view of the prevalence of violations of law and from the point of view of the public control of corporations. The suggestion is sometimes made that our system of free competition and free enterprise, which has been emasculated by the large corporations, might be salvaged if corporations were subjected to rigorous and detailed regulation. In the utility industry we have an example of an attempt to regulate corporations. These corporations have been refractory and ungovernable, and by clever manipulation have reversed positions so that the utility corporations have been more successful in regulating the public than the public has been in regulating the corporations. Nothing in this experience with regulation of utility corporations gives assurance that other corporations can be regulated in the public interest.

Public utility corporations differ from most other corporations in that they are "vested with public interest." As a result, they have unusual rights and duties. They have the right of eminent domain, through which private property may be condemned for their use; they have monopoly rights in specific areas through franchises and certificates of convenience. In return for these and other privileges, they have, according to legal theory, high moral obligations; they are expected to abandon the ordinary competitive ideals and the strife for maximum profits, and to be diligent in rendering the maximum service at the lowest cost to the public.

The control of the utility industry has not been left to these high moral ideals. Regulatory commissions have been authorized to control this industry in accordance with the high moral standards. In the early history of this industry control was exercised by municipal agencies, later by state agencies, and still more recently these have been supplemented by federal commissions. The federal regulations have been increasingly important, first, because the utility industry has been integrated into interstate holding-company systems over which state commissions can have little control; second, because the state commissions proved to be ineffective for reasons other than the interstate character of the industry.

The utility corporations began in the United States as small companies, financed and managed locally. During the last fifty years they have been integrated into large interstate systems. This expansion has been facilitated by the improved technique for long-distance transmission of power and by the diffusion of knowledge that extraordinarily large and secure profits could be made by the promotion and management of these systems. These large systems began, with a few restricted precedents, when Electric Bond and Share was organized in 1905 under the control of General Electric. Other systems, rather small in size, followed this. The great expansion of these systems occurred in the decade of the twenties. For instance, Associated Gas and Electric was organized as a local corporation in 1906 and remained in that class for the next fifteen years; its capital, which in 1922 was only $4 million, had swollen by 1930 to $835 million. Of the $20 billion in capital in utility systems in 1933, approximately half was in systems in which the top company was organized in the period 1923–30.

The second reason for the increased importance of federal regulation is the recognition that the state commissions are failing to hold the utility corporations to the high moral standards assigned to corporations vested with public interest. This failure was due in part to the interstate character of the utility systems, which prevented any state commission from securing correct knowledge of the operations of the corporations it was attempting to regulate. But it was due in part to the political patronage policies in the appointment of the regulatory commissions, and to the influence of the utility corporations, acquired through large campaign contributions, in the selection of the members of the commissions, and also to the bribery of such commissions. Within the last generation the Securities and Exchange Commission and the Federal Power Commission have initiated policies which give increased promise that this industry may be compelled to conform to the law.

In order to determine the nature and extent of the crimes of public utility corporations, an analysis has been made of the records of the 15 largest power and light corporations. These 15 corporations are all of the corporations in the power and light industry which are listed among the 200 largest nonfinancial corporations in the United States, with the following exceptions: 7 which are relatively independent local units confined to one municipality, 6 which have a large part of their business in other activities than power and light, and 1—the United Corporation— which is a financial organization with large minority holdings in several power and light systems. Thus these corporations are essentially unselected except on the basis of size and industry, and are in this respect coordinate with the 70 largest manufacturing and mercantile corporations which were analyzed in part II.

The evidence regarding the violations of law by these fifteen power and light corporations is secured from two types of sources: first, the decisions of courts and of regulatory commissions and especially of the Federal Power Commission, the Federal Securities and Exchange Commission, and the several state utility commissions;[1] second, the monumental report of the Federal Trade Commission on Utility Corporations[2] and to some extent the reports of other federal and state investigating commissions. The report of the Federal Trade Commission is of the greatest importance. The evidence in this report was secured principally by accountants who were authorized by Congress to examine the financial records and other records of these corporations. This investigation provided the principal evidence on which the Wheeler–Rayburn Holding Company Bill of 1935—popularly known as the "Death Sentence" bill—was enacted.

The present analysis of the violations of law by the power and light corporations is confined principally to the period ended in 1940, although some decisions subsequent to this are included if they refer to behavior which was under way in the preceding period. The reason for this limitation is that since 1940 the utility systems have been changing radically in their component parts, due to the law of 1935 which required reorganization.

If rate cases are excluded, we find that few decisions have been made against these 15 power and light corporations by courts, either under criminal or equity jurisdictions. These are presented in Table 18. This shows that 7 decisions have been made against 4 of the corporations or their officers by criminal courts; the charges in these cases include fraud, corrupt practices, and violations of the antitrust law. Thirteen decisions on charges of fraud were made by civil courts against 8 of the corporations and all of these cases might have been tried in the criminal

TABLE 18. Decisions (Including settlements) against 15 Power and
Light Corporations

| Corporation | Adverse decision by | | | Total |
	Criminal court	Civil court	Civil court settlements	
Associated Gas & Electric	2	1	5	8
Columbia Gas & Electric	—	3	—	3
Commonwealth & Southern	1	3	—	4
Central Public Service	—	1	—	1
Duke Power Co.	—	1	—	1
Electric Bond & Share	—	—	1	1
Engineers Public Service	—	—	—	—
Middle West Utilities	—	2	6	8
Niagara-Hudson	—	—	—	—
North American	3	1	—	4
Pacific Lighting	—	—	—	—
Southern California Edison	—	—	—	—
Standard Gas & Electric	—	—	4	4
United Gas Improvement	—	—	—	—
United Light & Power	1	1	2	4
Total	7	13	18	38

courts. Eighteen civil cases against 5 of the corporations were settled out of court, generally by payments to minority interests which claimed that they had been defrauded by the management of the corporations.

In addition, 388 orders of commissions have been enumerated, of which 71 were supported by court decisions and 315 were not referred to courts. These orders imply consummated or attempted fraud or false pretenses, but the commissions and courts made no explicit charge or finding of fraud or false pretense in these cases. These orders have been made against each of the 15 power and light corporations, with a range of 2 to 67 and an average of approximately 26 per corporation. This enumeration, however, is very incomplete, in that decisions against the several corporations are not reported uniformly, and also is subjective, in that the investigator must make a decision as to whether fraud is implied in the order. Consequently these orders are not submitted as firm proof of criminality.

Additional evidence is presented in the Report on Utility Corporations by the Federal Trade Commission and in a few other reports. These reports give 293 additional instances of violations of law, generally in the form of fraud, by these fifteen power and light corporations. These additional instances range from 1 each by Pacific Lighting Corporation and Southern California Edison to 86 by Associated Gas and Electric. This evidence, also, is not complete, since different accountants with different interests worked on the records of the several corporations and also covered the component parts of the several systems unequally.

These two enumerations—one based on decisions of courts and commissions and the other on reports of accountants for the Federal Trade Commission—do not provide an accurate index of the violations of law by these corporations. They are very far short of the total number of instances of violation of law, and are not reliable as a basis for comparing the several corporations as to the frequency of violations of law. However, these methods of enumeration agree in placing the following corporations above the average of the fifteen in frequency of violations of law, in the order named: Associated Gas and Electric, Middle West Utilities, Columbia Gas and Electric, Electric Bond and Share, and North American. Of the six corporations which are below the average by both methods of enumeration, four are substantially restricted to one state and have received little attention from the federal commissions; these four are: Duke Power Company, Niagara-Hudson, Pacific Lighting, and Southern California Edison.

The two principal crimes of power and light corporations are defrauding the consumers and defrauding the investors. Both of these are based on the inflation of property values and of other assets, while the fraud against consumers is based in addition on misrepresentation as to the necessary costs of the operating companies which provide the service to consumers. Before presenting a logical analysis of the methods of fraud used by the power and light corporations, a particular case will be presented in order to make the procedures as concrete as possible. This is the early record of the Pike Rapids Power Company, a subsidiary of Electric Bond and Share, as reported by accountants of the Federal Trade Commission and the Federal Power Commission.

Pike Rapids Power Company

In 1923 James C. Heyworth organized the Pike Rapids Power Company in Minnesota for the purpose of constructing two hydroelectric plants on the Mississippi River near Blanchard, Minnesota. For a few dollars he secured a license from the Federal Power Commission to construct this plant and took the initial steps toward construction. This project was an intrusion on territory which the Electric Bond and Share Company believed it had preempted. In December 1923 the American Power and Light Company, a subholding company in the Electric Bond and Share system, purchased the stock of the Pike Rapids Power Company at a profit to Heyworth of about $25,000 for a few months' work and with an understanding that he should have the contract for the construction of the plants, from which during the next two years he derived an additional profit of about $300,000. The first conclusion is that Electric Bond and Share paid this high price in order to avoid competition in its territory. After the Pike Rapids Power Company, under this new ownership, completed the construction of these plants, it sold them on December 20, 1925, to the Minnesota Power and Light Company, a company wholly owned by the American Power and Light Company, for $3,797,000. A formal certificate was made that this sum was the actual cost of construction of the plants. Examiners for the Federal Trade Commission, after examining the records, concluded that the actual cost of construction was $1,490,000 less than the sum certified and questioned the following items. First, the certified cost of construction included an item of $600,000 for interest and discount on funds borrowed by the Pike Rapids Power Company from the American Power and Light Company; this had an effective rate of interest of 20 percent, when American Power and Light was borrowing funds for other purposes for 5 to 6 percent, and the officers of Pike Rapids Power Company and American Power and Light Company were the same persons. Second, the Pike Rapids Power Company was recorded as paying $292,000 for undeveloped water lands for the hydroelectric plants. This land was bought from an affiliated company in the Electric Bond and Share system, the same persons signed the deed as buyers and sellers, and no revenue stamp was placed on the deed on the ground that it was not a commercial transaction. No objective appraisal of the land had been made, but the price paid was sixty-two times the assessed value of the land made by the assessor the following year. Third, the cost of investigating to determine whether American Power and Light should buy this project in 1923, amounting to $20,000, was charged against the cost of construction. Fourth, fees for supervision and management amounting to $260,000 were charged to construction of the plants.

No evidence was secured as to the actual cost of this supervision and management, but for the system as a whole a profit of more than 100 percent was made on the cost of services and doubtless the cost of supervision was greatly exaggerated in this case. The second conclusion from this evidence is that this certificate of actual cost of construction included entries which were not actual costs, and in that case the certificate was a formal perjury, committed for the purpose of deceiving the state utilities commission and thus defrauding consumers whose rates would be determined in part by these misrepresentations, and further designed to defraud the federal government in case the latter desired at a later date to purchase this project, as it had a legal right to do, and finally designed to defraud investors in the bonds issued against this property. In 1926 the Minnesota Power and Light Company applied for permission to issue bonds against this property, with a principal value of $3,700,000, or approximately a million and a half dollars more than the costs of construction according to the judgment of the examiner for the Federal Trade Commission. In its request the utility corporation not only stated the cost of this property (which was represented to be the cost of construction), but also made certifications regarding its earnings in order to show that the income of the corporation was sufficient to pay the interest of the bonds. The formal certification regarding earnings was regarded by the examiner for the Federal Trade Commission as questionable in at least three respects. First, it included $161,000 of "putative interest" in the earnings for the first year. This was interest on an investment of a few dollars in undeveloped water lands and was "putative" in the sense that no one paid the interest and no one received it and in the sense that it was not in the form of dollars in the cash register which could be used to pay interest on bonds, if they were issued. Second, hypothetical earnings from a net balance of sales of electricity between the Minnesota Power and Light Company and its wholly owned subsidiary in Wisconsin, the Great Northern Power Company, were recorded in the sum of $227,000 for this year. This amount, also, was never rung up on the cash register or deposited in a bank. It was not accounted as a part of the gross revenue on which fees were paid to the Electric Bond and Share Company or recorded in the books for any other purpose than this projected bond issue. It was a fictitious income which could not be used to pay interest. Third, service fees amounting to $100,000 were paid to Electric Bond and Share for this year; these were not entered as operating costs but as a part of fixed capital. The effect of this was to decrease the recorded operating costs and thus increase the net earnings. If these three items of putative interest, hypothetical earnings from sale of electricity to an affiliated company, and service fees recorded as fixed capital had not been included, the income would obviously be insufficient to pay interest on the bonds. The state utilities commission, not having access to this detailed information which was discovered later by the accountant for the Federal Trade Commission, accepted the sworn statement of the Minnesota Power and Light Company regarding the earnings and granted permission to issue the bonds. The statements, therefore, were misrepresentations which deceived the commission and doubtless, also, many investors. The third conclusion, therefore, is that this transaction involved fraudulent misrepresentations regarding the earnings of this company which were designed to deceive investors and the regulatory commission.

Defrauding the Consumers

It is ordinarily assumed that a business corporation will keep its costs at a minimum and its net profits at a maximum. This policy is reversed as to the operating companies in the utility systems—the plants which provide services to the consumers in the local communities. These operating companies are under the control of a holding company and the holding company loads every possible cost on the operating company and drains off all possible earnings from the operating company. The reason for this reversal of ordinary business policy is found in the fact that the rates which may be charged for services are based on costs and earnings. The legal criterion of a fair rate, as used generally until 1940, is this: the rates should be sufficient to yield a net income (that is, gross income minus necessary costs) sufficient to pay a return of 6 to 8 percent on the property used in operations. Higher rates will be authorized insofar as the utility corporation can effectively exaggerate the value of the property and the costs of operation, and can effectively minimize the net earnings. The result has been that the top holding company has "milked its subsidiaries" in every possible way. The misrepresentations which have been used have yielded millions of dollars of fraudulent profits during the last generation, and these millions of dollars have been paid in large part by consumers.

Two principal methods have been used by holding companies in "milking their subsidiaries," namely: first, taking from its operating companies a profit on construction, management, income taxes, loans, and security issues; second, depleting the assets of the operating company by dividends, loans, transfer of assets, and a few other methods. A total of 359 incidents of these two types have been enumerated, ranging from 1 for Pacific Lighting to 95 for Associated Gas and Electric.

The most clear-cut evidence regarding misrepresentation as to construction costs, which provide evidence as to the values of property, is provided in the reports of federal projects. Any utility system which constructs a hydroelectric plant on a navigable stream must secure a license from the Federal Power Commission. This license contains a provision that the corporation must make a sworn statement of the actual costs of construction, which if allowed by the commission, are to be entered on the books of the utility corporation as the original cost. Nine of the fifteen power and light corporations have made such sworn statements of bona fide costs on 26 federal projects, which the Federal Power Commission, after an investigation, has refused to allow in part. In 13 of these projects for which financial data are available, the amounts claimed as bona fide costs of construction were $183,109,797, and the amounts allowed by the commission were 30 percent less than this. Niagara-Hudson claimed a cost of $57,314,863 on project no. 16 and was allowed only $24,680,680. Electric Bond and Share, which has had several federal projects, has rejections ranging from 6 percent to 50 percent of the claims. If these fraudulent claims had been approved, fictitious values would have been entered on the books and the state commissions would have been compelled to authorize rates sufficient to pay returns of 6 to 8 percent on these fictitious values. In view of the extensive misrepresentation of costs of construction on these federal projects, on which the utility corporations knew that the claims would be investigated by the Federal Power Commission, the misrepresentation on construction of projects not under federal control must be enormous.

A part of the misrepresentation on costs of construction is the service fee charged to the operating company by the holding company. These service fees apply not only to construction, but also to management and other services. Thirteen of the fifteen power and light corporations have charged such fees and most of them have organized service companies under the control of the top holding company through which the services are rendered. These systems have usually claimed that they perform these services to the operating companies at cost. The investigation by the Federal Trade Commission provided certain evidence that these claims were false and that the fees yielded immense profits to the holding companies. Electric Bond and Share collected more than $50,000,000 in fees from its subsidiaries in 1905–29; in 1931 it collected $9,335,445 for services to operating companies which cost it only $3,634,682. Associated Gas and Electric in 1924–27 charged its operating subsidiaries $9,970,944 for services which had cost only $3,397,204. Standard Gas and Electric charged $3,358,884 for legal services alone, although these services cost the top holding company only $1,280,012. The fraudulent profits on these services to utility corporations in a year have probably been as great as the losses to the public from all the robberies, burglaries, and larcenies, and are equally criminal. These fees for services have generally included the expenditures by the holding companies for political lobbies and for defense of the management of the holding company against suits by minority stockholders. Thus the public ultimately pays for the subversive programs of the utility corporations.

Associated Gas and Electric has had the greatest proliferation of these services and fees. It organized special corporations for construction, for management, for purchases and supplies, and for the sale of appliances. To each of these special corporations it gave contracts to a total charge of $28,247,400 for privileges which cost the system nothing, therefore making a paper profit of that amount. The operating companies and ultimately the consumers, of course, had to pay for these contracts. Associated Gas and Electric in 1926 purchased the J. G. White Management Corporation, which had been employed on a fee basis previously as a management company for the Associated system. After this company became a part of the Associated system, its rates were increased and some of the operating companies were required to pay additional fees for the services of the preceding year, amounting to the excess of the new fees over the old fees. Some of the service companies which worked for this system were owned personally by Hopson, who was the dictator of the system; his personal service companies made profits of $3,187,064 in 1929–33, while the system as a whole had no profits whatever.

Somewhat related to these service charges were the intercompany charges. Columbia Gas and Electric had a series of "paper companies" intervening between the producing company and the final distributing company. One of these companies purchased gas from the producing company at 26.5 cents per mcf, which sold it to an affiliated company for 45 cents, which sold it to the distributing company at 64.77 cents. These intervening companies had the same offices and officers as the producing and distributing companies; they rendered no services and were merely a device by which the costs to the operating company could be increased and the procedure concealed and kept outside of the jurisdiction of the state commission. Standard Gas and Electric used somewhat similar methods in the sale of electricity. In the Associated Gas and

Electric system, the operating companies near Johnstown, Pennsylvania, were required to purchase their coal at $3.80 a ton from the Penelec Coal Company, which was owned by the Associated system, while coal of the same quality could be secured from other coal companies at $1.50 a ton. The Johnstown Fuel Supply Company, in turn, paid rent of $61,160 a year to an affiliated company, although the same quarters had rented for only $21,426 before they were purchased by the Associated system.

The enormous profits on these services and on intercompany transactions have now generally ceased. When the facts as reported by the Federal Trade Commission became known to the state commissions, they refused to authorize these charges as necessary costs. This demonstrates that they had been deceived by the previous claims of the utility corporations. Furthermore, the Federal Power Commission and the Securities and Exchange Commission have ordered the utility systems to put their service policies on an actual cost basis and to place control of these service companies in the hands of the operating companies.

A third method of adding fictitious costs to the expenses of operating companies and thus defrauding consumers was by taking a profit on federal income taxes. The top holding company charged each operating subsidiary for income taxes on an individual basis and paid income taxes to the Bureau of Internal Revenue on a system basis and kept the balance in the treasury of the holding company. Five of the fifteen power and light companies are reported to have used this method and the practice was probably more extensive than these reports indicated. Associated Gas and Electric made a net income of $750,000 a year in this manner in 1926–29, and the North American Company $500,000. Of the entire income of North American 1.6 percent was from such profits on federal income taxes. Furthermore, Associated Gas and Electric charged each of its subsidiaries monthly for federal income taxes, with interest at the rate of 8 percent, although the subsidiaries, if they had paid taxes directly to the Bureau of Internal Revenue, would not have needed to pay the taxes until the following year and could have paid then in quarterly installments without interest. This practice of taking profits on federal income taxes was explicitly prohibited early in the decade of the thirties, but even prior to that it was fraudulent because these profits were included as a part of the necessary costs of the operating companies and were therefore paid by consumers.

A fifth method of adding fictitious costs to the operating companies was by interest charges. Nine of the fifteen power and light corporations were reported to have used this method, with a total of 28 instances. The Washington Power Company borrowed money from banks at 4 percent when it was independent, but it paid Electric Bond and Share 6 percent after it was brought under the control of that system. The operating companies in the Associated system paid the holding company 8 percent, compounded monthly, on open accounts and received no interest whatever on reverse accounts. The Pennsylvania Electric Company, a subholding company in the Associated system, made a profit of $1,237,500 by borrowing money from banks at 4½ to 6 percent and lending it to operating companies at 8 percent. Standard Gas and Electric on several occasions made loans to subsidiaries without the required authorization of state commissions; when these loans became known to the state commissions, they were canceled and lower interest rates ordered.

A sixth method of adding fictitious costs to the expenses of the operating company was by high charges for security issues. Seven of the fifteen power and light corporations are reported to have made such charges, with a total of 37 instances. Electric Bond and Share had a general policy of exacting commissions from subsidiaries for negotiating the sale of securities or "finding a purchaser." The Minnesota Power and Light Company paid Electric Bond and Share a commission of 10 percent for "finding a purchaser" for its stock; Electric Bond and Share found as a purchaser the American Power and Light Company; the officers and directors of Electric Bond and Share were identical to those of American Power and Light, and with a few exceptions, the officers and directors of the Minnesota Power and Light were identical to those of the two corporations which controlled it. The recent requirement by the Securities and Exchange Commission that these security issues be sold by competitive bidding aroused great opposition from the holding companies, obviously because this prevented them from adding these fictitious costs to the expenses of the operating companies.

The fictitious costs which have been described previously constitute one method of "milking the subsidiaries." The second general method of "milking the subsidiaries" is by depleting the assets of those subsidiaries. This method, like the first, is a method of defrauding consumers.

The first of these methods of depleting the assets of the subsidiaries is by misapplication of the funds of the subsidiaries. Evidence indicates that eight of the fifteen power and light corporations have used this procedure, with Associated Gas and Electric and Middle West Utilities tying for the largest number of instances. Associated Gas and Electric, without the required authorization of the state commission, transferred most of the assets from the Owego Gas Corporation to other corporations within the system, leaving the minority stockholders of Owego Gas with little property. The New York State Commission in 1937 and the Securities and Exchange Commission in 1939 ordered this system to restore the financial structure of Owego Gas Corporation as it had been in 1931. Associated Gas and Electric similarly drained off the assets of General Gas and Electric Company by transferring its most valuable properties to other corporations within the system. In this case, however, one of the minority stockholders was the United Gas Improvement Company, which is one of the fifteen largest power and light corporations. This corporation brought suit against Associated Gas and Electric for fraud, and a settlement was reached by which United Gas Improvement sold its holdings in General Gas and Electric to Associated Gas and Electric at an enormous profit. Hopson, the manager of the Associated system, was convicted of fraud in connection with other transfers of the assets of the corporations in this system and sentenced to prison. Similar charges were made against Samuel Insull in the Middle West Utilities. Although he was acquitted in the criminal courts, decisions were made in civil courts which required the bonding companies to reimburse the receivers for the losses due to Insull's illegal appropriations of the securities of the subsidiaries. Also, six officers of the North American Light and Power Company made personal profits of approximately $1 million while administering a fund from 1917 to 1919 for the purchase of operating companies.

A second method of depleting the assets of the subsidiaries is by requiring them to issue excessive dividends, which customarily go to the top holding company. These excessive dividends are issued generally at the expense of the depreciation reserve. Middle West Utilities, as a system, had on December 31, 1930, a reserve for depreciation of $4,500,000; the accountants for the Federal Trade Commission calculated that this reserve should have been $21,400,000. The reserve was kept at this low point principally because the subsidiaries issued dividends in such amounts as to prevent them from accumulating a reserve. Only when the power and light corporations were making income tax reports did they make adequate provision, on paper, for depreciation. Oklahoma Gas and Electric, a subsidiary of Standard Gas and Electric, claimed $7,667,662 for depreciation in its income tax report, but actually set aside only $4,280,000 for this purpose.

Finally, the operating subsidiaries are required to issue securities and make loans in the interest of the holding company, which further depletes the assets of the subsidiaries. Twenty-three instances of such practices have been enumerated for 9 of the power and light corporations. After the Metropolitan Edison Company was acquired by the Associated Gas and Electric Company, its bonded indebtedness was increased in one year by $10 million. The money thus secured was used by the holding company to pay the debts of other subsidiaries; the notes of these other subsidiaries, which had little commercial value, were the collateral for these loans. Nebraska Power Company issued notes which, with discount, had an effective interest rate of 20 percent and lent the proceeds to American Power and Light, a subholding company in the Electric Bond and Share system, for no consideration whatever.

In addition to the frauds against consumers through fictitious charges for property and fictitious costs, and through depletion of the assets of the subsidiaries, the utility corporations have made illegal charges to consumers. Such illegal rates have been reported in 47 instances for 12 of the 15 power and light corporations. Overcharges are reported by 7 of the corporations in 11 cases. Three corporations in 11 cases failed to give information, as required by law, regarding alternate rates available to consumers; on complaint by these consumers, the corporations were ordered to reimburse the consumers. The other illegal rates consisted principally of discriminations in favor of affiliated companies.

Defrauding Investors

The second general crime of power and light corporations is fraud against investors. Instances of such frauds have been discussed previously in connection with the depletion of the assets of subsidiary corporations. More general methods of fraud are used and some of these will be discussed.

One of the general methods of defrauding investors is the inflation of assets. All of the 15 power and light corporations, according to reports of investigating commissions, have inflated their assets. Although the Federal Trade Commission was unable to investigate all of the constituent parts of any one utility system, it found a total write-up of approximately one and a half billion dollars. Approximately two-thirds of the write-up was in the assets of operating companies. The write-up of the property values of operating companies has the objective, which was described above, of securing higher rates than could be secured if property values were reported honestly. This inflation of assets has the second general objective of deceiving investors. The accountants of the Federal Trade Commission concluded that no one of the utility systems has a financial structure which made investments in that corporation safe. Utility corporations have been able to sell securities principally because they deceived the prospective investors as to their financial situation. One of the subsidiaries of Associated Gas and Electric desired to sell securities in New York State and for this purpose proposed a financial statement which showed their assets to be $125,011,655. The Securities and Exchange Commission ruled that this corporation must either eliminate a write-up of $32,375,153 from their financial statement or explain clearly that $32,375,153 of their assets, as advertised, was due to write-up. The corporation chose to eliminate the write-up.

The procedure used in the inflation of assets may be illustrated in the origin of Electric Bond and Share. General Electric turned over to this corporation in 1905 securities and cash valued at $1,300,000 as paid-in capital. Against this were issued $2,000,000 par value common stocks and $2,000,000 par value preferred stocks. The preferred stock and a part of the common stocks were sold to the public for $1,300,000, which entirely repaid General Electric for its investment, while it still retained a majority of the common stocks at no net cost. Other utility systems have been organized on the same principle, with inflation ranging from almost nothing to 100 percent or more.

When Electric Bond and Share wrote up its assets at the time of its organization, it made no explanation or excuse. In subsequent inflations of assets, it frequently offered no explanation, and likewise many other corporations made no explanation. Some corporations, however, have attempted to conceal the write-up, or at least give it some plausibility. Associated Gas and Electric employed Cheney, who purported to be an independent appraiser, but was actually Hopson's partner in private companies, to make appraisals of the physical properties. Some corporations have inflated their assets by keeping on the books much property which has been discarded or has become obsolete. Niagara-Hudson carried in its fixed capital until 1932 the cost of a hydroelectric plant which had been retired in 1923. The receivers of Middle West Utilities at the end of 1932 wrote off $18,700,000 book value of properties which had been retired from service, much of it many years before, and at the end of 1933 wrote off $12,000,000 more, and reported that the process of retiring obsolete property was still incomplete. Another method of inflating assets of the system is by transfer of securities from one subsidiary to another at a profit. Electric Bond and Share acquired the assets of the Utah Securities Company for $3,854,263 and sold them to another subsidiary for $33,373,243, recording a profit of approximately $30,000,000. National Electric Power Company in 1925–30 made paper profits from intercompany transfer of $5,500,000, or 31 percent of its total income in these years. Middle West Utilities in the same manner realized profits of $17,700,000 in 1912–30, or 16 percent of its total income for the period. Other methods of inflating assets are the payment of huge sums for promotion, recording "going-concern" values, capitalizing service fees, interest on construction, and discounts.

Practically all of the 15 power and light corporations have paid dividends on these inflated assets. Snyder has pointed out that the payment of dividends on watered stocks would be legal only if (a) stockholders need not contribute equally to the assets of the corporation; (b) creditors may not oppose the impairment of capital; (c) directors have no duty of safeguarding the property of the corporation. These three legal principles are generally accepted as obligations, and all three are violated by payment of dividends on inflated assets.[3] Nevertheless, the courts seldom take action to enforce these principles. While the dividend payments on the book values have been relatively moderate, the dividends on the actual cash investment have in many cases been enormous. The Birmingham Electric Company in 1928 paid 67.4 percent on the cash investment, the Nebraska Power Company from 112 to 338 percent a year in 1926–30, and the Southeastern Power and Light Company 3,102.6 percent in 1927. Such instances could be multiplied many times.

Furthermore, many of the dividends have been paid from capital. Of the dividends of $32,143,311 paid by Associated Gas and Electric in 1922–29, at least half were paid from capital according to the appraisals of the accountants for the Federal Trade Commission. Middle West Utilities paid dividends of $27,000,000 in 1931–1932, of which $22,500,000 was paid from capital, according to the calculations of the accountants for the Federal Trade Commission. Associated Gas and Electric claimed a surplus of $669,791 in 1940 and proposed to pay dividends from this surplus; the Securities and Exchange Commission decided from an inspection of the books that this corporation had a deficit of at least

$70,000,000 and prohibited payment of dividends, whereupon the system went into bankruptcy.

The state and federal commissions have been much more rigorous during the last decade regarding the inflation of assets of utility corporations. The Federal Power Commission has insisted that these corporations adopt uniform accounting practices, which are designed to prevent payment of dividends from capital. This forced several of the utility corporations into bankruptcy. Standard Gas and Electric was ordered to write off $115 million and this turned a ledger surplus of $124 million into a deficit. The Montana Power Company was ordered to write off $51,978,025; its plant account had been carried at $58,023,509, of which $46,891,597 was ordered written off. The number of such orders in the period subsequent to 1940, which is not directly included in the present study, is enormous.

A second general method of defrauding investors is by illegal securities. Fourteen of the 15 power and light corporations have 59 recorded instances of illegal securities or attempts to issue such securities. In 30 cases courts or commissions have ruled that proposed security issues of 12 of the corporations were financially unsound. Included among the illegal security issues were violations of the par value laws of the states in 5 cases, excessive interest rates in 3 cases, violations of prior rights of other securities in 5 cases. Also, a commission held that the trust company provided in one security issue was not impartial. Investigating commissions have reported 4 security issues which had not been authorized, as required by law, by the state commission, and 1 issue which had not been authorized by the corporation's board. Finance companies affiliated with 4 of the 15 corporations have been deprived of state licenses because of fraudulent behavior. When Electric Bond and Share was organizing the Utah Power and Light Company in 1922, gold notes were sold to acquire the money with which to purchase the securities which were the collateral for the gold notes. This is the principle of "check kiting," which is one of the techniques of professional thieves.

The third method of defrauding investors is the policy of "rigging the market." This has been reported against 7 of the 15 power and light corporations, so far as discovered. Fictitious sales of securities give prospective investors an impression that the securities have sound values. These methods, like some other methods which have been described, are now generally prohibited by the Securities and Exchange Commission.

Restraint of Trade and Unfair Competition

Almost all of the 15 corporations have engaged in illegal restraint of trade and unfair competition. The operating company is generally given a monopoly within a restricted area, but the holding company system acquires many operating companies and looks upon a certain region as its territory within which no competing system may intrude. Sixteen reports have been made regarding violation of the antitrust law by utility corporations. Two adverse decisions were made by courts against Columbia Gas and Electric, and one against Commonwealth and Southern, while commissions have made similar decisions in one case each against Columbia Gas and Electric, Middle West Utilities, and United Gas Improvement. Investigating commissions have reported 9 additional violations of the antitrust law by 4 of the 15 corporations.

Unfair competition by 11 of the 15 power and light corporations has been reported in 29 instances, with commission orders in 27 of these. Unfair methods of competition have usually been of two kinds: first, refusing or failing to serve cooperative or municipal utility companies in 19 cases; second, discrimination in favor of affiliated companies in 6 cases.

Unfair Labor Practices

Utility corporations, like other corporations, have violated the National Labor Relations Law. The National Labor Relations Board has made 21 decisions against subsidiaries of 7 of the 15 power and light corporations; 4 of these decisions have been affirmed by courts and the others have not been referred to courts. These 7 corporations are, in order of the number of adverse decisions, Commonwealth and Southern, Electric Bond and Share, North American, Engineers Public Service, Standard Gas and Electric, and United Light and Power.

Summary

The preceding descriptions refer to investigations and decisions which demonstrate the great frequency of violations of law by the 15 power and light corporations. Included in the preceding descriptions are 44 cases in which power and light corporations took actions without securing the

authorization of state commissions, as required by law. These unauthorized actions include extension of services, cessation of services, fore-
closures, contracts, security issues, and regulations for customers. Associated Gas and Electric has been most unruly in this respect, with 10
of the 44 incidents. Franklin D. Roosevelt, before he became president
of the United States, referring to the findings of the Federal Trade Commission regarding utility corporations, said:

> Nothing more atrocious in the way of thievery inside the law has
> ever been successfully attempted against the American public.[4]

This appraisal is probably accurate except that the phrase "inside the
law" is ambiguous. In fact, the behavior has been in violation of law, but
the agencies of criminal justice have done little or nothing about it. Furthermore, many of the private communications among employees lead
one to believe that the dishonesty and illegality of the utility systems are
recognized within the systems. The Federal Trade Commission found in
the files of the utility corporations letters such as the following:

> John Colton of the American Electrical Railway Association wrote to
> J. B. Sheridan, director of the Missouri Committee on Public Utility
> Information, "The thing about the utility industry which disgusts
> me is the lying, trimming, faking, and downright evasion of trust or
> violation of trust that marks the progress toward enormous wealth
> of some of the so-called big men of the industry. There are utility
> companies that try to play the game honest and with whom I would
> be glad to be associated. I do not believe that this type of utility com-
> pany is representative of 90 per cent of the industry by any means: I
> think it is about 10 per cent. I would enjoy being linked up with
> even so small a minority if it could impress upon the 90 per cent a
> realization of its responsibilities to the public and inculcate in it a
> few germs of ordinary garden-variety of honesty." Sheridan replied
> to Colton, "I agree with everything you say, but I have found more
> honest people in the industry than you have. The trouble with them
> is that they are so timid and fearsome. Of course, the biggest of
> them are merely messenger boys of money, and all slaves of money
> are timid."[5]

These widespread violations of law by the 15 power and light corporations have been possible only because of the intricacies of the corporate
and financial structure of these systems. In 1928 Associated Gas and

Electric had a profusion of security issues, the objective of which could have been nothing other than obfuscation. It had 3 classes of common stock, 6 classes of preferred stock, 4 classes of preference stock, 7 classes of secured bonds and notes, 24 classes of debentures, and 4 classes of investment certificates.

The profusion of corporations within a utility system, similarly, is designed to deceive. Mention has been made of the "paper companies" in the Columbia Gas and Electric system, each of which added a profit on the gas which was to be distributed to the consumers. Mention has been made, also, of the Pike Rapids Power Company and the transactions between this corporation and other corporations in the same system, which had identical officers and directors. The function of these corporate personalities is essentially the same as the function of the alias of the hoodlum criminal, namely, concealment and secrecy. This manipulation of corporate personalities is now being eliminated in the reorganization of the utility systems.

The corporations in this industry have customarily been organized as pyramids, with a holding company at the top, with subholding companies, and with operating companies at the bottom. One operating company in the Associated Gas and Electric system was separated from the top holding company by ten intervening units and six operating companies by eight intervening units. In the Middle West Utilities system, Insull's top holding company was able to control the West Florida Power Company with ownership of only 0.05 percent of the securities of that operating company.

Interpretation

The 15 power and light corporations have violated many laws with great frequency. Nevertheless few decisions have been made against them by courts or commissions on explicit charges of violations of the criminal law. The following are some of the reasons why these corporations which in fact have a high incidence of criminal behavior have a low incidence of official decisions against them.

First, the state commissions, which have had jurisdiction over the utility corporations during most of their history, have been ignorant of the policies which were being used by these corporations and were unable to deal effectively with the violations of law which were known. Fraud was a crime, however, even though the society did not have an effective organization for enforcement of the law.

Second, the utility corporations have fought every bill which was designed to implement the law of fraud as applied to utility systems. They fought with particular vigor and by illegal methods against the Wheeler–Rayburn bill. Professional thieves would not be able to fight effectively against a bill designed to stop professional theft, but the utility corporations have been more powerful than the professional thieves and more effective in their efforts.

Third, the utility corporations for two generations or more have engaged in organized propaganda designed to develop favorable sentiments. They devoted much attention to the public schools in the effort to mold the opinion of children. Probably no group except the Nazis has paid so much attention to indoctrinating the youth of the land with ideas favorable to a special interest and it is doubtful whether even the Nazis were less bound by considerations of honesty in this propaganda. The Federal Trade Commission reported that these utility corporations spent approximately $30 million a year in newspaper advertising alone and that this expenditure was designed to create good will rather than sell electricity or gas. In some states the utility corporations built summer camps for newspaper editors, and in others gave annual banquets to editors. They have subsidized college professors, made contributions to chambers of commerce and other community organizations, and in general charged these expenditures to the operating companies, so that the consumers pay for this propaganda. Another device, said to have originated with Pacific Gas and Electric, was the customer-ownership campaign. This consisted of selling corporate securities to as many customers in the local community as possible, in order that the customers' interests in higher dividends might counteract their interest in lower rates. This device, like many other practices of utility corporations, involved fraud, since the securities were seldom stocks, which would give nominal ownership, but were bonds or debentures.

Fourth, the utility corporations have fought with energy against every effort of local communities or larger groups to provide themselves with power and light by methods that were more economical than those of the utility corporations. The Federal Power Commission reported that utility corporations filed 278 petitions in the years 1888–1935 against 195 public authorities who were attempting to organize municipal power plants, and that 242 of these petitions caused delays totaling 289 years, with an average direct expense to the community of $1,900 and an indirect expense of $73,582.[6] The utility corporations were not content to permit municipalities to experiment with municipal ownership and let the best system win, presumably because they suspected their own system would not win. Similarly they have fought against the larger development of public power in the later period, such as Muscle Shoals, TVA, and other regional developments, and against the Rural Electrification policy.

Fifth, the utility corporations have used illegal methods of influencing elections and appointments. Three officers of the Union Electric Company in St. Louis, a subsidiary of the North American system, were convicted and imprisoned for maintaining a "slush fund" for influencing elections. This fund was raised principally by "kickbacks" from firms which provided supplies for the operating companies in that system, and consequently the consumers provided the money for the bribery of their public officials in the interest of the utility corporation. Convictions were secured in this case principally because of the vigorous campaign of the *St. Louis Post-Dispatch*. Doubtless the same practices have prevailed in many other places where no newspaper, equally vigorous in fighting political corruption, was located. Frank L. Smith, after being elected to the Senate from Illinois, was refused a seat because of the contribution to his campaign fund made by Samuel Insull while Smith was a member of the state utilities commission. W. J. Thayer was alleged to have been receiving payments from the Associated Gas and Electric Company while he was chairman of the New York Senate Committee on Utilities. The Department of Justice found that the United Gas Improvement Company had paid $125,000 to Tom Hill, a gambler in New Orleans, who had passed a part of it on to Governor Dick Leche and William Feazel, and that the governor was convicted in a conspiracy regarding gas, in which Feazel was said to be a participant.

Finally, many persons who are in legislative, administrative, or judicial positions are closely related to the utility corporations, although no implication of illegality is involved in these relationships. President Hoover's first Secretary of War was James W. Good, who had been counsel for the Alabama Power Company, and his solicitor general had been a member of the firm which acted for Electric Bond and Share in most of its mergers. William Hickey, for several years chief of the registration division of the Securities and Exchange Commission, became president of Standard Gas and Electric and held a series of important positions in the federal government during the Second World War. George Otis Spencer, who had been vice-president and treasurer of the New England Public Service Corporation, a subsidiary of Middle West

Utilities, was appointed in 1937 as chief of the financial section of the Utility Holding Company of the Securities and Exchange Commission. After Cummings resigned as attorney general of the United States he organized a law firm, which defended Columbia Gas and Electric against the United States in the antitrust suit which had been initiated while Cummings was attorney general. Also, he acted as one of the attorneys to defend the Union Electric Company in the bribery suit. The Power Branch of the War Production Board during the Second World War was composed almost entirely of men who had been and were still receiving salaries from utility corporations.

The Federal Power Commission and the Securities and Exchange Commission have forced the utility corporations to a considerably higher plane of honesty since 1935. But the conflict is not ended and it is yet uncertain whether the federal commissions or the utility corporations will win. At the present moment the members of the Federal Power Commission are divided fifty–fifty on a proposal which, if authorized, would emasculate the commission, with one member about to be appointed to fill a vacancy.

PART IV

INTERPRETATION

14

WHITE COLLAR CRIME
AS ORGANIZED CRIME

The preceding descriptions of the crimes of corporations have shown that these corporations have committed crimes against one or more of the following classes of victims: consumers, competitors, stockholders and other investors, inventors, and employees, as well as against the state in the form of tax frauds and bribery of public employees. These crimes are not discrete and inadvertent violations of technical regulations. They are deliberate and have a relatively consistent unity. They are in agreement with the general characterization by Veblen:

> The ideal pecuniary man is like the ideal delinquent in his unscrupulous conversion of goods and persons to his own ends, and in a callous disregard of the feelings and wishes of others and of the remoter effects of his actions, but he is unlike him in possessing a keener sense of status and in working more far-sightedly to a remoter end.[1]

The "ideal delinquent" of whom Veblen writes is best represented by the professional thief. The behavior of the "ideal pecuniary man" exemplifies the special culture of the business world, just as the "ideal delinquent" exemplifies the special culture of the underworld. The principal specifications of white collar crime in comparison with professional theft are elaborated below, with certain points of similarity and certain points of difference.

First, the criminality of the corporations, like that of professional thieves, is persistent: a large proportion of the offenders are recidivists. Among the 70 largest industrial and commercial corporations in the United States, 97.1 percent were found to be recidivists in the sense of having two or more adverse decisions. None of the official procedures used on businessmen for violations of law has been very effective in rehabilitating them or in deterring other businessmen from similar behavior.

227

Second, the illegal behavior is much more extensive than the prosecutions and complaints indicate. Samuel Insull is reported to have remarked during his trial that he could not understand why he was being prosecuted since he had done only what all other businessmen were doing. Many types of violation of law are industry-wide in the sense that practically all firms in the industry violate the law. This has been demonstrated by many investigations of the Commissioner of Corporations, the Federal Trade Commission, and the various Congressional committees. Lowell B. Mason, a member of the Federal Trade Commission, stated in a recent magazine article that

> about the only thing that keeps a business man off the wrong end of a federal indictment or administrative agency's complaint is the fact that, under the hit-or-miss methods of prosecution, the law of averages hasn't made him a party to a suit.[2]

President Truman, accepting the conclusion that violations of law are industry-wide, announced in his 1947 message to Congress that the Federal Trade Commission hereafter will attack violations of law through trade conferences which will be aimed at the modification of industry-wide practices. The trade conference policy was used also at the end of the decade of the twenties and was based on the same belief in the industry-wide character of many violations of law.

Third, the businessman who violates the laws which are designed to regulate business does not customarily lose status among his business associates. Although a few members of the industry may think less of him, others admire him. This may be illustrated by reference to a few cases. Leonor F. Loree, chairman of the Board of Kansas City Southern Railway, in accordance with instructions of the board, appointed a committee in 1924 to purchase shares of the Missouri, Kansas, and Texas Railway. Prior to this and with knowledge of the plan of his corporation, he purchased 14,000 shares of Missouri, Kansas, and Texas for his own account, and sold them later at a profit of $144,707. Thus he made a profit at the expense of the corporation which he directed. After he had been requested to explain this action and when a suit was about to be filed, he turned over his private profits to his corporation. After this whole transaction had received considerable public attention, Loree was elected president of the New York Chamber of Commerce.[3] When Sloan and his colleagues in General Motors were ordered by the court to return to the corporate treasury more than $4 million which they had taken illegally in bonuses, they were not dismissed from their executive positions and their prestige in the business world was not reduced. When Seiberling was ordered to repay almost $4 million which he had taken illegally from the Goodyear corporation, he continued to secure credit from banks and soon built the Seiberling Rubber Company into a prosperous business. When it became known that Clarence Dillon, as agent of Dillon Read and Company, had enriched himself enormously and illegally while in control of Goodyear Tire and Rubber Company until the court ordered modification of the method of control, his reputation as a shrewd manipulator was made. Such illustrations could be multiplied many times. They amount to the general principle that a violation of the legal code is not necessarily a violation of the business code. Prestige is lost by violation of the business code, but not by violation of the legal code except when the legal code coincides with the business code.

Fourth, businessmen customarily feel and express contempt for law, for government, and for governmental personnel. In this respect, also, they are similar to professional thieves, who feel contempt for law, policemen, prosecutors, and judges. Businessmen customarily regard governmental personnel as politicians and bureaucrats and the persons authorized to investigate business practices as snoopers. Businessmen characteristically believe that the least government is the best, at least until they desire special favors from government, and in many cases regard the enactment of a law rather than the violation as the crime. The businessman's contempt for law, like that of the professional thief, grows out of the fact that the law impedes his behavior.

White collar crimes are not only deliberate; they are also organized. Organization for crime may be either formal or informal. Formal organization for crimes of corporations is found most generally in restraint of trade, as illustrated by gentlemen's agreements, pools, many of the practices of the trade associations, patent agreements, and cartels. Formal organization is found, also, in conferences of representatives of corporations on plans regarding labor relations. They are organized formally also for the control of legislation, selection of administrators, and restriction of appropriations for the enforcement of laws which may affect themselves. While some associations have developed codes of business ethics and many of the representatives have been sincere in their formulations of such codes, the actual effect of the codes is not different from what it would have been if the codes had been written by men with their tongues in their cheeks.

The informal organization for crimes by corporations consists in con-

sensus among businessmen. While businessmen, with consensus, give
lip service to free competition and free enterprise, they also, with consensus, practice restraint of trade. They are not willing to bear the bur-
dens of competition or to permit the economic system to regulate itself
in accordance with the laws of supply and demand, but they adopt the
method of industrial planning and manipulation. While corporations
seldom insist that their advertising agencies engage in misrepresentation, they reward the agencies which increase sales with little regard for
the honesty of the methods which are employed. They have a high degree of consensus regarding the patent laws, as restrictions which are to
be disregarded or circumvented. The chief executive of a corporation
stated confidentially:

> If an inventor has secured a patent on a process in our field and his
> invention has merit, we buy the patent if he is willing to sell it for a
> reasonable sum. But if he tries to hold us up, we refuse to buy it and
> "invent around" his patent, which we can easily do after we have
> examined the plans which he has submitted to us for sale.

The points of similarity between white collar crime and professional
theft, which have been elaborated above, are not a complete statement
of the relationship between these two types of crimes. These types of
crimes are different as well as similar. The most significant point of difference lies in the offenders' conceptions of themselves and in the public's conceptions of them. The professional thief conceives of himself as
a criminal and is so conceived by the general public. Since he has no desire for a favorable public reputation, he takes pride in his reputation as
a criminal. The businessman, on the other hand, thinks of himself as a
respectable citizen and, by and large, is so regarded by the general public. The federal court, when imposing sentences on the members of the
firm of H. O. Stone & Company in Chicago in 1933 for fraudulent transactions in real estate, said to the defendants:

> You are men of affairs, of experience, of refinement, and of culture,
> and of excellent reputation and standing in the business and social
> world.

The characterization of the white collar criminals in this case would
apply to practically all of the men in the corporations which have been
described as violating the law. Even when they violate the law, they do
not conceive of themselves as criminals.

This problem of the conception of one's self as a criminal is an important problem in criminology. Some criminologists have insisted that the white collar criminal is not "really" a criminal since he does not conceive of himself as a criminal. This contention is based on two logical fallacies: taking the part for the whole and taking the word for the essence. The general problem of criminology is the explanation of criminal behavior. Some persons who engage in criminal behavior conceive of themselves as criminals and some do not. The origin and development of the conception of one's self as a criminal is an important problem, but it is not the entire problem of criminology. Those criminologists who limit their attention to this problem and draw conclusions regarding all criminal behavior are taking the part for the whole.

One's conception of himself as a criminal is based on a general characterization and on an ideal type. Many persons who have been convicted of crime and committed to prison say, "But I am not really a criminal." Such persons do not identify themselves with the ideal type. Two of the principal factors in the identification of self with ideal type are official treatment as a criminal and intimate personal association with those who conceive of themselves as criminals. The white collar criminal does not conceive of himself as a criminal because he is not dealt with under the same official procedures as other criminals and because, due to his class status, he does not engage in intimate personal association with those who define themselves as criminals.

Furthermore, many variations are found in the identification of self with others even among those who conceive of themselves as conforming to the ideal type of criminals. The word "criminal" may be applied to all of them, but the essence varies. Prisoners generally constitute a hierarchy, with high-class confidence men at the top at present and with the "yegg" or safe-breaker at the top in earlier generations. One of these classes of prisoners does not identify itself with the others and those in the upper criminal class look with contempt upon the lower criminal class. They place in the lower class of criminals the small number of businessmen who have been convicted and committed to prisons. The failure of the white collar criminal to identify himself with other criminals is in part an instance of the general process of stratification and segregation among criminals.

While white collar criminals do not conceive of themselves as conforming to the stereotype of "criminal," they do customarily think of themselves as "law violators." This is another aspect of a different word for the same essence. In their confidential relations businessmen speak with pride of their violations of law, and regard the enactment of the law rather than the violation as reprehensible. Their consciences do not ordinarily bother them, for they have the support of their associates in the violation of the law. The feeling of shame at their business practices is probably found more frequently among younger businessmen who have not thoroughly assimilated the culture and rationalizations of business. A radio announcer made the following statement of his disgust at the practices in which he participated:

> In order to hold my job I am compelled to make the most extravagant statements regarding cigarettes, toothpaste, toilet paper, cathartics, and other products which are on the program. I have to consider the various appeals and use the one which will produce the largest sales. After I have made my statement, I sometimes feel like going outside and vomiting or getting drunk, because I am so disgusted with the statements I am compelled to make.

The public, likewise, does not think of the businessman as a criminal; that is, the businessman does not fit the stereotype of criminal. This public conception is sometimes referred to as "status." Although the concept of "status" is not entirely clear it seems to be based principally upon power. The local community studies at least show that a person may have high status while being recognized as a profligate. Similarly, the businessman is often appraised lowly as to honesty, even while he has a high social status. Trade unions, farmers, and organized consumers are certainly not convinced that businessmen have high standards of honesty or that they are meticulous in the observance of law.

In order that businessmen may maintain their conceptions of themselves as not-criminal and their public status, public adherence to the law is necessary. The policy of corporations is general public adherence to the law and secret defections from the law. In this respect the businessman is quite different from the professional thief. In professional theft the fact of crime is a matter of direct observation, and the important problem for the thief is to conceal his identity in order to avoid punishment but not in order to maintain his status in the general public. In white collar crime, on the other hand, the important problem for the criminal is to conceal the fact of crime, since the identity of the firm which violates the law is generally known.

Secrecy regarding the fact of white collar crime is facilitated by intricacy of the processes and the wide scattering of effects in time and place. Consumers who are dissatisfied with the price of a commodity may not become aware for many years that the price is being manipulated by price agreements. Customers who read the claims presented on a label or in an advertisement may not become aware until scientific tests are made that the claims are fraudulent.

Businessmen develop rationalizations which are designed to conceal the fact of crime. Fraud in advertising is rationalized by the statement that every one puffs his wares. Businessmen fight whenever words that tend to break down this rationalization are used. A food manufacturer who had been ordered to desist from misrepresentations in his advertisements employed a chemist as adviser on proposed advertisements. This chemist described his experiences with his firm as follows:

> In my first associations with this firm I referred either by word of mouth or by letter to proposed statements as "dishonest" or "fraudulent." The manager of my department objected to my use of these words and ordered me to phrase my objections in other words, such as "It would not be good policy to make such claims," or "This claim does not agree with scientific findings."

With the same objective of protecting their reputations the business organizations have worked for a different implementation of the laws which apply to them. They do not want to be arrested by policemen, hauled before the criminal court, and convicted of crimes. Substitutes for these procedures have been found in orders to appear at a hearing, decisions by administrative commissions and cease and desist orders. The essential similarity between white collar crimes and other crimes has been partially concealed by this variation in procedure.

Secrecy regarding the violators of law is secured also by juggling corporate personality and brand names. This policy has the same function as the alias of the professional thief, namely, anonymity. The policy appears in at least three forms. First, a subsidiary of a corporation conceals its connection with that corporation. A cooperative plant which was purchased by a large meat-packing corporation continued to represent itself as a cooperative. An independent manufacturer of farm machinery was purchased by a near-monopolistic corporation but continued to represent itself as "independent" and as "fighting the trust." Clarence Dillon of Dillon Read and Company organized a dummy corporation by the name of Leonard Kennedy & Company and gave to this corporation at a considerable profit contracts with the firms which he was managing or advising. Associated Gas and Electric had most of the appraisals of its property made by Cheney, with the representation that Cheney was an independent appraiser when in fact Cheney was a partner of the manager of Associated Gas and Electric. Many corporations have organized dummy corporations for one or more of three purposes: to conceal transactions which would require payment of large income taxes, to increase the number of firms which may successively take profits, or to avoid laws which prohibit a corporation from owning more than a specified percentage of the stock of a public utility corporation. Second, corporations which are known to be subsidiaries are presented as distinct legal personalities. The objective in this case is to produce obfuscation as to responsibility. Electric Bond and Share has three subholding companies, each of which occupies the same offices as the parent company and has the same officers and directors. Each of these subholding companies, in turn, has regional companies subsidiary to it, with control over the operating companies in the region. Third, corporations juggle brand names as occasion requires. Some of the large dairy companies, while engaged in price wars, maintained the standard price for their milk under the regular brand name but sold the same milk under a different brand name at a lower price in order to meet the price of competitors. During World War II, when price ceilings were imposed on old brands, many corporations through subsidiaries not known to be connected with the parent company produced the old commodities with new brand names and claimed higher prices than the ceilings for the old brands.

With the objective of maintaining status and conception of self as noncriminal, the corporations employ experts in law, public relations, and advertising. These agencies are the corporate equivalent of the professional thief's "mouthpiece." The "mouthpiece" of the professional thief had as his principal function the defense of his client against specific charges. The function of the "mouth piece" of the white collar criminal is much more inclusive. He has the function of influencing the enactment and administration of the law as it applies to his clients, of advising his clients in advance as to the methods which may be used with relative impunity, as well as defending his clients before the courts and before the public when specific charges are made against them. Perhaps most important of all is the effort of the associations of businessmen to build up and maintain their status before the public. Cohen makes the following generalization which applies to such activities:

The efficiency with which a ruling class can secure popular recognition of their claims depends upon the popular stereotypes of that class. If ruling class membership suggests merit and ability entitling one to positions of public trust and authority, this recognition will be forthcoming. The ruling class will, accordingly, promote an ideology which incorporates such a stereotype, and will actually put some pressure on its members to conform, at least publicly, to the stereotype. If single members deviate grossly and publicly, conducting themselves in a manner "unbecoming a gentleman," such conduct reflects not only on the culprit but on the validity of the stereotype and thus threatens the standing of all who share his status and rule by virtue of the acceptance of that stereotype.[4]

The activities of Insull, Hopson, and others who committed gross violations of law were not so much offensive to the sentiments of businessmen as threats to the generalized and simplified stereotypes in terms of which the public evaluates businessmen as a group. This policy of condemning the gross violators of law, whose offenses have become publicly known, enables corporations to carry out a general attitude of public adherence to the law while they are engaged in secret defections from the law.

The characteristics of white collar crime, as they have been described above, depend to some extent on the corporate form of business organization. The statement is frequently made that big business is more legal and more honest than small business. No organized research has demonstrated the truth or falsity of this claim. Research on violations of price ceilings during World War II indicated but did not prove conclusively that no significant difference was found between large and small firms.[5] At any rate, the corporate form of organization which is generally used in big business has two advantages over other forms of organization from the point of view of violations of law: anonymity of persons so that the location of responsibility is impeded, and increased rationality in behavior.

The policies of a business which has corporate form are actions of a corporate unit. Responsibility is divided among directors, executives, subordinates, and stockholders. A director loses his personal identity in this corporate behavior and in this respect, but in no other respect, corporate behavior is like the behavior of a mob. Persons do not act in these situations as they would act if segregated from each other. This is true even when the corporation is essentially a dictatorship, like the American Sugar Refining Company under Insull, or Associated Gas and Electric under Hopson. The difficulty of locating responsibility and the resulting security to individuals are exemplified in the decision in the 6 percent case, in which General Motors Corporation was convicted of a crime but all of the directors and executives were acquitted: the corporation was guilty of a crime but no person directing the corporation was guilty of the crime.

The corporate form of business organization has, also, the advantage of increased rationality. The corporation probably comes closer to the "economic man" and to "pure reason" than any person or any other organization. The executives and directors not only have explicit and consistent objectives of maximum pecuniary gain but also have research and accountancy departments by which precise determination of results is facilitated and have discussions of policies by directors with diverse abilities and diverse interests so that the sentiments of one person are canceled by those of others. This general advantage does not deny the disadvantages of corporate organization. Two principal disadvantages have been pointed out in the literature. First, the directors do not necessarily have their attention fixed on the balance sheet of the corporation, but often engage in logrolling for personal advantages. Second, the corporation, like a government, tends to become bureaucratic with all of the limitations of bureaucratic organization.

The rationalistic, amoral, and nonsentimental behavior of the corporation was aimed in earlier days at technological efficiency; in later days more than previously it has been aimed at the manipulation of people by advertising, salesmanship, propaganda, and lobbies. With this recent development the corporation has developed a truly Machiavellian ideology and policy. It has reached the conclusion that practically anything is possible if resources, ingenuity, and strenuous effort are used. It has appropriated the physical and biological sciences and applied them to its objectives of technological efficiency and in the process has made significant contributions to those sciences. Similarly, it has appropriated the social and psychological sciences and applied them to the objective of manipulating people.

Three aspects of the rationality of the corporation in relation to illegal behavior may be mentioned. First, the corporation selects crimes which involve the smallest danger of detection and identification and against which victims are least likely to fight. The crimes of corporations are similar in this respect to professional thefts: both are carefully selected and both are similar to taking candy from a baby in that the victim is a weak antagonist. The advantage of selecting weak victims was stated explicitly by Daniel Drew in the decade of the eighties:

> I began to see that it is poor policy for big men in Wall Street to fight each other. When I am fighting a money-king, even my victories are dangerous. Take the present situation. I had scooped a fine profit out of the Erie deal and it was for the most part in solid cash. But— and here was the trouble—it had all come out of one man—Vanderbilt. Naturally it had left him very sore. And being so powerful, he was able to fight back. As has been seen, he did fight back. He had put me and my party to a lot of inconvenience. That always happens when you take money from a man on your own level. On the other hand, if I had taken these profits from outsiders, it would in the aggregate have amounted to the same sum, but the losers would have been scattered all over the country and so wouldn't have been able to get together and hit back. By making my money from people on the outside, an insider like myself could make just as much in the long run, and not raise up any one enemy powerful enough to cause him discomfort.[6]

The victims of corporate crimes are seldom in a position to fight against the management of the corporation. Consumers are scattered, unorganized, lacking in objective information as to qualities of commodities, and no one consumer suffers a loss in a particular transaction which would justify him in taking individual action. Stockholders seldom know the complex procedures of the corporations which they own, cannot attend annual meetings, and receive little information regarding the policies or the financial status of the corporation. Even if stockholders suspect illegal behavior by the management, they are scattered, unorganized, and frequently cannot even secure access to the names of other stockholders. In their conflicts with labor, the corporations have the advantage of a friendly press and of news commentators whose salaries are paid by business corporations, so that their unfair labor practices can be learned generally only by consulting official reports.

The ordinary case of embezzlement is a crime by a single individual in a subordinate position against a strong corporation. It is, therefore, one of the most foolish of the white collar crimes. The weakness of the embezzler, in comparison with the corporation, is illustrated in the case of J. W. Harriman. He was indicted for embezzlement in 1933 and later convicted. No criminal complaint was made against the banks which were accessory to this crime, and which were discovered in the investigation of this crime, namely, loans to one corporation in excess of the limit set by law, a pool formed by the officers of the bank to trade in the stock of the bank, concealment of the embezzlement by officers of the bank and of the clearing house, and refusal by many of the banks to meet the losses of Harriman's bank which they had agreed to do on condition that the embezzlement was concealed.

A second aspect of corporate rationality in relation to crime is the selection of crimes on which proof is difficult. In this respect, also, white collar crime is similar to professional theft. The selection of crimes on this basis is illustrated by advertising: since a little puffing is regarded as justifiable, the proof of unreasonable puffing is difficult. Again, a corporation organizes a company union under its own domination because proof that this is an unfair labor practice is difficult.

Third, the rational corporation adopts a policy of "fixing" cases. This is similar to the professional thief who maintains that if he has money and good standing with the "fixer" he can fix any case anywhere, since it is always possible to find a weak link in the chain of persons necessary for a conviction. The former officer of the federal Food and Drug Administration has described the pressures on that organization to prevent the execution of the law on particular offenders.[7] These pressures include threats by senators and congressmen that appropriations for the Food and Drug Administration will be cut unless charges against a constituent are withdrawn. When the Federal Trade Commission after the First World War was active in the enforcement of the law, representatives of large corporations went to the president of the United States, who replaced some of the commissioners with others who were more sympathetic with business practices; this resulted in the dismissal of complaints which had been made against many corporations. When minority stockholders bring suit against the management of the corporation, a customary procedure is to make a settlement. This is similar to the reimbursement by the professional thief of the victim of the theft in order to stop prosecution.

The "fixing" of white collar crimes, however, is much more inclusive than the fixing of professional thefts. The corporations attempt to prevent the implementation of the law and to create general goodwill, as well as deal with particular charges. An instance of this broader policy is by the fire insurance companies of Missouri, which had agreed to pay

Tom Pendergast a bribe of $750,000 to intervene in a rate case. Four of these companies which were proved to have paid shares of this bribe immediately appointed George Allen as vice-president. Allen was a person of great influence in Washington and his influence continued to increase. While Pendergast was promptly convicted and sentenced to prison, almost ten years elapsed before the fire insurance companies were convicted and their sentences were limited to fines.

The preceding analysis justifies the conclusion that the violations of law by corporations are deliberate and organized crimes. This does not mean that corporations never violate the law inadvertently and in an unorganized manner. It does mean that a substantial portion of their violations are deliberate and organized.

15

A THEORY OF WHITE COLLAR CRIME

A complete explanation of white collar crime cannot be derived from the available data. The data which are available suggest that white collar crime has its genesis in the same general process as other criminal behavior, namely, differential association. The hypothesis of differential association is that criminal behavior is learned in association with those who define such criminal behavior favorably and in isolation from those who define it unfavorably, and that a person in an appropriate situation engages in such criminal behavior if, and only if, the weight of the favorable definitions exceeds the weight of the unfavorable definitions. This hypothesis is certainly not a complete or universal explanation of white collar crime or of other crime, but it perhaps fits the data of both types of crimes better than any other general hypothesis.

This hypothesis or other hypotheses can be tested adequately only by research studies organized specifically for this purpose and by firsthand acquaintance with the careers of businessmen. In the absence of such studies, it is necessary for the present to fall back upon data now available. The available data provide two types of documentary evidence, namely, biographical or autobiographical descriptions of the careers of businessmen and descriptions of the diffusion of criminal practices from one situation to another. These two types of evidence will be illustrated in the following paragraphs.

Personal Documents

A young businessman in the used-car business in Chicago described the process by which he was inducted into illegal behavior.

When I graduated from college I had plenty of ideals of honesty, fair play, and cooperation which I had acquired at home, in school,

and from literature. My first job after graduation was se
writers. During the first day I learned that these machine
sold at a uniform price but that a person who higgled
could get a machine at about half the list price. I felt th
unfair to the customer who paid the list price. The othe. ___
laughed at me and could not understand my silly attitude. They told
me to forget the things I had learned in school, and that you
couldn't earn a pile of money by being strictly honest. When I replied that money wasn't everything they mocked at me, "Oh! No?
Well, it helps." I had ideals and I resigned.

My next job was selling sewing machines. I was informed that
one machine, which cost the company $18, was to be sold for $40
and another machine, which cost the company $19, was to be sold
for $70, and that I was to sell the de luxe model whenever possible
in preference to the cheaper model, and was given a list of the reasons why it was a better buy. When I told the sales manager that the
business was dishonest and that I was quitting right then, he looked
at me as if he thought I was crazy and said angrily, "There's not a
cleaner business in the country."

It was quite a time before I could find another job. During this
time I occasionally met some of my classmates and they related experiences similar to mine. They said they would starve if they were
rigidly honest. All of them had girls and were looking forward to
marriage and a comfortable standard of living, and they said they
did not see how they could afford to be rigidly honest. My own feelings became less determined than they had been when I quit my
first job.

Then I got an opportunity in the used-car business. I learned that
this business had more tricks for fleecing customers than either of
those I had tried previously. Cars with cracked cylinders, with half
the teeth missing from the fly wheel, with everything wrong, were
sold as "guaranteed." When the customer returned and demanded
his guarantee, he had to sue to get it and very few went to that
trouble and expense: the boss said you could depend on human nature. If hot cars could be taken in and sold safely, the boss did not
hesitate. When I learned these things I did not quit as I had previously. I sometimes felt disgusted and wanted to quit, but I argued
that I did not have much chance to find a legitimate firm. I knew
that the game was rotten but it had to be played—the law of the

jungle and that sort of thing. I knew that I was dishonest and to that extent felt that I was more honest than my fellows. The thing that struck me as strange was that all these people were proud of their ability to fleece customers. They boasted of their crookedness and were admired by their friends and enemies in proportion to their ability to get away with a crooked deal: it was called shrewdness. Another thing was that these people were unanimous in their denunciation of gangsters, robbers, burglars, and petty thieves. They never regarded themselves as in the same class and were bitterly indignant if accused of dishonesty: it was just good business.

Once in awhile, as the years have passed, I have thought of myself as I was in college—idealistic, honest and thoughtful of others—and have been momentarily ashamed of myself. Before long such memories became less and less frequent and it became difficult to distinguish me from my fellows. If you had accused me of dishonesty, I would have denied the charge, but with slightly less vehemence than my fellow business men, for after all I had learned a different code of behavior.

A graduate student in an urban university, in order to supplement his income, took a job as an extra salesman in a shoe shore on Saturdays and other rush days. He had no previous experience as a shoe salesman or in any other regular business. He described his experience in this store as follows:

One day I was standing in the front part of the store, waiting for the next customers. A man came in and asked if we had any high, tan, button shoes. I told him that we had no shoes of that style. He thanked me and walked out of the store. The floor-walker came up to me and asked me what the man wanted. I told him what the man asked for and what I replied. The floor-walker said angrily, "Damn it! We're not here to sell what they want. We're here to sell what we've got." He went on to instruct me that when a customer came into the store the first thing to do was to get him to sit down and to take off his shoe so that he couldn't get out of the store. "If we don't have what he wants," he said, "bring him something else and try to interest him in that style. If he is still uninterested, inform the floor-walker and he will send one of the regular salesmen, and if that doesn't work, a third salesman will be sent to him. Our policy is that no customer gets out of the store until at least three salesmen have worked on him. By that time the customer feels that he must be a crank and he will generally buy something whether he wants it or not."

I learned from other clerks that if a customer needed a 7-B shoe and we did not have that size in the style he desired, I should try on an 8-A or 7-C or some other size. The sizes were marked in code so that the customer did not know what the size was, and it might be necessary to lie to him about the size; also his foot might be injured by the misfit. But the rule was to sell him a pair of shoes, preferably a pair that fit but some other pair if necessary.

I learned, also, that the clerks received an extra commission if they sold the out-of-style shoes left over from earlier seasons, which were called "spiffs." The regular salesmen made a practice of selling spiffs to anyone who appeared gullible and generally had to claim either that this was the latest style or that it had been the style earlier and was coming back this season, or that it was an old style but much better quality than present styles. The clerk had to size up the customer and determine which one of these lies would be most likely to result in a sale.

Several years later I became acquainted with a man who had worked for several years as a regular salesman in shoe stores in Seattle. When I described to him the methods I had learned in the shoe store where I worked, he said, "Every shoe store in Seattle except one does exactly the same things and I learned to be a shoe salesman in exactly the same manner you did."

Another young man who was holding his first position as a shoe salesman in a small city wrote an autobiographical statement in which he included the following statement made to him by the manager of the store:

My job is to move out shoes and I hire you to assist in this. I am perfectly glad to fit a person with a pair of shoes if we have his size, but I am willing to mis-fit him if it is necessary in order to sell him a pair of shoes. I expect you to do the same. If you do not like this, some one else can have your job. While you are working for me, I expect you to have no scruples about how you sell shoes.

A man who had been a schoolteacher and had never been officially involved in any delinquencies secured a position as agent of a book publishing company and was assigned to public school work. He soon

learned that the publishing companies bribed the members of the textbook committees in order to secure adoptions of their books. With considerable shame he began to use the same method of bribery because he
felt it was necessary in order to make a good record. Partly because he
disliked this procedure but principally because this work kept him away
from home much of the time, he decided that he would become a lawyer. He moved to a large city, registered for night courses in a law
school, and secured a daytime job as a claim agent for a casualty insurance company. About two years later he was convicted of embezzling
the funds of the insurance company. A portion of his autobiography describes the process by which he got into this difficulty.

> Almost immediately after I got into this business I learned two
> things: first, the agents who got ahead with the company were the
> ones who make settlements at low figures and without taking cases
> into court; second, the settlements were generally made by collu-
> sion with the lawyers and doctors for the claimants. Most of the law-
> yers for the claimants were ambulance-chasers and were willing to
> make settlements because they got their fees without any work.
> The claim agent for the insurance company got a secret kick-back
> out of the settlement. When I learned that this was the way to get
> ahead in the casualty insurance business, I went in for it in a big
> way. Accidentally I left some papers loose in my office, from which it
> was discovered that I was "knocking down" on the settlements. The
> insurance company accused me of taking money which belonged to
> them, but actually I was taking money which belonged to the claim-
> ants.

The following statement was made by a young man who had graduated from a recognized school of business, had become a certified public accountant, and had been employed for several years in a respected
firm of public accountants in a large city.

> While I was a student in the school of business I learned the
> principles of accounting. After I had worked for a time for an ac-
> counting firm I found that I had failed to learn many important
> things about accounting. An accounting firm gets its work from
> business firms and, within limits, must make the reports which
> those business firms desire. The accounting firm for which I work is
> respected and there is none better in the city. On my first assign-

ment I discovered some irregularities in the books of the firm and these would lead anyone to question the financial policies of that firm. When I showed my report to the manager of our accounting firm, he said that was not a part of my assignment and I should leave it out. Although I was confident that the business firm was dishonest, I had to conceal this information. Again and again I have been compelled to do the same thing in other assignments. I get so disgusted with things of this sort that I wish I could leave the profession. I guess I must stick to it, for it is the only occupation for which I have training.

The documents presented above were written by persons who came from "good homes" and "good neighborhoods" and who had no official records as juvenile delinquents. White collar criminals, like professional thieves, are seldom recruited from juvenile delinquents. As a part of the process of learning practical business, a young man with idealism and thoughtfulness for others is inducted into white collar crime. In many cases he is ordered by managers to do things which he regards as unethical or illegal, while in other cases he learns from those who have the same rank as his own how they make a success. He learns specific techniques of violating the law, together with definitions of situations in which those techniques may be used. Also, he develops a general ideology. This ideology grows in part out of the specific practices and is in the nature of generalization from concrete experiences, but in part it is transmitted as a generalization by phrases such as "We are not in business for our health," "Business is business," and "No business was ever built on the beatitudes." These generalizations, whether transmitted as such or constructed from concrete practices, assist the neophyte in business to accept the illegal practices and provide rationalizations for them.

All the preceding documents came from young men in subordinate positions and are in no sense a random sample of persons in such positions. Unfortunately, similar documents even of a scattered nature are not available for the managers of large industries. No firsthand research study from this point of view has ever been reported. Gustavus Meyer in his *History of American Fortunes,* and Lundberg in his *America's Sixty Families* have demonstrated that many of the large American fortunes originated in illegal practices. On the other hand, they pay little attention to the process by which illegal behavior develops in the person. Bits of information may be gleaned from biographies of men like Ar-

mour, DuPont, Eastman, Firestone, Ford, Gary, Guggenheim, Havemeyer, McCormick, Marshall Field, Mellon, Morgan, Rockefeller, Seiberling, Swift, Woolworth, and others. Many of the biographies are sub-
scription books written on order of the businessmen for advertising
purposes; criminal behavior is seldom admitted and never explained.
Bouck White's *The Book of Daniel Drew* is a forthright description of an
actual person but is classed in the *Dictionary of American Biography* as
semifiction.

One illustration of the types of materials which may be found in the
biographies of managers of industry will be presented, as evidence of the
process of differential association. Coleman DuPont, after being inducted into the methods used in the public utilities, including an immense inflation of capital, returned to the powder industry, and with
two cousins changed the simple financial structure of the DuPont company into an intricate financial structure with $50 million capital with
the expenditure of a few thousand dollars in cash.[1]

Diffusion of Illegal Practices

The diffusion of illegal practices is the second type of evidence that
white collar crime is due to differential association. Business firms have
the objective of maximum profits. When one firm devises a method for
increasing profits, other firms become aware of the method and adopt it,
perhaps a little more quickly and a little more generally if the firms are
competitors in the same market than if they are not competitors. The
diffusion of illegal practices which increase profits is facilitated by the
trend toward centralization of the control of industry by investment
banks and by the conferences of business concerns in trade associations. The process of diffusion will be considered first in relation to competition, and subsequently with reference to other relations.

The diffusion of illegal practices among competitors is illustrated in
the following incident in a food manufacturing concern. A chemist who
had been employed to advise this firm as to the scientific basis for claims
in advertising made the following statement regarding his experiences
with the firm.

> When I got members of the firm off in a corner and we were talking
> confidentially, they frankly deplored the misrepresentations in their
> advertisements. At the same time they said it was necessary to ad-
> vertise in this manner in order to attract the attention of customers

and sell their products. Since other firms were making extravagant statements regarding their products, we must make extravagant statements regarding our products. A mere statement of fact regarding our products would make no impression on customers in the face of the ads of other firms.

A few other illustrations of the diffusion of illegal claims in advertising will be given. These are all described in greater detail in the preceding chapters of this book. General Motors devised the fraudulent advertisement of its interest rate on installment purchases at 6 percent, when in fact the rate was more than 11 percent. The other automobile companies also had interest rates of about 11 percent, but they advertised their interest rate as 6 percent as soon as General Motors began to do so. Again, when one automobile company published an advertisement of the price and specifications of a certain model, together with a picture of a more expensive model, thus misrepresenting their products, the other companies in the automobile industry generally published similar advertisements with similar misrepresentations. Within a few months after the tire dealers had solemnly adopted a code of ethics in advertising, including a pledge not to use misrepresentations, one tire manufacturer announced a special cut-rate price for tires on the Fourth of July and Labor Day, in which the savings were grossly and fraudulently misrepresented; the other tire manufacturers promptly made similar announcements of cut-rate sales with similar misrepresentations.

Thus competition in advertising drives the participants to the extremes and when one corporation violates the law in this respect other corporations do likewise.

Practices in restraint of trade are similarly diffused. A detailed description has been given of the conspiracy in restraint of trade between Goodyear and Sears Roebuck and of the diffusion of the same conspiracy among other rubber manufacturers.[2] More frequently practices in restraint of trade are diffused by conferences and agreements among competitors. Sometimes definite coercion is employed in forcing competitors into illegal practices in restraint of trade. This is illustrated by the case in which the Aluminum Company of America, after failing to persuade the Dow Chemical Company to enter into an illegal agreement regarding magnesium, initiated an infringement suit against the latter company; this suit was withdrawn as soon as Dow Chemical Company agreed to enter into the illegal conspiracy.[3]

Illegal practices are diffused, also, when competition is not involved.

This will be illustrated by the diffusion of misrepresentations in regard to the quality of gas sold by public utility corporations. The heating value of gas is customarily measured in terms of British thermal units, or BTUs. A BTU is the amount of heat that will raise the temperature of 1 pound of water 1 degree under standardized conditions. Until 1921 the Public Service Company of Colorado, a subsidiary of Cities Service, furnished gas in Denver with 600 BTUs. In that year this company secretly reduced the heating value of the gas, without reducing the price, until it had only 400 BTUs. The company made a statement to the Colorado state commission that the experiment demonstrated that families consumed no more gas with the reduction of BTUs, and asked for authorization to adopt such heating values as they found to be most economical and efficient. This request was granted without an inspection of the detailed evidence and without a consultation with other authorities. This practice of reduction of BTUs, with the accompanying argument, then spread to other gas companies. In June 1924 the executive committee of the American Gas Association adopted a resolution that, since the Denver experiment showed no decrease in efficiency with the reduction of BTUs, the state utility commissions should generally authorize the reduction of BTUs to as low as 300 without change in rates. In 1925 the Spokane Gas and Fuel Company requested authorization to reduce their gas to 450 BTUs, giving as supporting evidence the testimony of the Public Service Company of Colorado that the consumption of gas had not increased when BTUs were reduced, and with the further explanation that Alabama had adopted this standard and Illinois was considering it. The state commission of Washington, with no conflicting evidence available, granted the request. In May 1926 the Iowa Committee on Public Utilities published a pamphlet for use in the public schools which contained the statement: "Government research has shown that the lower British Thermal Unit produces the same results in practical operation and can be much more economically manufactured." In the meantime the Bureau of Standards of the United States had been collecting evidence on this topic. In 1925 it wrote a report to the effect that the efficiency of gas for heating purposes was directly proportional to the BTUs and that a decrease in BTUs was equivalent to an increase in price. This government report was discussed in 1924, before publication, with the members of the American Gas Association. The president of this association wrote to the director of the Bureau of Standards: "Many members of the Gas Association would not want to send out a report that would indicate that the charge for gas should be inversely proportional to the calorific value of gas." Gordon King, a service engineer of the Gas Association, stated: "The more I study this (government) document the less value or good to any one I see in it, and if it were possible I believe it should be suppressed." The Bureau of Standards in 1926 asked permission to examine the data on which the Public Service Company of Colorado based their conclusions, but this request was refused. A paper on this subject was written by a gas engineer for the Bureau of Standards which dealt specifically with the Denver situation. This paper was submitted to the Public Service Company of Colorado for criticisms. The officers of this corporation wrote to the officers of the National Electric Light Association, who wrote a personal letter to Paul S. Clapp, assistant to Secretary Hoover of the Department of Commerce, urging that the Secretary prohibit publication. Although consent to publish the paper was given to the author, both the *Gas Age Record* and the *American Gas Journal,* which had given space to the Denver claims, refused to publish this paper. It was not published anywhere until placed in evidence in 1935 by the Federal Trade Commission. This paper stated that the Public Service Company of Colorado had refused to make available the data on which they based claims that reduction of BTUs did not increase consumption of gas, that the evidence of the Bureau of Standards demonstrated the exact opposite of this, and that if the policy used in Denver were extended to the United States consumers would pay $490 million a year more for their gas. In 1927 the directors of the American Gas Association informed the Bureau of Standards that they did not approve of a reinvestigation of this question. In July 1928 the Association issued a newsletter to the effect that the Illinois Commerce Commission had conducted an investigation which sustained the Denver conclusions. The Bureau of Standards appraised this Illinois survey, which was made under conditions very favorable to the gas companies, as "a beautiful demonstration of an almost exact inverse proportion between the heating value and the volume of gas demanded by domestic consumers." The continued diffusion of these claims which the Bureau of Standards held to be misrepresentation was stopped by the trend toward natural gas; in fact with the new developments, the gas companies have tended to reverse the position which they had taken during the decade of the twenties. The misrepresentation stopped as soon as it ceased to have economic value to the gas companies.[4]

Other illustrations of the diffusion of criminal practices are found in the customer-ownership campaigns of utility companies and in the sales quota system of many manufacturing companies. It is not necessary to describe the details of these practices or of their diffusion. These practices are not in themselves criminal, but they have been used so frequently for fraudulent purposes that their significance is practically comparable to that of the burglar's "jimmy."[5]

Not only do specific practices become diffused but also more general attitudes or mental sets are diffused. This is illustrated in the following statement by Daniel Drew:

> With this panic year of which I am now writing (1857) a new state of affairs came about in financial circles. The panic was known as the "Western Blizzard." It put old fogeyism out of date forevermore. The men who conducted business in the old-fashioned slow-poke method—the think-of-the-other-fellow method—were swept away by this panic, or at least were so crippled up that they didn't figure much in the world of affairs afterwards. A new generation of men came in—a more pushful set. I was one of them. We were men who went ahead. We did things. We didn't split hairs about trifles. Anyhow, men of this skin, with a conscience all the time full of prickles, are out of place in business dickerings. A prickly conscience would be like a white silk apron for a blacksmith. Sometimes you've got to get your hands dirty, but that doesn't mean that the money you make is also dirty. Black hens can lay white eggs. . . . It isn't how you get your money but what you do with it that counts.[6]

Isolation

Businessmen are not only in contact with definitions which are favorable to white collar crime but also they are isolated from and protected against definitions which are unfavorable to such crime. Most of them, to be sure, were reared in homes in which honesty was defined as a virtue, but these home teachings have little explicit relation to business methods. The persons who define business practices as undesirable and illegal are customarily called "communists" or "socialists" and their definitions carry little weight.

The public agencies of communication, which continually define ordinary violations of the criminal code in a very critical manner, do not make similar definitions of white collar crime. Several reasons for this difference may be mentioned. The important newspapers, the motion picture corporations, and the radio corporations are all large capitalistic enterprises and the persons who own and manage them have the same standards as the persons who manage other corporations. These agencies derive their principal income from advertisements by other business corporations and would be likely to lose a considerable part of this income if they were critical of business practices in general or of particular corporations. Finally, these public agencies of communication themselves participate in white collar crimes and especially in restraint of trade, misrepresentation in advertising, and unfair labor practices.

Businessmen are shielded against harsh criticisms by persons in governmental positions. Congress provided special implementation of the Sherman Antitrust Act and of many subsequent laws so that the stigma of crime would not be attached to businessmen who violated these laws. This special implementation is almost if not wholly an exclusive feature of the laws which apply to businessmen. Moreover, the administrators select the less critical procedures in dealing with businessmen. They generally select equity procedures for businessmen accused of restraint of trade, and criminal procedures for trade unionists accused of restraint of trade.[7]

The less critical attitude of government toward businessmen than toward persons of lower socioeconomic class is the result of several relationships. (a) Persons in government are, by and large, culturally homogeneous with persons in business, both being in the upper strata of American society. (b) Many persons in government are members of families which have other members in business. (c) Many persons in business are intimate personal friends of persons in government. Almost every important person in government has many close personal friends in business, and almost every important person in business has many close personal friends in government. (d) Many persons in government were previously connected with business firms as executives, attorneys, directors, or in other capacities. In times of war, especially, many persons in government retain their business connections. (e) Many persons in government hope to secure employment in business firms when their government work is terminated. Government work is often a step toward a career in private business. Relations established while in government, as well as inside information acquired at that time, carry over after the person joins a business firm. (f) Business is very powerful in American society and can damage or promote the governmental programs in which the governmental personnel are interested. (g) The program of the government is closely related to the political parties, and for their success in campaigns these political parties depend on contributions of large sums from important businessmen. Thus, the initial cultural homogeneity, the close personal relationships, and the power relationships protect businessmen against critical definitions by government.

The United States Steel Corporation, organized in 1900 by J. P. Morgan after he had directed the combinations of many of the constituent parts, was the largest merger that had occurred in American industry. This merger was protected against prosecution under the antitrust law for many years. Amos Pinchot described some of the connections between this corporation and the government which assisted in shielding the corporation, and many additional connections could be discovered by a thorough search of the directories of corporations.

Philander C. Knox, former counsel for the Carnegie Steel Company and close personal friend of U.S. Steel director Henry Clay Frick, was U.S. Attorney-General when the company was formed. Steel was well represented in high places throughout the administrations of Theodore Roosevelt and W. H. Taft. Elihu Root, former attorney for the Carnegie Steel Company, was Secretary of State under Roosevelt and was succeeded by Knox, while Knox was replaced as Attorney-General by George F. Wickersham, formerly attorney for the U.S. Steel Corporation. Truman Newberry, president of a subsidiary of U.S. Steel, was Secretary of the Navy, an important post in steel politics. Herbert Saterlee, son-in-law of J. P. Morgan, was assistant secretary of the Navy. Robert Bacon, a partner of J. P. Morgan and a director of U.S. Steel, was for a time Secretary of State.[8]

Although the Aluminum Company of America had the most complete monopoly of any corporation in the United States and for several decades ruthlessly stamped out all competitors, the many complaints did not result in effective suits against this corporation. The principal power in this corporation was Andrew Mellon, who was an extremely important member of the Republican Party and a Secretary of the Treasury: it has been said that three presidents served under him. When the Democrats came into power in 1932, this corporation was not left without influence in the federal government. Oscar Ewing, who had been counsel for the Aluminum Company for many years, had been treasurer of the Democratic Party and was at the time a vice-president of this party. It was understood prior to the death of President Roosevelt that Ewing was to be appointed Solicitor General of the United States. That plan did not materialize, perhaps because Truman, as a member of a Senate Committee, had been extremely critical of the contracts secured by the Aluminum Company for the production of war materials. Other important persons were ready to assist this corporation to maintain its monopolistic position, despite the fact that it had been convicted of participating in cartels which were a serious handicap to the efficiency of the United States in its preparation for war. The Reynolds Metal Company had developed in this emergency period to assist in the production of aluminum but great pressure was placed on the administration to restrict the sale of public power to the Aluminum Company of America. Secretary Ickes testified that Averell Harriman, Robert R. Patterson, William S. Knudsen, and others appealed to him not to sell Bonneville power to the Reynolds Metal Company, although the Bonneville Act prohibited sale of this power under conditions which would tend to create a monopoly.[9]

Harold Judson was appointed assistant solicitor general of the United States and in that capacity had the duty, among others, of representing the government in suits regarding the submerged oil lands of California. Judson had been an attorney for the oil companies of California and he appeared on the record as contributing $380,500 in the California campaign of 1939. When an inquiry was made regarding this, he testified that he had not contributed any of that amount himself but all of it for oil companies in California. Although the law requires that the names of all persons making contributions either directly or indirectly be listed, Judson's name was the only one that appeared. He retained his position despite this evidence.[10]

The businessman who has probably had the most extensive connections with government is Victor Emanuel. He is or has been the controlling power in Standard Gas and Electric, American Aviation, Consolidated Vultee, Station WLW in Cincinnati, Republic Steel, and other corporations. He has been affiliated, also, with a banking firm which has been reported to have connections with I. G. Farben under the Nazi regime. After Pearl Harbor, General Aniline and Film, the principal American subsidiary of I. G. Farben, was indicted for a cartel in war materials. The German-owned patents of that corporation were seized by the Alien Property Custodian, as were other German-owned patents. The Alien Property Custodian at that time was Leo Crowley, who was also chairman of Standard Gas and Electric. In a conference of federal

departments the recommendation was made that all German-owned patents be made freely available to American industry. This recommendation was unanimously approved by all participants in the conference except James E. Markham, who had become Alien Property Custodian and
who was a director of Standard Gas and Electric, in which Emanuel was
a powerful influence. Markham appealed to George Allen, an influential
person in Washington, to oppose the recommendation of this interde-
partmental committee, and Allen also was a director of several of Emanuel's corporations. Also, Crowley, as chairman of the Export-Import
Bank, lent 14 percent of that bank's capital to the International Telephone and Telegraph Company, in which Emanuel's banking affiliate
was interested.

In some cases persons have been nominated for important positions
in the government but have not been appointed when their business
connections were discovered. Charles Beecher Warren was nominated
for the position of Attorney General of the United States in 1925, in
which position he would control prosecutions under the antitrust law. It
was revealed in Congressional hearings that Warren had been indicted
(but not convicted) in 1910, along with the American Sugar Refining
Company, that he had been an attorney for the American Sugar Refining Company, which was convicted on several occasions of violations of
the antitrust law, and that he had acted as an agent of that corporation
from 1906 to 1925 in purchasing the stock of competing sugar corporations. His nomination was not confirmed. Also, Edwin Pauley was
nominated in 1946 for the position of Undersecretary of the Navy, which
had jurisdiction over the oil reserves. Pauley had been engaged in the oil
industry in California and had worked strenuously in opposition to the
United States in the suits regarding submerged oil lands. He was treasurer of the Democratic Party. Secretary Ickes testified that Pauley had
promised that $300,000 would be contributed to the campaign by Cali-
fornia oil men if the government dropped the suit on submerged oil
lands. Because of the publicity, Pauley's name was withdrawn.

Although some individuals may be sacrificed, those of greater power
are protected. Richard Whitney, president of the New York Stock Exchange, was indicted on March 12, 1938, for stealing securities from
trust funds of the Exchange, and was committed to prison on April 12,
1938. Subsequent investigations revealed that this crime was known
three months before the indictment to other officers of the Exchange
and to two partners of J. P. Morgan. At that earlier date Whitney made

restitution to the trust funds by borrowing more than a million dollars from his brother, who was a partner of J. P. Morgan, and his brother, in turn, borrowed most of this amount from another partner, both knowing that this loan was for the purpose of restoring to the trust funds the securities which had been stolen. The New York statutes define the concealment of such knowledge as a felony. The prosecutors in the case knew that restitution had been made but made no inquiry as to the source of funds used in the restitution or as to financiers who might have been accessory to this act. Also, the New York Stock Exchange, presumably with the hope of restoring public confidence, appointed Robert M. Hutchins, president of the University of Chicago, as a public representative on the Board of Governors of the Exchange. Within a short time Hutchins resigned from this board with the public explanation that he did so because the Board of Governors refused to assist in the search for others who were implicated in the Whitney crime.[11]

Social Disorganization

Differential association is a hypothetical explanation of crime from the point of view of the process by which a person is initiated into crime. Social disorganization is a hypothetical explanation of crime from the point of view of the society. These two hypotheses are consistent with each other and one is the counterpart of the other. Both apply to ordinary crime as well as to white collar crime.

Social disorganization may be either of two types: anomie, or the lack of standards which direct the behavior of members of a society in general or in specific areas of behavior; or the organization within a society of groups which are in conflict with reference to specified practices. Briefly stated, social disorganization may appear in the form of lack of standards or conflict of standards.

Two conditions are favorable to disorganization of our society in the control of business behavior: first, the fact that the behavior is complex, technical, and not readily observable by inexperienced citizens; second, the fact that the society is changing rapidly in its business relations. In any period of rapid change, old standards tend to break down and a period of time is required for the development of new standards.

The anomie form of social disorganization is related to the change from the earlier system of free competition and free enterprise to the developing system of private collectivism and governmental regulation of business. The tradition has been that a government should not intervene in the regulation of business but that free competition and supply and demand should regulate economic processes. This tradition was generally held by the people of the United States in the earlier period. While that tradition has been largely abandoned in practice, it retains great force as an ideology, which has been designated "the folklore of capitalism." In practice businessmen are more devoted than any other part of current society to the policy of social planning. This is social planning in the interest of businessmen. Social planning for the more inclusive society is criticized by businessmen as "regimentation," "bureaucracy," "visionary," and "communistic." In this transition from one social system toward a different social system, anomie has existed in two forms. First, the businessmen passed through a period of uncertainty and conflict of standards. They were dissatisfied with the system of free competition and free enterprise and had no substitute on which they could reach consensus. This period cannot be sharply limited but is located within the three to six decades after the Civil War. Second, the general public has passed or is passing through the same uncertainty and conflict of standards, starting at a later period than the businessmen did and continuing after businessmen had reached a new general consensus.

Conflict of standards is the second form of social disorganization. This is similar to differential association in that it involves a ratio between organization favorable to violations of law and organization rather than social disorganization. Business has a rather tight organization for the violation of business regulations while the political society is not similarly organized against violations of business regulations.

Evidence has been presented in previous chapters that crimes of business are organized crimes. This evidence includes references not only to gentlemen's agreements, pools, trade associations, patent agreements, cartels, conferences, and other informal understandings, but also to the tentacles which business throws out into the government and the public for the control of those portions of the society. The definition of specified acts as illegal is a prerequisite to white collar crime, and to that extent the political society is necessarily organized against white collar crime. The statutes, however, have little importance in the control of business behavior unless they are supported by an administration which is intent on stopping the illegal behavior. In turn the political administration has little force in stopping such behavior unless it is supported by a public which is intent on the enforcement of the law. This calls for a clear-cut opposition between the public and the government, on the one side, and the businessmen who violate the law, on the other. This clear-cut opposition does not exist and the absence of this opposition is evidence of the lack of organization against white collar crime. What is, in theory, a war loses much of its conflict because of the fraternization between the two forces. White collar crimes continue because of this lack of organization on the part of the public.

The explanation of crime in general in terms of social disorganization has been at the focus of attention of many criminologists for at least a generation. This has not proved to be a very useful hypothesis up to the present time. A precise definition of social disorganization has been lacking, and the concept has often included ethical implications which interfered with its utility as an analytical concept. Also, this hypothesis cannot be tested for validity. Finally, it does not explain the content of the criminal behavior or the reasons for the conflicts of standards; the hypothesis points to and describes the conflicts of standards but provides no explanation of the genesis of the conflicts.

16

VARIATIONS IN THE CRIMES OF CORPORATIONS

The suggestion is frequently made that crime must be explained by the psychological characteristics of the offenders. Explanations of crime by psychological characteristics have a long and varied history. One school of thought has placed the emphasis on physical deviations from type, another on lack of intelligence, and a third on emotional disturbances. All of these schools use the same logic and differ only in the characteristics which they believe to be important in the causation of criminal behavior. As research work on each of these types of characteristics has continued, the difference between criminals and noncriminals in respect to that characteristic has proved to be insignificant and inconsistent. The current tendency is to advocate emotional instability as the psychological characteristic which explains ordinary criminal behavior, and this explanation has been presented particularly by psychiatrists and psychoanalysts. Even these advocates, however, would suggest only in a jocular sense that the crimes of the Ford Motor Company are due to the Oedipus complex, or those of the Aluminum Company of America to an inferiority complex, or those of U.S. Steel to frustration and aggression, or those of the DuPonts to traumatic experience, or those of Montgomery Ward to regression to infancy. Some analogical support might be found in the last-mentioned case from the fact that the chief executive of that corporation was carried from his office in the arms of the agents of parental authority.

If personal characteristics play an important part in the causation of white collar crimes, they should appear especially in the variations among the corporations in their frequency of violations of laws. These 70 corporations do vary widely in the number of decisions against them and have a range of 1 to 50 adverse decisions. Also, some of these corporations have violated one law and none of the other laws, while other corporations have violated all of the laws which have been considered.

These variations in the number of decisions seem to be due to four types of factors, namely, age of the corporation, size of the corporation, position of the corporation in the economic structure, and personal traits of the executives of the corporations.

First, since the number of decisions covers the lifespan of the corporations, variations in the ages of corporations may account for some of the variations in the number of decisions. Some of the corporations are only 18 years of age, while others are nearly 150 years of age. These variations in age, however, seem to be of slight importance in explaining variations among the corporations. Most of the decisions were rendered in the last fifteen years and very few indeed more than thirty years ago. The rank order of the corporations would remain generally the same if the period within which decisions were enumerated were restricted to the last eighteen years although a few corporations would change positions to a very great extent.

Second, variations in the number of decisions per corporation are related to the size of the corporations. The larger corporations generally have more subsidiaries and more specialized divisions than the smaller corporations and each of these subsidiaries and divisions may become involved with the law. In the list of the 70 large corporations the 15 which have the largest assets have twice as many adverse decisions as the 15 smallest corporations. However, some small corporations in this list have as many adverse decisions as some larger corporations and the coefficient or correlation between size and number of decisions is not large enough to be statistically significant. Here again, however, this variation in size is important in some cases.

Third, position in the economic structure has great significance in the variations among the corporations as to the number of violations of law. While the range of decisions against the 70 corporations is 1 to 50, the corporations in one industry are not scattered evenly over this range but tend to cluster at certain points. Of the three motion picture corporations in the list of 70 large corporations, Loew's has 31 adverse decisions, and Paramount and Warner 25 each. The two dairy companies—Borden and National Dairy Products—tie with 12 decisions each. Sears Roebuck and Montgomery Ward tie with 39 adverse decisions each. Of the four rubber companies, Goodrich has 7, Firestone 8, U.S. Rubber 10, and Goodyear 14 adverse decisions. When industries show a wider range of decisions, this may generally be explained by differences in the age and size of the corporations. Among the meat packers, Armour and

Swift tie with 50 adverse decisions, while Wilson has only 19. The smaller number of decisions against Wilson is explained principally by the fact that it does not engage in several branches of the industry, e.g., dairy products, in which the other meat packers have a large number of decisions. Again, U.S. Steel has 26 adverse decisions, while the nine other steel corporations range between 5 and 14. This is explained by the fact that U.S. Steel has a wider range of specialties than any of the other steel corporations and also by the fact that decisions have been made against U.S. Steel as the dominant corporation in the industry for practices in which the other steel companies participated, even though they were not named in the complaints or decisions.

The position of a corporation in the economic structure affects its crime rate in comparison with other corporations in one or both of two ways. First, position in the economic structure determines in a gross sense the opportunity and need for violation of the law. This proposition is illustrated by the fact that U.S. Steel and General Motors have no adverse decisions under the Pure Food and Drug Law, while Armour and Swift have many such decisions. A corporation does not search for opportunities to violate any law whatever. Rather it is carrying on certain activities for the purpose of profits and finds itself impeded by a specific law and it violates that law. This will be illustrated by a brief elaboration of several of the laws which are included in this study.

The violations of the antitrust laws are affected by the economic positions of the several corporations. Economists have defined the conditions which facilitate monopoly price as including, among other things, a large capital investment or other conditions which impede the entrance of new competitors into the industry. The significance of this is seen in the difference between the mercantile corporations on the one hand, and the manufacturing and mining corporations, on the other hand, as to violations of the antitrust law. The mercantile corporations as a class have few adverse decisions on charges of fixing uniform prices. Of the eight mercantile corporations only three have adverse decisions under the antitrust laws, with a total of 10 decisions. Of these 10 decisions only 2 relate to price uniformity and the others to price discriminations. If the large mercantile corporations were so unwise as to make agreements to fix uniform prices on their commodities at a point significantly higher than the prices in smaller stores, the customers would shift their trade to the smaller stores. Mercantile corporations do not enter into conspiracies to fix uniform prices because they cannot increase their profits thereby. On the other hand, of the 62 manufacturing and mining corporations all except 5 have decisions against them under the antitrust law and evidence has been presented above that these 5 probably participated in violations of this law.[1] These corporations violate the antitrust law because they occupy an economic position which enables them to increase their profits in this manner. Although practically all of the large manufacturing and mining corporations have engaged in illegal restraint of trade, many of them have done so only in peripheral and specialized branches of their industries. For instance, competition has been keen in the automobile tire industry and no one of the 4 principal rubber manufacturing corporations in the list of 70 large corporations has adverse decisions on charges of fixing uniform prices on tires. All of them, however, have adverse decisions for restraint of trade on other rubber products, including golf balls, rubber hose, rubber tubing, and rubber-covered wire and cable.

Variations among the corporations in the frequency of patent infringements are likewise related to economic position. It has been shown that the large corporations which are protected by huge capital investments against the entrance of new competitors into their industry secure few patents on their inventions, initiate few infringement suits, and are seldom sued by others for infringement in comparison with corporations which do not have their protection against competition.[2]

Position in the economic structure likewise affects fraud in advertising. Adverse decisions on this complaint have been made principally against the mercantile corporations. Eight mercantile corporations have a total of 49 adverse decisions by the Federal Trade Commission on charges of misrepresentation in advertising, while 62 manufacturing and mining corporations have a total of only 36 such decisions. Manufacturing and mining corporations seldom violate laws regarding advertising because they seldom engage in advertising for sales purposes.

The position of a corporation in the economic structure is related also to the number of its violations of the National Labor Relations Law. The corporations which have engaged in unfair labor practices under this law had generally been engaged in vigorous opposition to collective bargaining before the enactment of the law; their violations of this law were merely a continuation of this opposition. It is presumably not chance that makes one corporation accept collective bargaining with equanimity and another fight it vigorously. It has been suggested that industries which are more favorable to collective bargaining have characteristics such as the following: labor costs are a relatively small part of total costs, and the corporation is able to pass on additional labor costs to consumers. While these characteristics do not explain all of the variations among the 70 large corporations in their unfair labor practices, they illustrate the relation between external position and violations of the law.

The second way in which the position of a corporation in the economic structure determines its crime rate is by determining the other corporations with which it interacts. The corporations in one industry tend to have approximately equal numbers of adverse decisions for three principal reasons. First, all of the corporations in one industry may agree to fix prices or to engage in unfair labor decisions. They have the same number of adverse decisions because they have participated together in the violations of the law. Second, when one corporation in an industry uses an illegal method, the other corporations in that industry adopt the same illegal method in order that the first may not have a competitive advantage over them. Third, the corporations in an industry or a branch of an industry belong to trade associations in which policies are discussed and adopted. These associations through conferences, publications, and other means act as centers for the diffusion of techniques of violations of law and of a common ideology regarding the violation of law. Consequently, the corporations which belong to a trade association tend to act in a uniform manner and to have approximate equality in the number of decisions against them.

Variations among persons in the lower socioeconomic class in the frequency of violations of particular laws may be similarly affected by their economic positions. Unskilled laborers do not violate the antitrust law or commit fraud in advertising. Negroes have a very low rate of embezzlement because they seldom occupy positions of financial trust.

The preceding analysis has reached the conclusion that variations among corporations in the violations of law are due principally to position in the economic structure. This implies that the variations are not due to personality. The corporations which are in similar positions have a high degree of similarity in behavior. Two facts are especially significant. First, many corporations violate the antitrust law in certain industrial areas and not in others, although the officers and directors are the same for all areas. That is, behavior as to violation of law varies without variations in persons. Second, many corporations which violated the antitrust law forty years ago are still violating that law, although the personnel of the corporation has changed completely. That is, variations in persons occur without variation in behavior as to violation of law.

The data which are available as to the violations of law by the 70 large corporations are inadequate.[3] As indicated above, they are not a precise index of the comparative criminality of the several corporations. Moreover, the data were not collected with the objective of testing hypotheses as to the causation of crime. It is therefore imperative to consider the hypothesis of personality characteristics as an explanation of white collar crimes. This hypothesis has been developed to some extent by Clinard.[4] His argument is that personal traits should be included in the explanations of criminal behavior as supplements to rather than substitutes for the cultural definitions which have been discussed under the headings of differential association and social disorganization. Certainly white collar crimes, like other crimes, are not adequately explained by differential association and social disorganization. In that sense supplements to the hypotheses are needed.

Several questions arise when personality traits as supplements to a general theory of criminal behavior are considered. First, what are the personality traits which should be added? No one can give a definitive answer to this question. That is, the hypothesis of personality traits has not been implemented but is left as a vague orientation. It is recognized that some executives of corporations are high-minded, public-spirited citizens and others are dishonest, narrowly selfish, and even asinine. It is questionable, however, whether the crime rates of corporations vary on account of these personal variations. In one area two corporations doing the same kind of work and of approximately the same size have exactly the same number of adverse decisions. The chief executive of one of these is a philanthropic, public-spirited citizen, while the chief executive of the other is generally regarded as cantankerous, narrow-minded, and self-seeking.

Second, it is probable that many persons who insist that personality must be included have not properly understood differential association and especially have limited their conception of it to the associations with criminal patterns and have neglected the association with anticriminal patterns. If personal traits are to be used as supplements to differential association, they should be traits which are not already included under differential association.

Third, it is questionable whether a logical combination can be made of differential association, which is essentially a process of learning, and of personal traits, which are presumably the product of learning. It is not satisfactory to combine two types of explanations which are constructed on different principles.

Conclusion

This study has attempted to do two things: first, present evidence that persons of the upper socioeconomic class commit many crimes and that these crimes should be included within the scope of the general theories of criminal behavior; second, in the light of this evidence present some hypotheses that may explain all criminal behavior, both white collar and other.

The first of these objectives has been realized in that a sample of large corporations is found to have violated laws with great frequency. The evidence does not justify a conclusion that the upper class is more criminal or less criminal than the lower class, for the evidence is not sufficiently precise to justify comparisons and common standards and definitions are not available.

The explanation of criminal behavior has not been developed in this book in a positive manner. Quite obviously, the hypothesis that crime is due to personal and social pathologies does not apply to white collar crimes, and if it does not explain these crimes such pathologies are not essential factors in crimes in general. In contrast with such explanations the hypothesis of differential association and social disorganization may apply to white collar crimes as well as to lower class crimes.

NOTES

Notes to Chapter 1

1. Sheldon Glueck and Eleanor Glueck, *One Thousand Juvenile Delinquents* (Cambridge, 1934); *Five Hundred Criminal Careers* (New York, 1930); *Five Hundred Delinquent Women* (New York, 1934).

2. United States Bureau of the Census, *The Prisoner's Antecedents* (Washington, D.C., 1923), p. 32.

3. Clifford R. Shaw and Henry D. McKay, *Juvenile Delinquency and Urban Areas* (Chicago, 1943).

4. An excellent analysis of a group of this nature is given in Pauline V. Young, *Pilgrims of Russian Town* (Chicago, 1932).

5. These studies are summarized by Thorsten Sellin, *Research Memorandum on Crime in the Depression* (New York, 1937).

6. See Edwin H. Sutherland, *The Professional Thief* (Chicago, 1937).

7. The term "white collar" is used here to refer principally to business managers and executives, in the sense in which it was used by a president of General Motors who wrote "An Autobiography of a White Collar Worker."

8. F. P. McEvoy, "The Lie Detector Goes Into Business," *Reader's Digest,* February 1941, p. 69.

9. Roger W. Riis and John Patric, *The Repairman Will Get You If You Don't Look Out* (Garden City, 1942).

Notes to Chapter 3

1. W. Y. Elliott and others, *International Control in the Non-Ferrous Metals* (New York, 1937); Harvey O'Connor, *The Guggenheims* (New York, 1937), p. 104.

2. U.S. Industrial Commission, *Report,* 1901, vol. 13, p. 93.

3. O'Connor, *The Guggenheims,* pp. 106–24; Donald vs. American Smelting and Refining Co., 61 NJE 458, 49 A 771; 82 NJE 729, 48 A 786 (1901).

4. O'Connor, *The Guggenheims,* pp. 401–09.

5. Securities and Exchange Commission, *Annual Report,* 4:139 (1937).

6. Frank A. Fetter, *The Masquerade of Monopoly* (New York, 1931), pp. 192–305.

7. Federal Trade Commission, *Decisions* 19:94 (1934). Reference will be made to this series hereafter as FTC.

8. *New York Times,* February 16, 1943, p. 9.

9. FTC 39:259 (1944).

10. Interstate Commerce Commission, *Annual Report,* 48:84 (1934); 49:101 (1935). Reference will be made to this series hereafter as ICC.

11. ICC 58:107 (1944).

12. Carson vs. American Smelting and Refining Company, 293 F 771 (1923), 4 F 2nd 463 (1925), 11 F 2nd 764 (1925), 25 F 2nd 116 (1928).

13. National Labor Relations Board, *Decisions,* 16:437–60 (1939). Reference will be made to this series hereafter as NLRB.

14. NLRB 29:360–90 (1941); 126 F 2nd 680 (1942).

15. NLRB 34:968–83 (1941); 128 F 2nd 345 (1942).

16. NLRB 44:646–53 (1942).

17. O'Connor, *Guggenheims,* p. 304.

18. Ibid., p. 314.

19. American Smelting and Refining Co. vs. Industrial Commission of Utah, 250 P 651 (1926); American Smelting and Refining Co. vs. Industrial Commission of Utah, 69 P 2nd 271 (1937); State ex rel Federated Metals Corp. et al. vs. Nelson et al., 117 SW 2nd 361 (1938); American Smelting and Refining Co. vs. Industrial Commission of Arizona, 123 P 2nd 163 (1942).

20. Godfrey et al. vs. American Smelting and Refining Co., 158 F 225 (1907); Riverside Dairy & Stock Farm vs. American Smelting and Refining Co., 236 F 510 (1916); American et al. vs. Anderson Smelting and Refining Co., 265 F 928 (1919).

21. Hicks et al. vs. American Smelting and Refining Co. et al., 172 P 1055 (1918).

22. Federal Trade Commission, *Report on Profiteering,* 65th Cong., 2nd sess., Sen. Doc. 248, 1918, p. 10.

23. Charles R. Flint, *Memories of an Active Life* (New York, 1923), pp. 297–99.

24. Hood Rubber Co. vs. U.S. Rubber Co., 229 F 583 (1916).

25. FTC 1:506–15 (1919).

26. FTC 28:1489–506 (1939).

27. FTC 21:176–85 (1935).

28. FTC 306–25 (1936).

29. FTC 26:826–51 (1938).

30. *New York Times,* March 6, 1940, p. 40.

31. Ibid., August 19, 1947, p. 1.

32. Metallic Rubber Tire Co. vs. Hartford Rubber Works Co., 189 F 402 (1911), 200 F 743 (1912), 245 F 860 (1915), 266 F 543 (1920), 275 F 315 (1921).

33. *Official Gazette,* 530:277, September 1941.

34. ITS Rubber Co. vs. U.S. Rubber Co., 278 F 978 (1922), 288 F 786 (1923). FTC 21:161–62 (1936).

35. FTC 21:161–62 (1936).

36. NLRB, old ser., vol. 2, pp. 499–505 (1935); NLRB 2:148–58 (1936).

37. American Oak Leather Co. vs. C. H. Fargo Co., 77 F 671 (1896), 82 F 248 (1897), 96 F 891 (1899), 181 US 434 (1901).

38. Theobald vs. U.S. Rubber et al., 142 NYS 187 (1913), 146 NYS 597 (1914); *New York Times,* May 21, 1913, p. 4; December 24, 1913, p. 18.

39. *New York Times,* March 22, 1928, p. 40.

40. Ibid., May 6, 1936, p. 40; January 4, 1939, p. 32; January 10, 1939, p. 31; January 13, 1939, p. 33.

41. Ibid., April 15, 1941, p. 38.

42. Diamond vs. Davis et al., 38 NYS 93, 103 (1941); *New York Times,* July 24, 1941, p. 30; August 14, 1941, p. 30; October 1, 1941, p. 38; February 14, 1942, p. 27.

43. W. W. Ayer & Son vs. U.S. Rubber Co., 282 Pa 404 (1925); *Printers' Ink,* 123:17–20, April 26, 1923; 130:10, January 15, 1925.

44. Blackburn Tire Co. vs. Fisk Tire Co., 60 SW 2nd 838 (1933).

45. FTC 8:450–616 (1925).

46. U.S. Industrial Commission, *Report,* 1910, vol. 13, pp. cxi–cxii; vol. 19, pp. 229–30; Harvey O'Connor, *Mellon's Millions* (New York, 1933), pp. 66, 73.

47. *New York Times,* October 13, 1919, p. 1; June 29, 1923, p. 1.

48. Ibid., December 20, 1916, p. 19.

49. O'Connor, *Mellon's Millions,* p. 299.

50. *New York Times,* November 25, 1919, p. 3.

51. U.S. Coal Commission, Report on Civil Liberties, 1925, 68 Cong., 2nd sess., Sen. Doc. 195.

52. *New York Times,* July 24, 1945, p. 19.

53. O'Connor, *Mellon's Millions,* pp. 224–25; John J. Casey, *Congressional Record,* March 8, 1928, pp. 4496–538; National Committee for the Defense of Political Prisoners, *The Harlan Miner Speaks: Report of Terrorism in the Kentucky Coal Fields,* 1932.

54. U.S. Coal Commission, *Report,* 68 Cong., 2nd sess., Sen. Doc. 195, part I, pp. 1435–537.

Notes to Chapter 4

1. The most thorough analysis of crime from the point of view of the legal definition is Jerome Hall, *Principles of Criminal Law* (Indianapolis, 1947). He lists seven criteria of crime: "(1) certain external consequences ('harms'), (2) which are legally forbidden (principle of legality); (3) conduct; (4) *mens rea;* (5) the fusion, 'concurrence,' of *mens rea* and conduct; (6) a 'causal' relationship between the legally forbidden harms and the voluntary misconduct; and (7) (legally prescribed) punishment" (p. 11). The position taken in the present chapter is in most respects consistent with Hall's definition; certain differences will be considered later.

2. U.S. vs. Swift, 188 F 92 (1911).

3. Some of the antitrust decisions were made against meat packers under the Packers and Stockyards Act. The penal sanctions in this act are essentially the same as in the Federal Trade Commission Act.

4. Violations of the federal Fair Labor Standards Act and of most of the state labor laws are defined as misdemeanors.

5. For a list of such states, see Walter J. Derenburg, *Trade Mark Protection and Unfair Trading* (New York, 1936), pp. 861–1012.

6. Orville C. Snyder, "Criminal Breach of Trust and Corporate Mismanagement," *Miss. Law Jour.,* 11:123–51, 262–89, 368–89, December 1938 and April 1939; A. A. Berle, "Liability for Stock Market Manipulation," *Columbia Law Rev.,* 31:264–79, February 1931; David L. Dodd, *The Judicial Valuation of Property for Stock-Issue Purposes* (New York, 1930).

7. Lowell B. Mason, "FTC Stipulation—Friend of Advertiser?" *Chicago Bar Record,* vol. 26, pp. 310 f., May 1945.

8. Paul E. Hadlick, *Criminal Prosecutions under the Sherman Antitrust Act* (Washington, 1939), pp. 131–32.

9. Livingston Hall, "Statutory Law of Crimes, 1887–1936," *Harvard Law Rev.,* 50:616–53, February 1937.

10. Hall, *Principles of Criminal Law,* ch. x.

11. Wendell Berge, "Remedies Available to the Government under the Sherman Act," *Law and Contemporary Problems,* 7:111, January 1940.

12. On the role of the stranger in punitive justice, see Ellsworth Faris, "The Ori-

gin of Punishment," *Intern. Journ. of Ethics,* 25:54–67, October 1914; George H. Mead, "The Psychology of Punitive Justice," *Amer. Journ. Sociol.,* 23:577–602, March 1918; Florian Znaniecki, *Social Actions* (New York, 1936), pp. 345–408.

13. Percentages compiled from cases listed in the report of the Department of Justice "Federal Antitrust Laws, 1938."

14. The trend away from penal methods suggests that the penal sanction may not be a completely adequate criterion in the definition of crime.

15. *New York Times,* March 26, 1948, pp. 31, 37.

16. George F. Canfield, "Corporate Responsibility for Crime," *Columbia Law Rev.,* 14:469–81, June 1941; Frederic P. Lee, "Corporate Criminal Liability," ibid., 28:1–28, February 1928; Max Radin, "Endless Problem of Corporate Personality," ibid., 32:643–67, April 1932.

17. For a summary of classical theories of corporate personality, see Frederick Hallis, *Corporate Personality* (London, 1930). See also Henri Levy-Bruhl, "Collective Personality in the Law," *Annales Sociologique,* ser. C, fasc. 3, 1938.

18. Robert A. Gordon, *Business Leadership in the Large Corporation* (Washington, D.C., 1945).

Notes to Chapter 5

1. This total includes three judicial opinions that corporations had engaged in restraint of trade. In dissolution suits against the American Can Company and the U.S. Steel Corporation, the courts expressed the opinions that these corporations had violated the antitrust law at an earlier time but that dissolution was not necessary since competition increased subsequently (U.S. vs. American Can, 230 F 859 [1916], 234 F 1019 [1916], 256 U.S. 706 [1920]; U.S. vs. U.S. Steel, 223 F 55 [1915], 251 U.S. 417 [1920]. A suit by the National Lead Co. to collect a debt was dismissed by the court, with the opinion that the contract under which the debt was claimed was void, since it was in violation of the state antitrust law (80 Mo. Ap. 247 [1899]).

2. Maloney vs. American Tobacco Co., 72 F 801 (1896); Stockton vs. American Tobacco Co., 55 N.J. Eq 352 (1897); John Wilbur Jenkins, *James B. Duke* (New York, 1927), pp. 94, 98–99.

3. People vs. Duke et al., 44 NYS 336 (1897).

4. Vol. 13, pp. lxxiii–lxxix.

5. State vs. Continental Tobacco Co., 75 SW 737, 745 (1903).

6. Commonw. vs. Strauss, 74 NE 308 (1905), 78 NE 136 (1905).

7. U.S. vs. McAndrews & Forbes et al., 149 F 823 (1906), 149 F 836 (1907), 212 US 585 (1908).

8. *Report on the Tobacco Industry,* 1909.

9. Commonw. vs. American Tobacco Co., 115 SW 754, 756 (1909), 116 SW 1176 (1909), 180 SW 58 (1915).

10. U.S. vs. American Tobacco Co., 164 F 700, 1024 (1908), 191 F 3711 (1911), 221 US 106 (1911).

11. U.S. Tobacco Co. vs. American Tobacco Co., 163 F 701 (1908); Weisert Tobacco Co. vs. American Tobacco Co., 163 F 712 (1908); Larus Bros. vs. American Tobacco Co., 163 F 712 (1908); Monarch Tobacco Co. vs. American Tobacco Co., 165 F 774 (1908); People's Tobacco Co. vs. American Tobacco Co., 170 F 117 (1909); 204 F 58 (1913); Ware–Kramer Tobacco Co. vs. American Tobacco Co., 178 F 117 (1910), 180 F 160 (1910); Simon et al. vs. American Tobacco Co., 192 F 662 (1912).

12. FTC 1:538 (1918).

13. Federal Trade Commission, *Report on the Tobacco Industry,* 1920.

14. Federal Trade Commission, *Letter from the Chairman on Prices of Tobacco Products,* 1922.

15. FTC 7:255, 351, 541, 546 (1924); 9:504, 514 (1925); American Tobacco Co. vs. FTC, 9 F 2nd 570 (1925), 274 US 543 (1927).

16. FTC 11:144 (1927); 38 F 2nd 547 (1927).

17. Porto Rican American Tobacco Co. vs. American Tobacco Co., 30 F 2nd 234 (1929).

18. U.S. vs. American Tobacco Co., 147 F 2nd 93 (1945); 324 U.S. 836 (1946); *New York Times,* July 25, 1940, p. 19.

19. *New York Times,* June 12, 1925, p. 5.

20. FTC 12:510 (1928).

21. Lord vs. RCA et al., 24 F 2nd 565 (1928), 28 F 2nd 257 (1928), 278 US 648 (1928), 35 F 2nd 962 (1929), 283 US 847 (1930).

22. U.S. vs. General Electric et al., cited in 3 F Sup 23 (1933).

23. U.S. Special Service Committee (Black, chairman), *Investigation of Air Mail and Ocean Mail Contracts,* 73 Cong., 2nd sess., Hearings, 1933; *Congressional Record,* 1933–34, index "Air Mail Contracts."

24. Pick Manufacturing Co. vs. General Motors, 80 F 2nd 641 (1934), 299 US 3 (1935).

25. *New York Times,* October 18, 1936, pp. 18, and III, p. 1; October 20, p. 34; October 31, p. 27.

26. FTC 24:1401 (1937); 30–34 (1939); 31–1852 (1940).

27. *Chicago Tribune,* October 22, 1937.

28. U.S. vs. General Motors et al., 121 F 2nd 376 (1941).

29. U.S. vs. Ethyl Gasoline Corp., 27 F Sup 959 (1939), 309 US 436 (1940).

30. Federal Trade Commission, *Report on the Motor Vehicle Industry* (1939).

31. TNEC, *Monograph* 36, pp. 261 ff.

32. FTC 34:58 (1941), 35:955 (1932).

33. Minneapolis Gasoline and Fuel Co. vs. Ethyl Gasoline, 38 F Sup 454 (1941), 2 FRD 307 (1941); Emich Motor Corp. vs. Ethyl Gasoline, 2 FRD 552 (1942); Sinaiko Bros. Coal and Oil Co. vs. Ethyl Gasoline, 2 FRD 305 (1942); Ulrich et al. vs. Ethyl Gasoline, 2 FRD 357 (1942).

34. *New York Times,* October 5, 1940, p. 17.

35. 66 F Sup 714 (1944).

36. *New York Times,* September 23, 1947, p. 37.

37. Ibid., August 22, 1947, p. 22.

38. Ibid., November 20, 1942, p. 17.

39. Sears Roebuck vs. Winchester Repeating Arms Co., 178 Ill App 318 (1913).

40. FTC 1:163 (1918).

41. *Report on Household Furnishings,* 1924, vol. 3, p. 230.

42. Ibid., pp. 168–71.

43. FTC 22:233 (1936), 25:1707 (1937), 26:1521 (1938); *Business Week,* February 10, 1934, p. 12.

44. Federal Trade Commission, *Report on Chain Stores,* 73 Cong. 2 sess., Sen. Doc. 4, pp. 27–28, 63–65; Sen. Doc. 94, pp. 65, 69, 96, 98.

45. TNEC, *Hearings,* part 19, pp. 10681–684.

46. Federal Trade Commission, *Annual Report,* 1936, pp. 31–32.

47. U.S. vs. E. C. Knight, 156 US 1.

48. Multon Handler, ed., *The Federal Anti-Trust Law* (Chicago, 1932), p. 175.

On this trend in general, see Frank A. Fetter, *The Masquerade of Monopoly* (New York, 1931), ch. 24, "Mergers Multiply in Judicial Sunshine."

49. U.S. Industrial Commission, *Report,* 1901, vol. 13, p. 474.

50. Charles A. Pearce, "Trade Association Survey," TNEC, *Monograph* 18, 1941, pp. 67–68.

51. U.S. Federal Trade Commission, *Preliminary Report on Competitive Conditions in Flour Milling* (Washington, D.C., 1926), p. viii.

52. TNEC, *Monograph* 21, p. 122.

53. For an illustration of the details covered in these regulations, see U.S. vs. Sugar Institute, 15 F Sup 817 (1934), 297 US 553 (1936).

54. TNEC, *Monograph* 18, 1941, p. 395.

55. FTC 22:232 (1936); 25:1707 (1937); 26:1521 (1938); 28:1489, 1899 (1939); Howard Wolf and Ralph Wolf, *Rubber* (New York, 1936), pp. 467–87.

56. Kenneth F. Crawford, *The Pressure Boys* (New York, 1939), pp. 21–22.

57. TNEC, *Hearings,* part 25, p. 13324.

58. Lincoln Steffens, *Autobiography* (New York, 1931), part III.

Notes to Chapter 6

1. For instances see the case of American Can Company (pp. 88–89) and of Sears Roebuck (pp. 89–90).

2. William Z. Ripley, *Railroads: Rates and Regulations* (New York, 1912), pp. 188–89.

3. The statistics on rebates were secured from the list of suits published in the Annual Reports of the Interstate Commerce Commission. The references to these Annual Reports will be given as ICC, while the separate series of Decisions of the Interstate Commerce Commission will be referred to as ICC Decisions.

4. Pp. 16–18.

5. ICC, *Decisions,* 22:51 (1911).

6. ICC 55:148 (1911).

7. U.S. Senate Committee, *Report on Transportation and Sale of Meat Products,* 51 Cong., 1st sess., Senate Report no. 829, 1890.

8. "The Greatest Trust in the World," *Everybody's Mag.,* 12:291 ff., 1905.

9. ICC 32:64 (1918); *New York Times,* August 6, 1918, p. 6.

10. FTC 16:67–76 (1932).

11. FTC 15:232–48, 1931.

12. Ripley, *Railroads,* p. 208.

Notes to Chapter 7

1. Pp. 50–51.

2. The statistics regarding infringement have been compiled from cases in the *Federal Reporter* and from the lists of infringement suits published in the *Official Gazette* of the Patent Office. Little information is available regarding the content of the stipulations and consent decrees and these, consequently, provide little evidence as to the criminality involved in the violations of these laws.

3. Howe et al. vs. Underwood et al., Fed. Case 6775 (1854). This report refers to a decision in 1853 which is apparently not reported.

4. Pittsburgh Reduction Co. vs. Cowles Electric Smelting and Aluminum Co., 55

F 30 (1893), 64 F 125 (1894); Electric Smelting and Aluminum Co. vs. Pittsburgh Reduction Co., 111 F 742 (1902), 125 F 926 (1903); H. T. Warshow, *Representative Industries in the United States* (New York, 1928), pp. 8, 45.

5. Goodyear Tire and Rubber Co. vs. Consolidated Rubber Co., 26 Ohio Circuit 269 (1905).

6. Consolidated Rubber Co. vs. Finley Rubber-Tire Co., 106 F 175 (1901).

7. Howard Wolf and Ralph Wolf, *Rubber* (New York, 1936), p. 421.

8. Overman Cushion Tire Co. vs. Goodyear Tire and Rubber Co., 34 F 2nd 508 (1929), 66 F 2nd 361 (1933), 95 F 2nd 879 (1937), 306 US 665 (1938).

9. Electric Vehicle Co. vs. C. A. Duerr & Co. et al., 172 F 923 (1909), 184 F 893 (1911). See also U.S. Board of Tax Appeals, 9:1107–13 (1928).

10. Parker Rustproof Co. vs. Ford Motor Co., 6 F 2nd 649 (1925), 23 F 2nd 502 (1928), 41 F 2nd 1010 (1930).

11. Bucher and Gibbs vs. International Harvester Co., 211 F 473 (1913).

12. Mathey vs. United Shoe Machinery Co., 32 F Sup. 684 (1940), 117 F 2nd 331 (1941).

13. Bemis Box Car Co. vs. J. G. Brill Company, 200 F 749 (1912), 226 US 614 (1913).

14. Douglas Pectin Co. vs. Armour & Co., 14 F 2nd 768 (1926), 21 F 2nd 584 (1927), 27 F 2nd 814 (1928).

15. U.S. vs. Procter & Gamble, 47 F Sup 676 (1942).

16. Lever Brothers vs. Procter & Gamble, 38 F Sup 680 (1941), 49 F Sup 444 (1943), 139 F 2nd 633 (1943). See also *Time*, March 13, 1944, p. 90.

17. Mishawaka Rubber & Woolen Co. vs. Kresge, 119 F 2nd 316 (1941), 316 US 203 (1942).

18. Winget Kickernich Co. vs. Kresge, 96 F 2nd 878 (1938), 102 F 2nd 740 (1939), 308 US 557 (1939).

19. No-D-Ka Dentifrice Co. vs. Kresge, 24 F 2nd 726 (1928).

20. O'Cedar Corporation vs. F. W. Woolworth, 66 F 2nd 363 (1933), 73 F 2nd 366 (1934), 291 US 666 (1934).

21. Best Foods vs. Wilson & Co., 300 F 484 (1924).

22. Sheldon vs. Metro-Goldwyn Pictures Corp. et al., 26 F Sup 134 (1938), 106 F 2nd 45 (1939), 309 US 390 (1940); Young vs. Loew's, 2 FRD 350 (1942); Stonesifer vs. Twentieth Century Fox, 46 F Sup 196 (1942), 140 F 2nd 579 (1944); *New York Times*, March 11, 1938, p. 15.

23. On the general relation between patents and restraint of trade, see Wendell Berge, *Cartels* (Washington, D.C., 1944), ch. iv.

24. The registration of trademarks is not nearly so prevalent among the 70 large corporations as the registration of patents, but trademark registration shows the same trend toward increase and among manufacturing corporations trademark registrations are closely associated with patent registrations.

25. See p. 23.

26. TNEC, *Monograph* 31, 1941, p. 133.

27. See p. 101.

28. 1 Daly Reports 209.

29. TNEC, *Monograph* 31, 1941, pp. 47 ff.

30. U.S. vs. Eastman Kodak Company, 226 F 62.

31. U.S. vs. Motion Picture Patents Co., 225 F 899.

32. David O. Woodbury, *Beloved Scientist: Elihu Thompson* (New York, 1944), pp. 165, 167.

33. Ibid., p. 290.

34. General Electric vs. Winsted Gas Co., 110 F 963 (1901).

35. N. R. Danielian, *A T and T* (New York, 1939).

36. *PM,* February 3, 1947, p. 6.

37. U.S. Senate Committee on Patents (Bone chairman), 77th Cong., 2nd sess., 1942, *Hearings,* part I, p. 630.

38. Berge, *Cartels,* pp. 44–45.

39. *New York Times,* January 19, 1939, p. 10.

40. American Cutting Alloys Co. vs. General Electric, 135 F 2nd 502 (1943). On the cartel in tungsten carbide see U.S., 77 Cong., 2nd sess., Senate Com. on Patents, 1942, *Hearings,* part I, pp. 39–520.

41. U.S. vs. Chemical Foundation, 294 F 300 (1924), 5 F 2nd 191 (1925), 272 US 1 (1926).

42. *New York Times,* November 16, 1944, p. 1; February 18, 1945, p. 35.

43. In his acceptance of this award in 1929 Garvan said, "I believe that modern chemistry plus modern aeronautics has made war impossible" (*Cong. Rec.,* 71: 4179, October 3, 1929). On the Chemical Foundation in general, see the court decisions referred to above and the indexes of the *Congressional Record* 1919–26.

44. Barge, *Cartels,* ch. VII; U.S., Report of Senate Committee on Military Affairs, Sub-Committee on Monopoly and Cartels (Kilgore chairman), 68 Cong., 1st sess., 1943, *Hearings* on "Monopoly and Cartel Practices: Vitamin D," part VI; *Time,* October 30, 1944, p. 88; *New York Times,* January 15, 1946, p. 16.

Notes to Chapter 8

1. See p. 49.

2. One decision against Sears Roebuck in 1918 involved four distinct counts and is counted as 4 cases; the number of decisions against this firm would be reduced to 15 if this were counted as one decision (FTC 1: 163–72 [1918]; 258 F 307 [1919]).

3. This distinction between advertising and nonadvertising corporations obviously cannot be made with precision.

4. U.S. Department of Agriculture, Bureau of Chemistry, Chemical Supplements, nos. 171–230.

5. *New York Times,* August 27, 1938, p. 24.

6. Cheney Brothers vs. Gimbel Brothers, 280 F 746 (1922).

7. *New Republic,* 86–369, May 8, 1936.

8. Quoted by Joseph B. Matthews and Ruth E. Shallcross, *Partners in Plunder* (New York, 1935).

9. *New Republic* 86:369, May 6, 1936.

10. Quoted by George Seldes, *Witch Hunt* (New York, 1940), pp. 134–35.

11. Federal Trade Commission, *Annual Report,* 1941, p. 132. The distribution of decisions was significantly different in 1945, with 94.4 percent in food and drugs (Federal Trade Commission, *Annual Report,* 1945, p. 74).

12. Harvey W. Wiley, *An Autobiography* (Indianapolis, 1930), pp. 261 ff.

13. E. Pendleton Herring, "The Balance of Social Forces in the Administration of the Food and Drug Law," *Social Forces,* 13:364–65, March 1935.

14. Edith Lucie Weart, "Milk: A Food or a Medicine?" *New Republic* 93:359–61, February 2, 1938.

15. Blake Clark, "Lifting the Cigarette Ad Smoke Screen," *Reader's Digest,* 43:17–21, July 1943.

16. FTC 32:1723, 1749–50, 1807–18 (1941).

17. FTC 26:1443 (1938).

18. Cheney Brothers vs. Gimbel Brothers, 280 F 746 (1922).

19. FTC 27:1617 (1938).

20. FTC 25:711–20 (1937).

21. See p. 68.

22. FTC 25:1523–24, 1526–27 (1937); 32:807–25, (1941); 33:1541–52 (1941).

23. FTC 33:176–85 (1935).

24. FTC 8:148–60 (1924), 10:661–64 (1926), 12:299–302 (1928), 19:523 (1934), 23:637–49 (1936), 27:1633–34 (1938), 28:1876 (1939), 29:1535 (1939), 29:1540 (1939), 31:1761 (1946).

25. *PM,* May 16, 1944, p. 10.

Notes to Chapter 9

1. See p. 49.

2. Commonwealth vs. Hunt, 4 Metcalf 111.

3. U.S., Report of Senate Committee on Education and Labor, *Violations of Free Speech and Rights of Labor,* 76 Cong., 1st sess., Senate Report no. 6, part I, pp. 139–48. The reference to this hereafter will be La Follette Committee Report.

4. Lewis L. Lorwin and Arthur Wubnig, *Labor Relations Boards: The Regulation of Collective Bargaining under the National Industrial Recovery Act* (Washington, D.C., 1935).

5. Ibid., pp. 354–55.

6. Herbert Harris, *American Labor* (New Haven, 1938), p. 301; *Congressional Record,* 75 Cong., 1st sess., p. 7148, July 13, 1937.

7. NLRB vs. Jones & Laughlin, 301 US 11 (1936).

8. U.S., *Investigation of the National Labor Relations Board,* 76 Cong., 3rd sess., House Report no. 1902, 1940.

9. D. O. Bowman, *Public Control of Labor Relations: A Study of National Labor Relations Boards* (New York, 1942), pp. 407–08.

10. Bowman, *Public Control of Labor Relations,* p. 409.

11. H. A. Millis (Research Director), *How Collective Bargaining Works* (New York, 1942), p. 513.

12. H. J. Heinz vs. NLRB, 311 US 514 (1941).

13. Texas and New Orleans RR Co. vs. Brotherhood of Railway and Steamship Clerks, 281 US 548 (1930).

14. "Characteristics of Company Unions, 1935," *U.S. Bur. Labor Statistics,* no. 634, 1937, pp. 51, 86, 117, 143. See also National Industrial Conference Board, *Collective Bargaining through Employee Representation* (New York, 1933).

15. La Follette Committee, *Hearings,* part 6, pp. 2255–66.

16. La Follette Committee, *Hearings,* part 4, pp. 1194 ff.

17. La Follette Committee, *Report,* part 2, p. 113.

18. La Follette Committee, *Hearings,* part 6, p. 2069.

19. La Follette Committee, *Report,* part 3, pp. 46–47.

20. NLRB 14:113–68 (1939); La Follette Committee, *Hearings,* part 6, p. 2300.

21. NLRB 4:647 (1937).

22. When Henry Ford retired, Harry Bennett was dismissed and the Service Department abandoned. Thereafter no cases of violence against the Ford Company were reported.

23. NLRB 4:621–78 (1937).

24. NLRB 26:322–400 (1940). See also Charles R. Walker, "The Ford Way of Doing Business," *New Republic,* 102:666–69, 723–25, May 20–27, 1940.

25. See, especially, regarding Jones & Laughlin, NLRB 1:503–18 (1936); regarding Republic Steel, NLRB 9:219–404 (1938); regarding Weirton Steel, NLRB 32: 1145–267 (1941).

26. Carey McWilliams, "Racketeers and Movie Magnates," *New Republic,* 105:533–34, October 27, 1941. Both Bioff, of the union, and Schenck, of the picture corporation, were convicted of income tax evasion in this transaction.

27. See p. 84.

28. The Report of the La Follette Committee contains much information on these associations. A description of the antiunion association in California is given in brief form in NLRB 37:50–99 (1941).

29. La Follette Committee, *Report,* part 4, pp. 67–68.

30. C. L. Christenson, *Collective Bargaining in Chicago, 1929–1930* (Chicago, 1933).

31. Montgomery Ward vs. Lusk et al., 52 SW 2nd 1110 (1932).

32. State vs. Anaconda, 59 P 854 (1900).

33. U.S., House Committee on Labor, *Hearings on House Joint Resolution* 449, 74 Cong., 2nd sess.; Vito Marcantonio, "Dusty Death," *New Republic,* 86:105–06, March 4, 1936; Kenneth G. Crawford, *The Pressure Boys* (New York, 1939), pp. 234–42.

Notes to Chapter 10

1. See pp. 16–18.

2. Scott vs. Brown, 2 Queens Bench Div. 724 (1892).

3. A. A. Berle, "Liability for Stock Market Manipulations," *Columbia Law Rev.,* 31:264–79, 1931.

4. The public official has a similar position with multiple and conflicting interests and frequently places his party above the state. Lippmann has argued, however, that the standards of political behavior in this respect are higher than the standards of business behavior (Walter Lippmann, *Drift and Mastery* [New York, 1944], ch. 1).

5. Howard Wolf and Ralph Wolf, *Rubber* (New York, 1936), pp. 450–60.

6. Henry D. Lloyd, *Lords of Industry* (New York, 1910), pp. 218–19. Gates as a salesman for a barbed-wire company secured many orders and then organized his own company to fill the orders. Later he organized American Steel and Wire Co. with capital of $90 million. The Seligmans—bankers for the corporation—started suit against Gates when he could not account for $26 million of the capital stock. Gates closed 13 of the mills, sold his own shares short, and the stock plunged downward. The Seligmans, who had large holdings of this stock, rather than take a ruinous loss, withdrew the suit against Gates and no account was ever made of this $26 million (Harvey O'Connor, *Steel—Dictator* [New York, 1935], pp. 39–40). Frick, manager of Carnegie Steel Company during the absence of Carnegie, purchased land for $500,000 and sold it to the corporation for $1,500,000. This action was rescinded when Carnegie returned and learned the details (Clarence W. Barron, *More They Told Barron* [New York, 1931], p. 223). Frick and Phipps, executives of Carnegie Steel, presented to Carnegie a plan for the sale of his company. Although Carnegie was old and anxious to sell, he refused to do so when he learned that each of these promoters would make a profit of $2,300,000 on the transaction. However, Carnegie

himself, as majority stockholder of the Frick Coke Co., attempted to compel the coke company to sell coke to the Carnegie Steel Co. at half the price coke was sold to other steel companies (Burton J. Hendrick, *The Life of Andrew Carnegie* [Garden City, 1937], vol. 1, pp. 85–86).

7. John K. Winkler, *The Du Pont Dynasty* (New York, 1935), pp. 220–28; James Marquis, *Alfred I DuPont: The Family Rebel* (Indianapolis, 1941), pp. 279–325.

8. See pp. 26–29.

9. Charles P. Norcross, "The Trail of the Hunger Tax," *Cosmopolitan*, 47:588–97, October 1909.

10. Federal Trade Commission, *Report on the Meat Packing Industry*, 1919, part III, ch. V.

11. F. M. Leopold vs. Inland Steel Co., 125 F 2nd 369 (1942).

12. *New York Times*, June 11, 1942, p. 33.

13. M. Jacobstein, *The Tobacco Industry*, Columbia Studies in History, vol. XXVI, no. 3, 1907, pp. 133–34.

14. Wolf and Wolf, *Rubber*, p. 491; *Time*, vol. 26, pp. 48–52, July 29, 1935.

15. *New York Times*, February 23, 1943, to October 26, 1943.

16. Dunn vs. Wilson & Co., 51 F Sup 655 (1943).

17. *New York Times*, April 15, 1941, p. 38.

18. Victor House, "The Lowly Bondholder," *Harpers*, 168:418, March 1934.

19. John T. Flynn, *Graft in Business* (New York, 1931), pp. 125–39.

20. U.S. Commissioner of Corporations, *Reports on the Steel Industry*, 1911, ch. VII.

21. Wolf and Wolf, *Rubber*, pp. 450–60; U.S. Senate Committee on Banking and Currency, *Hearings on Stock Exchange Practices*, part IV, pp. 2133–38; John T. Flynn, "Other People's Money," *New Republic*, 6:333–34, November 1, 1933. The firm of Kennedy & Co., which was a corporation management firm in the Goodyear transaction, appeared as an expert engineering firm in the financing of municipal improvements in Rio de Janeiro by Dillon Read. U.S. Senate Committee on Banking and Currency, *Hearings*, pp. 1907–09.

22. Federal Trade Commission, *Report on Motor Vehicle Industry*, 1939, pp. 582–607; L. H. Seltzer, *Financial History of the Automobile Industry* (New York, 1928), pp. 234 ff.

23. John C. Baker, "Executive Compensation Compared with Earnings," *Harvard Bus. Rev.*, 14:223–24, 1936.

24. *New York Times*, April 28, 1945, p. 20; March 5, 1946, p. 30.

25. Alden Winthrop, *Are You A Stockholder?* (New York, 1937), pp. 68–71.

26. Ibid., pp. 97–100.

27. Winkelman et al. vs. General Motors et al., 44 F Sup 960 (1942).

28. R. R. Rogers vs. Hill, 60 F 2nd 106, 114 (1932), 288 US 586 (1933).

29. *Time*, November 27, 1939, p. 15; Mathews et al. vs. American Tobacco Co. et al., 130 NJE 470, 23 A 2nd 301 (1941).

30. Hiller vs. Boylan, 29 NYS 2nd 653 (1941); *New York Times*, May 27, 1941, p. 37; September 30, 1941, p. 35; December 25, 1941, p. 40.

31. O'Connor, *Steel—Dictator* (New York, 1935), p. 344.

32. Neuberger vs. Barrett, 39 NYS 2nd 575 (1942).

33. *New York Times*, October 26, 1935, p. 23.

34. Epstein vs. Schenck et al., 35 NYS 2nd 969 (1939).

35. David L. Dodd, *Stock Watering: The Judicial Valuation of Property for Stock Issue Purposes* (New York, 1930).

36. Federal Trade Commission, *Report on Motor Vehicle Industry,* 1939, ch. xiii.

37. Tooker vs. National Sugar Refining Co., 89 NJE 305, 84 Ath 10 (1912).

38. John K. Winkler, *The DuPont Dynasty* (New York, 1935), pp. 158–64; James Marquis, *Alfred I. DuPont: Family Rebel* (Indianapolis, 1941), pp. 170–75.

39. Arthur Pound, *The Turning Wheel* (Garden City, 1934), pp. 80–81.

40. Seltzer, *Financial History of the Automobile Industry,* pp. 148–90.

41. Ibid., p. 158; Federal Trade Commission, *Report on the Motor Vehicle Industry,* 1939, pp. 455–58.

42. Mandelbaum vs. Goodyear Rubber, 6 F 2nd 818 (1925).

43. Securities and Exchange Commission, *Annual Reports,* 2:93 (1935), 3:161 (1936), 4:138 (1937), 139 (1937), 6:236 (1940).

44. M. Jacobstein, *The Tobacco Industry* (New York, 1907), pp. 133–35; Charles Edward Russell, *Lawless Wealth* (New York, 1908), pp. 152–53.

45. John T. Flynn, *God's Gold* (New York, 1932), pp. 344–46; Thomas Lawson, *Frenzied Finance* (New York, 1905), passim.

46. F. Pecora, *Wall Street under Oath* (New York, 1939), pp. 78, 110–12; John T. Flynn, "The Bankers and the Crisis," *New Republic,* 74:158, March 22, 1933.

47. Quoted by John T. Flynn, *Graft in Business* (New York, 1932), pp. 14–15.

48. Alexander Noyes, *Forty Years of American Finance* (New York, 1909), p. 300.

49. William Z. Ripley, *Main Street and Wall Street* (Boston, 1927), ch. vii; Anderson F. Farr, "The Annual Corporate Report," *Harpers,* 168:421–32, March 1934; idem, "Give the Stockholders the Truth," *Scribners,* 93:232 ff., April 1933; Winthrop, *Are You a Stockholder?*

50. "Investigation of Labor Troubles in the Anthracite Regions of Pennsylvania, 1887–1888," 50 Cong., 2nd sess., House Report 4147, 1889, pp. ii, iv.

51. Ripley, *Main Street and Wall Street,* pp. 180–81.

52. FTC 24:1616–27 (1937); U.S. vs. National Biscuit Co., 25 F Sup 329 (1938), 109 F 2nd 66 (1940).

53. Clarence W. Barron, *They Told Barron* (New York, 1930), p. 133.

54. Farr, "The Annual Corporate Report," p. 429.

55. Ibid., pp. 427–28.

56. *New York Times,* February 26, 1933, II, p. 11.

57. Winthrop, *Are You a Stockholder?,* pp. 162–64.

58. Farr, "The Annual Corporate Report," p. 232; Winthrop, *Are You a Stockholder?,* pp. 14, 162, 225–28, 304–05; *New York Times,* April 5, 1936, III, p. 1; April 7, 1936, p. 37.

59. *New York Times,* May 1, 1935, p. 10; November 12–14, 1935.

60. "Report on Sale and Distribution of Milk," 74 Cong., 1st sess., House Doc. 152, pp. 146–47.

61. Flynn, *God's Gold,* pp. 344–45.

62. American Oak Leather Co. vs. C. E. Fargo Co., 77 F 671 (1896), 96 F 891 (1899), 181 US 434 (1901).

63. "Absorption of the Tennessee Coal and Iron Company," 62nd Cong., 1st sess., Sen. Doc. 44, 1911; U.S. Commissioner of Corporations, *The Steel Industry,* 1911, pp. 258–59; O'Connor, *Steel—Dictator,* pp. 54–57.

64. U.S. Department of State, *Report of the International Commission of Enquiry into the Existence of Slavery and Forced Labor in the Republic of Liberia,* Public no. 147, 1931; Raymond L. Buell, *The Native Problem in Africa* (New York, 1928), vol. ii, pp. 818–52; Arthur L. Hayman and Harold Freeze, *Lighting up Liberia* (New

York, 1943); Mauritz A. Wallgren, "Liberia in Shackles," *Nation,* 137:185–88, August 16, 1933; James C. Young, *Liberia Rediscovered* (Garden City, 1934).

Notes to Chapter 11

1. Committee on War Expenditures, *Hearings,* vol. XXII, pp. 6431–33.

2. Federal Trade Commission, *Report on War-Time Profits and Costs in the Steel Industry,* p. 29; TNEC, *Hearings,* part XVIII, p. 10424.

3. *Congressional Record,* 79:448–49 (1935); Federal Trade Commission, *War-Time Profiteering,* 65 Cong., 2nd sess., Sen. Doc. 248.

4. Federal Trade Commission, *Report on the Meat Packing Industry,* 1919, part I, p. 74.

5. Committee on War Expenditures, 66 Cong., 3rd sess., p. 18; House Rep. 1307, p. 21.

6. Harvey O'Connor, *Steel—Dictator* (New York, 1935), pp. 80–81.

7. U.S., Special Senate Committee (Nye chairman), *Investigation of the Munitions Industry,* 74 Cong., 1st sess., Sen. Rep. 944, part I, p. 9. This report will be referred to hereafter as Nye Committee.

8. U.S. vs. Bethlehem Steel Corp., 23 F Sup 676 (1938), 26 F Sup 259 (1938), 113 F 2nd 301 (1940), 315 US 289 (1942).

9. U.S. vs. Aluminum Company of America, 87 Ct. Cl. 96 (1938).

10. Nye Committee, *Hearings,* index "Old Hickory."

11. Federal Trade Commission, *Report on the Meat Packing Industry,* 1919, part I, p. 75.

12. Ibid., p. 76.

13. Marshall B. Clinard has written a detailed analysis of violations of price regulations in World War II, and this will be published in the near future under the title *The Black Market: A Study in White Collar Crime.* [New York, 1952]

14. *New York Times,* November 1, 1942, II, p. 7; December 4, 1942, p. 40.

15. *New York Times,* September 4, 1942, p. 1; December 11, 1942, p. 36; May 19, 1943, p. 12; August 31, 1943, p. 8; July 6, 1944, p. 16; September 22, 1945, p. 32; *PM,* October 31, 1946, p. 3.

16. *PM,* August 3, 1945, p. 11.

17. *New York Times,* June 13, 1943, p. 31; January 19, 1944, p. 17; March 1, 1946, p. 17.

18. Associated Press reports, March to October 1943, and May 1945. Damages were collected by the United States from the Carnegie Steel Company before it became a part of the U.S. Steel Corporation, for defective materials sold to the United States under fraudulent conditions (Committee on Naval Affairs, *Violation of Armor Contracts,* 53 Cong., 2nd sess., House Rep., 1468, 1894). Also, charges were made, without official decisions, that fraud had been used in the prewar years by DuPont in the sale of powder to the government and by the Goodyear Tire and Rubber Company in the construction of Zeppelins.

19. Federal Trade Commission, *Report on War-Time Profiteering,* 65 Cong., 2nd sess., Sen. Doc. 248, 1917; Nye Committee, *Report,* part 2.

20. *PM,* March 9, 1944, p. 6.

21. Routzahn vs. Aluminum Co., 23 F 2nd 230 (1927), 31 F 2nd 669 (1929).

22. U.S. vs. Aluminum Co., 2 F Sup 894 (1932), 67 F 2nd 172 (1933).

23. *Congressional Record,* 78:3675, February 16, 1934.

24. Ibid., 72:5326, 5743–66 (1930).

25. Harvey O'Connor, *Mellon's Millions* (New York, 1933), p. 148.

26. These are included in Table 3 as "Restraint of Trade."

27. Nye Committee, *Report,* part 3, p. 168.

28. Ibid., p. 164.

29. Ibid., pp. 260–62.

30. Ibid., p. 145.

31. Ibid., p. 167.

32. Nye Committee, *Hearings,* part 5, pp. 1112–13.

33. Nye Committee, *Report,* part 3, pp. 73–74.

34. Charles J. Post, "The Powder Trust," *Harper's Weekly,* 58:6–8, May 2, 1914; 58:19–21, May 9, 1914.

35. "Washington Merry-Go-Round," December 19, 1947.

36. *In Fact,* November 23, 1942, p. 3.

37. Nye Committee, *Report,* part 3, p. 171.

38. *In Fact,* November 23, 1942, p. 3.

Notes to Chapter 12

1. Wyman-Partridge & Co. vs. Boston Blacking Co., 175 F 834 (1909).

2. Dowling vs. Great A & P, 159 SE 609 (1931); Smith vs. Great A & P, 136 SW 2nd 759 (1939).

3. Smalley vs. Great A & P, 156 S 638 (1934); Majure vs. Great A & P, 167 S 637 (1936).

4. Medline vs. Montgomery Ward, 104 F 2nd 485 (1939); Hornin vs. Montgomery Ward, 120 F 2nd 500 (1941).

5. Wilkerson vs. Swift, 124 F 2nd 176 (1941).

6. Paddock vs. Goodyear, 40 NE 697 (1942).

7. *New York Times,* February 28, 1934, p. 4; September 22, 1934, p. 17; November 16, 1937, p. 26.

8. U.S. Attorney General, *Annual Report,* 1909, pp. 11–12; 1910, pp. 12–18; 1911, p. 20; 1913, p. 27; 1916, p. 59; H. J. Howland, "The Case of the Seventeen Holes," *Outlook,* 92:25–38, May 1, 1909; *Amer. Review of Reviews,* 40:644–50, December, 1909; *Independent,* 67:1111–12, 1155, November 18, 1909; pp. 1402–03, December 23, 1909; *World's Work,* 18:116–36, June 1909.

9. *Outlook,* 92:55–56, May 8, 1909.

10. Vandergriff vs. Goodyear Company, 184 SE 452 (1936).

11. Charles A. Myers Co. vs. Ford, 64 F 2nd 942 (1935).

12. Gloversville Silk Mills Co. vs. Gimbel, 176 F 219 (1910).

13. "The International Harvester Company," *Fortune,* 8:118, August 1933; William T. Hutchinson, *Cyrus Hall McCormick* (New York, 1935), vol. II, p. 550; Cyrus McCormick, *The Century of the Reaper* (New York, 1931), p. 92.

14. D. Taylor vs. Kresge, 194 F 379 (1912).

15. Hutchinson vs. Montgomery Ward, 159 S 862 (1935).

16. Columbia Railway Gas and Electric Co. vs. Swift & Co., 17 F 3rd 46 (1937).

17. Lynch vs. General Motors, 159 S 785 (1935); Bronnhill Realty vs. Montgomery Ward, 60 F 2nd 222 (1932).

18. West vs. Great A & P, 10 F 2nd 898 (1926); District of Columbia vs. Saks & Co., 263 F 1020 (1920), 253 US 479, 258 US 582 (1921).

19. Loomis Realty Co. vs. Goodrich Company, 42 Ohio Cir. 493 (1912).

20. Norton's Trustees vs. Montgomery Ward, 73 SW 2nd 41 (1934).

Notes to Chapter 13

1. Most of these decisions are published in the series known as Public Utility Reports, for which the abbreviation customarily used is PUR.

2. Federal Trade Commission, *Utility Corporations,* vols. 1–84D (1929–37).

3. O. C. Snyder, "Criminal Breach of Trust and Corporate Mismanagement," *Miss. Law Jour.,* 11:123–51, 262–89, 368–89, December 1938 to April 1939.

4. Report of Senate Committee on Interstate and Foreign Commerce, 73 Cong., 1 sess., 1933, p. 229.

5. Federal Trade Commission, *Utility Corporations,* vol. 72A, ex. 5–6.

6. Ibid., 84, xxv.

Notes to Chapter 14

1. Thorstein Veblen, *Theory of the Leisure Class* (New York, 1912), p. 237.

2. *Nation's Business,* vol. 35, no. 1, p. 38, January 1947.

3. *New Republic,* 56:33, August 29, 1928.

4. Albert K. Cohen, *Differential Implementation of the Criminal Law* (Bloomington, Indiana, 1942), pp. 36–37.

5. George Katona, *Price Control and Business,* Principia Press, Monog. no. 9, 1945.

6. Bouck White, *The Book of Daniel Drew* (New York, 1910), pp. 270–71.

7. See p. 128.

Notes to Chapter 15

1. See p. 164–65.

2. See pp. 89–90.

3. See pp. 80–81.

4. Federal Trade Commission, *Utility Corporations,* 81A:237–44.

5. Ibid., "Customer-ownership" in index, vol. 84.

6. Bouck White, *The Book of Daniel Drew* (New York, 1910), pp. 144–45.

7. See p. 57.

8. Amos Pinchot, "Walter Lippmann," *Nation,* 137:9, July 5, 1933.

9. *Indianapolis Star,* April 15, 1945.

10. *PM,* February 19, 1945, p. 3.

11. I. F. Stone, "Questions on the Whitney Case," *Nation,* 148:55–58, January 14, 1939; "Dewey vs. Prosecution," *New Republic,* 111:389–90, September 23, 1944.

Notes to Chapter 16

1. See p. 72.

2. See pp. 110–11.

3. See ch. 2.

4. Marshall B. Clinard, "Criminological Theories of Violations of Wartime Regulations," *Amer. Sociol. Rev.,* 11:258–70, June 1946.

INDEX

A. C. Spark Plug Company (subsidiary GM), 68

advertising, 25, 83, 108, 236, 238

advertising, misrepresentation in, x, 14, 15, 37, 39, 45, 53, 122–34, 233, 251, 261; laws against, 46–47, 49; prevalence, diffusion of, 126–27, 130, 246–47

advertising agencies, 57, 128, 133–34, 230

agreements in restraint of trade, 78–87, 91–92, 247

agricultural machinery industry, 82, 103

Alexander Milburn Company, 70

Allen, George, 239, 254

Allied Chemical and Dye Company, 78, 119, 120, 170

Aluminum Company of America, 85, 97, 101, 177, 182–83; cartels, 80–81, 189, 247; monopoly, 72, 77, 86, 185–86, 252–53

Aluminum Goods Manufacturing Company, 85

aluminum industry, 40, 77, 101

Amalgamated Copper Company, 171

American Aviation (company), 253

American Brass Company, 82

American Can Company, 73, 75–76, 88–89, 166

American Car and Foundry Company, 103, 156

American Dye Institute, 119

American Federation of Labor, 136

American Gas Association, 248–49

American Oil Company, 35

American Pharmaceutical Association, 128

American Pig Lead Association, 26

American Power and Light Company, 205–06, 212, 214

American Radiator and Standard Sanitary Manufacturing Company, 69–70

American Radiator Company, 69–70

American Sheet and Tin Plate Company, 75–76

American Smelting and Refining Company, 26–32, 155, 160, 166, 167, 169

American Snuff Company (subsidiary American Tobacco Co.), 67

American Sugar Refining Company, 154–55, 156, 160, 235–36, 254; financial manipulations, 164, 169; fraud, 194–95; rebates, 95, 98; restraint of trade, 74–75, 79

American Telephone and Telegraph, 117

American Tobacco Company, 95, 96, 107, 130; financial manipulations, 157, 161–62, 163, 167, 169; restraint of trade, 65–67, 77, 87, 88

American Woolen Company, 160, 169

Anaconda Copper Mining Company, 151–52, 158, 163, 166, 167, 169, 171, 175

Anaconda Wire and Copper Company, 181

anomie, 255–56

Anthony and Company, 115

antitrust laws, 47–49, 73, 84, 92, 93; violations of, ix, 30, 34–36, 39, 55, 260–61, 262. *See also* Sherman Antitrust Act of *1890*

Armour & Company, 77, 97–98, 104, 125, 156, 179; number of decisions against, 15–19, 65, 78, 95, 137, 142, 151, 192, 259–60; rebates, 95, 97–98

Associated Gas and Electric, 202, 222, 234, 236; fraud, 208, 209–14, 215, 216; violations of law, 204, 205, 219–20